# *TWISTING IN THE WIND*

## THE ANGLO-AMERICAN LEGAL TRADITION
## AND
## AFRICANS IN AMERICA
### EDITED BY PASTOR MICHAEL S. WILLIAMS, D.MIN.

Resource *Publications*

An imprint of *Wipf and Stock Publishers*
199 West 8th Avenue • Eugene OR 97401

Resource *Publications*
an imprint of Wipf and Stock Publishers
199 West 8th Avenue, Suite 3
Eugene, Oregon 97401

Twisting in the Wind
The Anglo-American Legal Tradition and Africans in America
By Williams, Michael S.
©2001 Williams, Michael S.
ISBN: 1-57910-679-X
Publication date: June, 2001
Previously published by , 2001.

**All rights reserved. No part of this publication may be reproduced, stored in a retrieval system, or transmitted, in any form or by any means, electronic, mechanical, photocopying, recording, or otherwise without the prior permission of The City Church Publication Society.**

**This book is sold subject to the condition that it shall not, by way of trade or otherwise, be lent, re-sold, hired out or otherwise circulated without the publisher's prior consent in any form of binding or cover other than that in which it is published and without a similar condition including this condition being imposed upon the subsequent publisher.**

**The City Church Publication Society
San Francisco, California**

**This BOOK is intended for CIVIL COMMENTARY** purposes *only*. It is an expression of the author's First Amendment rights, *should they actually exist*, under the **United States** Constitution. It is sold with the understanding that neither the publisher nor the author are engaged in the profession of providing advice in any manner, including, but not limited to: relationship counseling, therapy, psychological counseling, medicine, law, or any other manner of advice. **NOTHING** in this **BOOK** is intended to suggest an altering of the political establishment of the **United States** of America. If treasonous intend is read into this book, it will be done on Constitutional grounds. In other words, it treasonous intent will be culled from this book so as to pay for the luxurious lifestyle of Federal Agents, Marshals, Court Clerks, Judges, etc. They have and will always thrive at the expense of **AFRICAN** people.

First Printing
The City Church Publication Society
**San Francisco, CA**

E-Mail Address: PMSW46@AOL.com

## TABLE OF CONTENTS

Introduction .................................................................................. 7

Building The Scaffold ................................................................ 28

The Jamestown Laws: The Legal Noose (1630-1699) ............... 32

Benjamin Banneker's Appeal To Thomas Jefferson (1791) .... 49

Thomas Jefferson's Reply to Banneker (1791) ......................... 57

Guilty of Seeking Freedom: The Fugitive Slave Act of 1793 ... 60

An Appeal To Heaven: Nat Turner's Rebellion (1831) ............ 63

Henry Highland Garnett's Appeal To Open Revolt (1843) ... 101

Reconstruction's Collapse 1865-1877 And Southern "Redemption" (1877-1896) ..................................................... 115

Enforcement Act of 1870 ......................................................... 123

The Cruikshank Ruling (1875) ................................................ 139

The Civil Rights Act of 1875 ................................................... 177

The Civil Rights Act of 1875 Declared Unconstitutional (1883) ................................................................................................. 182

Booker T. Washington's Appeal to Pragmatism (1895) ......... 259

More Than A Street Car Ride: Plessy v. Ferguson (1896) ..... 263

Conclusion ................................................................................ 298

A Response by Rev. John Brinson, M.Div. ............................. 308

Biographical Sketch of Dr. Michael S. Williams .................... 310

# 6

*"[An AFRICAN] In America That Ain't Paranoid Is Crazy"*
*H. Rap Brown*

## Introduction

This book, *Twisting In The Wind: The **ANGLO-AMERICAN LEGAL TRADITION** and **AFRICANS** in America*, is a follow-up to my previous work, *No Rights and No Respect, A Documentary Commentary on **African** Life in America*[1] In the latter, I sought to critically examine the written texts that make America a "predastate," or *predatory state*,[2] in reference to the **AFRICAN**.[3] The historical phenomenon called

---

[1] Pastor Michael S. Williams, D.Min., ed., *No Rights and No Respect: A Documentary Commentary on African Life in America*, (San Francisco: The City Church Publication Society, 2000). In order to understand both works, I recommend that they be read together.

[2] The word "predastate" is a compound of the words "predator" and "state." America is a *predatory state*. America has a *parasitic* relationship with the world in general but with **AFRICANS**, within its sphere of influence, in particular. It exists for the sole purpose of eroding the humanity of anyone that it considers inferior. Ibid. 19.

[3] Anyone familiar with my writing slant knows that I am of the opinion that persons of African descent can never "do" enough to be allowed full participation in the American experience; therefore I do not consider them to be "Americans." I do not consider myself an "American." I will refer to them throughout this book as "**AFRICANS**." This is not a very farfetched proposition. African **SLAVES** arriving in America's British colonies in the Seventeenth and Eighteenth Centuries were well aware of their "inferior" status. Therefore, they made it a point to acknowledge their unique heritage. They called themselves "**AFRICANS**." Campbell notes that persons of African descent in this country, up until the mid-1820s and

"America" has a voracious appetite. It creates and then feeds off of human misery. Various European tribes, beginning in 1492, invaded the Western Hemisphere—where America is domiciled—and conquered various sections of this part of the world. The invading Europeans then proceeded to butcher the inhabitants of the land. These indigenous nations, somewhat condescendingly known as *tribes*, had been here for at least 12,000 years. Their land was stolen. They were nearly exterminated. **AFRICANS** were then brought to America by the European tribes to work and cultivate the lands wrestled from the original populations. However, out of all of the invading tribes, whether they were Dutch, French, or Spanish, no tribe did as much damage—especially in the name of civilization—than the English did! *Not only did the English begin the most destructive phase of the AFRICAN Slave trade, but their legal tradition audaciously gave them the written "authority" to decide the status of the Native American in general, but the AFRICAN in particular.*

---

late 1830s, referred to themselves as "**AFRICANS**," because the term "**Negro**" was equated with "**SLAVE**." Hence, most Black institutions contained the word "African," in their title, e.g., The *African* Free Lodge, The *African* Methodist Episcopal Church, The Free *African* Society, etc. The name fell into disuse by the 1830s due to attempts on the part of powerful interests in the **United States** that sought to deport *all "free" blacks* to Africa. James T. Campbell, *Songs of Zion: The African Methodist Episcopal Church in the **United States** and South Africa* (New York: Oxford University Press, 1995), vii, 73. Also, Richard B. Moore, *The Name "Negro," Its Origin and Evil Use*, ed., W. Burghart Turner and Joyce Moore-Turner (Baltimore: Black Classics Press, 1992), 62.

## *My Qualifications*

In a letter written to a Federal judge, in reference to a case I was intimately familiar with, I admitted, as I do now—*I possess no legal "credentials." Therefore, I am not "competent" to engage in the "practice" of law.* I am however an *AFRICAN*. I have felt the brunt of the **ANGLO-AMERICAN LEGAL TRADITION** since the day of my birth. By virtue of the fact of my **AFRICANITY**, I am not "presumed innocent until proven guilty beyond a reasonable doubt," I am *guilty*, with no hope of ever being declared innocent. This would be true— even if I were an attorney or Federal Judge. The **AFRICAN** attorney, Appellate, or **Supreme Court** Justice may wield a small degree of power within the confines of his or her courtroom or chamber! However, can that same person walk out of the courtroom, without being accompanied by a white janitor, and successfully hail a cab?

I am no *attorney*! I am *a pastor*. Many members of the "Bar" or academia, both European and **AFRICAN** *can* and *will* dismiss this book out of hand. But to tell the truth, I couldn't care less what they think or say! I have sat through more arraignments, sentencing hearings, trials, and pre-trial maneuvering sessions than I care to remember. I have sat in those sessions with relatives and parishioners. I have witnessed the overwhelming number of **AFRICAN** defendants, being escorted in by white defense attorneys, who reap the benefits from **AFRICANS** caught within the "system." It makes no difference whether the attorney is for the defense or the prosecution. The white attorneys all belong to the same synagogues, churches, and clubs. They may parry and thrust with each other during "business hours," all at the same time utilizing a mish-mash of Latin phrases judicial "codes," and citing "precedents." But after the **AFRICAN** has been re-shackled and sent back to "holding," or forced to endure the prospect of prison, the same attorneys go out for drinks or snort a few lines of "coke," that same day and toast their good fortune.

In many cases, these distinguished barristers are not the brightest of bulbs. But "membership" does have its privileges! A lack of pigmentation can clothe *cronyism* and call it *qualification*. In some instances all the person has to do is to "show up" and therefore claim his birthright! The late **AFRICAN** Federal Appellate jurist A. Leon Higginbotham, Jr., said this of former Vice-President Dan Quayle,

> [Dan Qualye] was vice-president under George Bush. Do you know how former vice-president and former senator Dan Quayle got into the University of Indiana Law School? He got in on affirmative action, on a special admissions program designed for people who did not score well on the LSATs and had substandard grades but had promise. The law school wanted to experiment, and they accepted twenty students under this program, sixteen of whom were white. So, Dan Quayle gets in on a special admissions program and nobody's arguing that he shouldn't be a lawyer now.... There's an awful lot of hypocrisy. Some of the people who are the most

hostile against affirmative action *are the individuals who have benefited the most from it in other ways!* [Italics Added][4]

The same goes for the "judges." The judges are addressed as "your Honor" in the courtroom, but on the golf course, or at the exclusive club—whose dues are paid at the expense of **AFRICAN** freedom of movement—s/he is "Bill," "Joe," or "Emily."[5] The high number of **AFRICANS** caught up in the American Legal System supports the Euro-American dominated legal profession, from **US Supreme Court** Chief Justice William H. Rehnquist, to the lowliest ambulance chaser! Far too many **AFRICANS** are ignorant of this fact!

What can be said about the attorneys could also be said of the "Law" enforcement persons that make a living by arresting **AFRICAN** persons. On a level social playing field, these white "officers of the court" would be destitute. Most come from mediocre and/or low achieving backgrounds. These "law" enforcement types are usually

---

[4] A. Leon Higginbotham, Jr., "Opening Argument," in *Black Judges on Justice*, edited by Linn Washington (New York: New Press, 1994), 13.

[5] Many of these persons have freakish lifestyles well known to their fellow "legal" operatives. But when they arrive in court, it's all "business." Ahhhhhhhh! What a life! Note the alleged corruption of one Judge Michael Dufficy's Marin County, (California) courtroom. His decisions in court allegedly went in favor of his friend's clients *if* the lawyers had been to one of his parties where he would allegedly parade around his opulent mansion wearing his judge's robe with nothing on underneath! Matt Issacs, "Odor! Odor In The Court," *The SF Weekly*, (San Francisco) 10 October 2000.

from trailer park or rural backgrounds. However, with foolish **AFRICANS** willing to live at variance with the "Law," these "officers of the court," will never worry about starving, missing child support payments, having their homes foreclosed, cars repossessed, or paying the "dope" man. This goes for prosecutors also.[6]

---

[6] One of the more famous instances of prosecutorial drug use was in the case of Assistant **United States** Attorney, Daniel Perlmutter. Perlmutter was a protégé of former New York Mayor, Rudolph Giuliani. He worked for Giuliani, during the mid-1980s, when Giuliani served as **United States** Attorney for New York State's Southern District. Perlmutter was a Phi Beta Kappa graduate of Williams College and New York University Law School. The 29-year-old prosecutor was known as "Mad Dog." He earned this nickname due to his vicious, as well as calculatingly, vindictive "take-no-prisoners" prosecutorial style—especially in *drug* cases. Like most prosecutorial zealots, he had a hidden side. Besides being mentally unbalanced, he free-based cocaine and shot heroin. In 1984, he began paying prostitutes for sex and stole drugs and cash from the evidence safe at the US Attorney's Office. He went so far as to ingest heroin from *one of the cases he was prosecuting*. He even used colleagues' names as he contracted with call girl services. He frequently missed work. For a *five-month period*, he came to work only *twenty five times* (what African Assistant US Attorney could *do that—and keep a job*?). When discovered by his supervisor, Giuliani, he was in his unheated apartment naked and shivering on the floor—*but he was not fired!* However in 1986, he was unceremoniously fired, indicted, tried, and convicted for stealing five pounds of heroin and $41,800.00 from the US Attorney's Office. He was sentenced to *three* (3) years in Federal Prison. Wayne Barrett and Adam Fifield, *Rudy: An Investigative Biography of Rudolph Giuliani*, (New York: Basic Books, 2000), 140-141. Parenthetically speaking, one wonders if he would have gotten as many breaks as he did, or the relatively short prison time—if he were *African*. The same goes for Federal Investigators; especially the Nation's "elite" law enforcement agency—*the FBI!* Of late, revelations have surfaced concerning alleged spying by a member one of the FBI's most secret directorates, counterintelligence. Special Agent Robert Phillip Hanssen, a veteran of nearly a quarter century with the Bureau was recently arrested after allegedly spying for the former Soviet Union and Russian

Said one **AFRICAN** prisoner,

> One thing to always keep in mind is that the Euro-American attorney who is supposed to defend and protect your rights is in fact a "sworn officer of the court." S/he is quick to advise you, "Why, you'll never see the light of day! *Take the deal! It's a good deal. With time off for good behavior you'll be back out in a few years,*" S/he is no more than an incompetent actor with mediocre legal abilities. S/he plays that part again and again. It's his or her job to ensure that the wheels of injustice continue to spin smoothly. S/he is the golfing buddy of the judge, the cousin of the prosecutor. S/he may have been a prosecutor once. They lunch together every afternoon. Their children attend the same private schools. They belong to the same exclusive social and civic clubs; they may even engage in group sex and other sexual deviancies during their "down time." When you deal with them, you may think you are dealing with *your* friend, but in reference to you, they are not dealing with *their* friend! You are fighting for your life, but to them, you represent a

---

Federation for fifteen years. He had *never* been given a polygraph test or been subject to internal oversight/review. After al, why should he have been? He was a member of the "club." A devout Roman Catholic, he even worshiped at the exclusive Saint Catherine of Siena Catholic Church located in Great Falls, Virginia with the likes of his supervisor former **FBI Director** Louis Freeh and **US Supreme Court** Justice Antonin Scalia. He was classified as being "one of us," (a trusted *white* insider), why should he have been a suspect? He fit the profile of a "loyal" agent. It was taken for granted that he was a "good guy!" He was virulently anti-Communist and a "prude." Whenever fellow agents would go to strip clubs, he would always absent himself! Phillip Shenon, "Colleagues Say the FBI Agent Accused of Spying Decried 'Godless Communists,'" (Reprinted from the *New York Times*), *San Jose Mercury News*, 25 February 2001, 20A. Space will not permit a comprehensive listing of "law breaking" law enforcers that arrest **AFRICANS** and commit crimes simultaneously.

mortgage payment, child support, an illicit drug payment or a vacation! If you refuse to accept the "deal," and have the effrontery to go to trial, there will be hell to pay for having the nerve to buck the accepted system of things. The wheels of "justice" will then begin to turn on you! You won't be dealt with fairly because you cannot afford adequate legal representation. Your defense counsel may even snooze in court during trial. You will not be afforded a jury of your peers. The legal terms they use are spoken in a language you don't understand—Latin. "Precedents" will be cited, your arresting officer will be afforded the opportunity to sit in court and intimidate witnesses. Witnesses will be coached in what to say. Hand signals are given and passwords are spoken. Objections are over-ruled by the judge with a nod and a sly wink. You sit in the midst of a Masonic style ritual. As Chief Justice Roger B. Taney said in the case of *Scott v. Sandford*, you have "no rights that are bound to be respected." (1856)

The American Legal System also has a profitable side to it. This same prisoner relates,

Today's modern prisons are factories. High-grade products are being assembled in America's prisons. Multinational corporations view prisons as being a cheap source(s) of labor. These facilities are non-union sweatshops! One good example of prisoner labor exploitation is Ohio Penal Industries (OPI). OPI maintains factories in nearly all of Ohio's twenty-seven prisons. It reaps huge profits from the products it sells to the public, because it pays prisoners substandard wages. It's supposedly a job "training" program, but it does not assist in job placement when the inmates are paroled. There are no unions, and there is no form of workman's compensation if prisoners are injured while working. The average pay for an inmate worker is less than $50 a month for 40 hours workweeks. Several volumes could be devoted to the practices of OPI, but let it suffice here to say that OPI's competitors complained that they could not compete with OPI's prices because OPI maintains an almost zero per cent labor cost.

Recently, analysis has shown it is more cost effective for the corporations to own the prisons (and the Black people in them). The advantage to these companies running these private prisons is that they can profit from the inmate labor pool. They may, in turn, contract with outside companies to produce goods using inmate labor. Since the majority of people incarcerated are Black, we can make the connection between this form of labor exploitation and the chain gangs of the past. Make no mistake about it—slavery lives! [7]

---

[7] There are definite economic benefits to be realized by increasing the African male jail and prison population. After all, there is money to be made and jobs to be created with the construction of additional jails and prisons! There are support services that go along with imprisonment, i.e., uniforms for prisoners and guards, janitorial supplies, food for the inmates and staff. Concrete, barbed wire, electronic surveillance systems, tear gas, firearms, and pepper spray must be purchased. Imprisonment is more than locking a person up. It is a very profitable enterprise. Jerome G. Miller calls this process, "the Cold War of the 1990s." This "Cold War" of the 1990s has its own version of the Military-Industrial Complex. Miller calls it the "Crime Control-Industrial Complex." With the collapse of Communism, a need arose to continue expenditures that had formerly been directed against the Soviet Union. The Cold War had produced jobs and profits for defense contractors. It was a simple matter then for some of those same contractors to seek conversion of their technologies to domestic use. With their resources now directed towards a domestic market, the target population became, instead of Russians, African Americans, specifically males. The new idea was to warehouse them in high-tech prisons. There is now a great demand for prisons to be built in rural areas. This is due to the economic boom caused by prison construction as well as vending opportunities. This

## *The Actual Texts*

Some of the texts I commented on carry no legal weight.[8] Others, to the detriment of the **AFRICAN** do.[9] The writings that carry, even to this day, *no* legal force, carried a more sinister intent! They laid the philosophical foundation for this documents that did/do carry legal force. The writings of the so-called "Founding Fathers,"[10]

---

assists the local population economically as well as the contractors that profit by warehousing African Men in prison. Jerome G. Miller, *Search and Destroy: African-American Males in the Criminal Justice System* (Cambridge, UK: Cambridge University Press, 1996), 228, 230-231.

[8] The Declaration of Independence (1776), Williams, *No Rights and No Respect*, 25-35, Thomas Jefferson's *Notes on the State of Virginia* (1781-1782), Ibid., 37-39, James Madison's Notes on the **SLAVERY** Debate at the Constitutional Convention (Tuesday, August 22, 1787), Ibid., 40-47, and Abraham Lincoln's Comments on the Dred Scott Decision (1857), Ibid., 138-159.

[9] The **United States** Constitution, Ibid., 48, The **Fugitive Slave Act of 1850**, Ibid., 63-75, The **United States Supreme Court**'s decision in the case of *Scott v. Sanford* (1856), 78, The Emancipation Proclamation (1863), Ibid., 160-168, General William T. Sherman's proclamation granting 40 Acres and a Mule (1865), Ibid., 170-176, The Freedman's Bureau Act (1865), Ibid., 179-182, and Amendments 13-15 to the Constitution (1865-1868), 183-187.

[10] I provided a listing of the "Founding " Fathers in **Appendix B** of *No Rights and No Respect*, 200. The Founding Fathers were a mixed collection of Southern planters and Northern merchants and bankers. A few of them were political "hacks," that, had it not been for the "Revolution," would have faded into historical obscurity. I also wrote, to some perhaps a bit harshly, that "[p]opular mythology would have us believe that the "Revolution" was fought by heroic/selfless individuals sickened by the

whether they are legal documents or not, in the strictest sense of the word, are but reflections of each other! You could not have a **United States** Constitution, and not have a Declaration of Independence, or Thomas Jefferson's *Notes*! After all, the same mind, Jefferson's, that produced the Declaration in 1776 authored the *Notes* from 1781-1782!

Without a Dred Scott Decision (1856), Lincoln would never have had opportunity or need to make his comments on the case in 1857. His discussion of the Dred Scott case in his famous debates with Stephen Douglas assisted him in his successful drive to the White House in 1860.[11]

---

injustice of British rule over its thirteen colonies. The lofty words calling for "Freedom," were qualified by the notion of the colonials that persons of **AFRICAN** descent were to be tolerated as necessary evils at best or thought to be sub-human beings fit only for cotton, tobacco, and sugar cultivation.... The familiar colonial cry of "taxation without representation is tyranny" rings a bit hollow when looked at closely. The taxes levied against the colonials by the British parliament were done for the sake of paying for the large contingent of British troops needed to protect the colonials from French and Native American attacks. Then there was the Spanish presence to be taken into consideration. The Spanish occupied territories such as Florida, which bordered Georgia and South Carolina, as well as vast tracts of land west of the Mississippi River. This meant that the British government was merely asking the colonials to assist in offsetting the cost of their *own* defense! By "doing the math," the colonials figured that they could displace the *British* colonial establishment with their *own*, tax their *own* people, provide for their *own* defense, produce their *own* goods, slaughter the Native American and enslave the **AFRICAN**—and most importantly, *not share the proceeds with anyone*! Ibid., 25-26.

[11] Ibid., 138-159.

## *Twisting In The Wind: The US Constitution and the AFRICAN*

The same could be said about the documents that *do* carry legal force. The **United States** Constitution serves as the legal template for American society. From this written text flow the draconian powers of the Federal Government.

## *The ANGLO-AMERICAN LEGAL TRADITION: A Definition*

The Anglo (English)-American Legal Tradition could be defined as follows. It is a government-sponsored system of "justice." It arose out of the English experience perhaps going as far back at the $12^{th}$ Century with the signing of the *Magna Carta* (Latin for the *Great Charter*). It also arose out the English tradition of "common law." It is adversarial in nature. This is why in court cases, you will see contending parties (adversaries) as *X v* (ersus) *Y* (for example—*Plessy v. Ferguson*).

In this system, a minimum of two parties, the "plaintiff" and the "defendant" stand before a "judge" and fight each other through legal representatives (lawyers). The "plaintiff" is usually the person or institution to file a "complaint" in "court." Either party can be an individual or a corporate body. The majority of times whenever an **AFRICAN** stands within the context of this system, s/he is the "defendant," the government, i.e., the "State of..." or the **United States** of America is the "plaintiff." The "defendant" has the choice as to whether to be "tried" by a jury (6-12 persons) or by the trial judge.

The "system" also has built into it a complex system of "appeals." An "Appeal," is made to a court of superior jurisdiction. Appellate Courts are superior to trial courts. The ultimate appellate court in the **United States** is the **US Supreme Court**. As we will see, the "appellate" system is no friend to the **AFRICAN**. Depending upon whom sits on the "bench," whether at the "trial" or "appellate" level, the **AFRICAN'S** "status" rests in their hands! *Twist! Twist! Twist!*

**AFRICANS** have attempted to address this sorry state of affairs in a variety of manners. As they addressed their condition, the response met with indifference (see Thomas Jefferson's response to Benjamin Banneker), armed force (as in the case of Nat Turner's insurrection in 1831), or the judicial process (see *Scott v. Sandford* and *Plessy v. Ferguson*)!

At the risk of redundancy, allow me to paraphrase with ***bold emphasis*** what I said previously! *What many **AFRICANS** fail to understand is that the <u>American legal system</u>, is the monstrous child of the <u>English system of law</u>. The <u>English</u> version is a Byzantine system of adversarial combat articulated through laws passed by the British Parliament, enforced by Royal Governors, and judges, arrests, arraignments, charges, juries, grand juries, verdicts, etc. <u>It was its transplantation onto American soil during America's colonial period (1607-</u>*

***1781) that set the tone for our awkward position (TWISTING IN THE WIND!).***

In such a system, someone must *win* and someone must *lose!* The stakes involved are granting or limiting physical movement (jail, prison, parole, or probation), seizure or attachment of assets (money or property), or termination of life by means other than natural (execution).

As you will see as we explore the various documents related to the "Tradition" the **AFRICAN**, by definition, is a non-person. This was perhaps best articulated by **United States Supreme Court**'s Chief Justice Roger Brooke Taney who piously, as well as *legally*, droned, as only a member of the Federal Judiciary could, in writing the majority opinion in the Dred Scott case (1856). In the Scott case, he declared that **AFRICANS** had no rights to be respected.[12]

Notice how he carefully designates the **AFRICAN'S** inferiority via English *Socio-Legal **TRADITION***:

> [**AFRICANS**] had for more than a century before been regarded as beings of an inferior order, and altogether unfit to associate with the white race, either in social or political relations; and so far inferior, that they had no rights which the white man was bound to respect; and that the [**AFRICAN**] might justly and lawfully be reduced to **SLAVERY** for his benefit. He was bought and sold, and

---

[12] For the full text of the Dred Scott Decision, see Williams, *No Rights and No Respect*, 77-136.

treated as an ordinary article of merchandise and traffic, whenever a profit could be made by it. This opinion was at that time fixed and universal in the civilized portion of the white race. It was regarded as an axiom in morals as well as in politics, which no one thought of disputing, or supposed to be open to dispute; and men in every grade and position in society daily and habitually acted upon it in their private pursuits, as well as in matters of public concern, without doubting for a moment the correctness of this opinion.

***And in no nation was this opinion more firmly fixed or more uniformly acted upon than by the English Government and English people***. They not only seized them on the coast of AFRICA, and sold them or held them in SLAVERY for their own use; but they took them as ordinary articles of merchandise to every country where they could make a profit on them, and were far more extensively engaged in this commerce than any other nation in the world.[13]

## *The Arbitrary Nature of the Tradition*

The "Tradition," as articulated through the American Legal System, is arbitrary. It can decide our status *at will*. It can designate us "slaves." It can designate us "free." It can designate us "guilty." It can designate us "innocent." In

---

[13] This is perhaps one of the more infamous passages in Chief Justice Taney's document. Based upon his careful reading of British and Colonial tradition, the relationship between **AFRICANS** and Europeans, and his understanding of the intent of the framers of the **CONSTITUION**, he boldly states that **AFRICANS** have absolutely no rights that a **WHITE** is bound to respect.

other words, via the **US Constitution** used as a rope, we *Twist* in American Society's *wind*!

Seven years after the Dred Scott decision (1856), with the authority vested in him as the President of the **United States**, Abraham Lincoln issued the Emancipation Proclamation (1863).[14] This was a politically inspired wartime measure, not a freedom charter for the slaves! It was issued so as to prevent France and Great Britain from entering the Civil War on the side of the rebellious Southern states![15] In fact, the proclamation *excluded* the so-called Border States (Delaware, Kentucky, Maryland, and Missouri). While they were slave-holding states, they were firmly under Union control! Lincoln's proclamation was to take "effect" only in those areas that were under Confederate control—where he had *no* authority![16] ***Twist! Twist! Twist!***

Twelve years later, Congress passed a sweeping piece of legislation entitled, the **Civil Rights Act of 1875**. President U.S. Grant signed this measure into law. Eight years later the **Supreme Court** declared the Act *unconstitutional* (1883). Thirteen years later the Court declared that it was Constitutional for the **AFRICAN** to be excluded from the mainstream of American life in the case of *Plessy v. Ferguson* (1896). Sixty years later, the same body

---

[14] For the full text, and analysis of the Emancipation Proclamation, see Williams, *No Rights and No Respect*, 160-168

[15] Ibid.

[16] Ibid.

effectively reversed itself in *Brown v. the Board of Education* (1954). ***Twist! Twist! Twist!***

For this cause, I call America's predatory, as well as capricious, system of "justice," the noose that we hang from as we ***literally twist in America's wind***. Like so many of our lynched brothers and sisters whose rotting corpses were left to "twist" in the wind from their broken necks, we also "swing." The simple fact is that if "rights" can be granted, they can also be taken away! "Rights" *granted*→***Twist***, "Rights" *taken away*, ***Twist! Twist! Twist!***

A scholar of rare objectivity, Carter G. Woodson (1875-1950), founder of the Association for the Study of Negro Life and History could, remark in 1921, as he took an objective look at the irony of America's high sounding phrases concerning "liberty and justice for all,"

> The citizenship of the [**AFRICAN**] in this country is a **fiction.** The Constitution of the **United States** guarantees to him every right vouchsafed to any individual by the most liberal democracy on the face of the earth [!]...but despite the unusual powers of the Federal Government, this agent of the body politic has studiously evaded the duty of safe guarding the rights of the [**AFRICAN**] {Italics Added}[17]

---

[17] Carter G. Woodson, "Fifty Years of Negro Citizenship as Qualified by the **United States Supreme Court**." *Journal of Negro History* 6:1 (January 1921): 1.

Far too many **AFRICANS** are ignorant of the fact that anything the Federal Government does is *legal, binding* and *authorized* if passed by Congress, signed into law by the President and never challenged in the **Supreme Court**! Even if it *is* challenged, if the **Supreme Court** declares the law to be constitutional, it stands! Many injustices that rival the horrors of Nazi Germany were/are carried on under the authority of the Federal Government, the Tuskegee Experiment, (1932-1972) is a prime example![18] ***Twist! Twist! Twist!***

It is a shame that **AFRICANS**, regardless as to what side of the "Law" they stand on, are by the fact of their **AFRICANITY**, targets for the "Law!" Every time an **AFRICAN** is arrested, does the arresting, is arraigned, presides over the arraignment, is tried, presides over the trial, is sentenced, or presides over the sentencing, the roles are irrelevant! America is a huge prison! So as the **AFRICAN** judge sentences the **AFRICAN** defendant, s/he is being sentenced also! One goes to jail or prison and the other can't get a cab or is stopped by a "Law" Enforcement

---

[18] In the "study," African men, infected with syphilis, were never told of their condition. Instead their condition was allowed to go untreated for nearly forty years, while the effects of the disease were "studied." They were only told that they had "bad blood." James H. Jones, *Bad Blood: The Tuskegee Syphilis Experiment* (New York: The Free Press, 1993), ix-x, 1. This revelation has caused many observers to believe that the AIDS virus was developed by the government to eradicate African peoples, Ibid. Also, Haki R. Madhubuti, *Black Men Obsolete, Single, Dangerous?: Afrikan-American Families in Transition: Essays in Discovery, Solution and Hope* (Chicago: Third World Press, 1991), 51-57.

official for ***Driving While Black*** (DWB)! Why? Because s/he fits the "profile." To illustrate this point even further, I am reminded of a movie I saw back in the 1970 entitled *The Watermelon Man*.

The title role was given to the late **AFRICAN** comedian, Godfrey Cambridge. Cambridge began the movie as a White Man. He was a salesman. He despised **AFRICANS**. He lived in the suburbs. He also had a White wife and children. He would often jog to the bus stop every day. One day he woke up and found that while sleeping, he turned black. As he jogged to the bus stop, his formerly friendly neighbors hollered, "get him! *He's running and he's a Negro! He musta done something!"* So it is, even to those **AFRICANS** that the system has afforded a bit of "authority," as they preside over trials or execute arrests. Behind the smiles of their white "colleagues," the thought persists; s/he's a Negro! *S/he musta done something!*

## *The Format*

I will use the same format in this work as was used in *No Rights And No Respect*. I will present the relevant document with commentary. The commentary will point out, through a brief historical sketch and social analysis of the words of the document, that **AFRICANS**, according to these assembled texts are considered to be *less* than nothing! I want to provide the reader with a historical and social ***context*** for understanding America's Sacred ***Texts***!

Persons familiar with my writing style will recognize my preference for "foot notes" over against "end notes."

Finally, as the documents suggest, the **AFRICAN**, via the **ANGLO-AMERICAN LEGAL TRADITION**, has been tried and convicted. S/he is a convict free to wander the grounds of this hi-tech prison called America. But as in any conviction, there is the right to appeal the sentence. At that point, as mentioned earlier, the case moves from the trial court to the appellate court. The appellate court reviews the case and puts its stamp of judicial finality upon the defendants life by, a) refusing to review the case, b) upholding the trial court's findings, c) reversing the conviction, or ordering a new trial. In the case of the **AFRICAN**, we will examine various *appeals*, Benjamin Banneker's *Appeal to Reason*, Nat Turner's and Henry Highland Garnett's *Appeal To Open Revolt*, and Booker T. Washington's *Appeal To America's Pragmatism.* As we will see, all of these *Appeals* fizzled and **AFRICAN** Americans were/are left to *Twist in the Wind* with America's Constitution wrapped around their collective necks.

Many will protest my views as being extreme. They will point to the fact that there are *AFRICAN* judges and justices sitting on various Federal and State benches. *AFRICAN* law enforcement officers, especially Federal! But this is nothing special! Some of the most vicious, as well as skilled, scouts the US Army had on the American Frontier were Native American! They were used to track their brothers and sisters! After they found their brethren, the Army disarmed the scouts and sent them to the reservation along with the Native Americans they had tracked! Jewish "Kapos" kept their Jewish brethren in line in the Nazi death camps! But in the end, they went to the ovens also! As soon as the White man is finished with those **AFRICANS** in the "Big" House, they will be dealt with! In fact they are being "dealt with" as you read these pages!

## Thanks

Last but certainly not least, I want to thank my wife Pat for her encouragement and support. I cannot mention the **AFRICAN** experience in America without extending to my long time friend, Rev. John Brinson, my deepest thanks for his critical review of my manuscript as well as points of discussion! A special thanks goes to the editorial staff, under the skillful supervision of Mrs. Tara Evans Bell of The City Church Publication Society for their patience and editorial skill!

*Pastor Michael S. Williams, D.Min.*
*Bayview Hunters Point*
*San Francisco, California*
*Juneteenth 2001*

## Building The Scaffold

The year was 1619. The place was Jamestown. Jamestown was the first permanent settlement in what would later become the English colony of Virginia. It was this place where **AFRICANS** first made contact with the **ANGLO-AMERICAN LEGAL TRADITION**. English colonists founded Jamestown in 1607. It was named *James*town in honor of the reigning English king, James I. James' name would later be associated with a rather faulty translation of the Bible first published in 1611. In our day, that rather flawed work is known as the *Authorized Version* of the Holy Bible, or *King James Version* of the Bible.

In 1619, a boatload of **AFRICANS**, aboard a Dutch warship, sailed into Jamestown's port and into history. The **AFRICANS** had been taken from a Spanish vessel and deposited by the Dutch at the nearest port of call, which happened to be Jamestown. The English did not immediately make the **AFRICANS** *slaves*, but *indentured servants*. The fact that they were "indentured" meant that they would work on a contract basis for an employer, usually a plantation owner, for a set number of years, usually between 5 and 10 years. After the set period was up, they would be free. In this aspect, they were no different that *white* English men and women that worked the various cotton and tobacco plantations that served as the basis for Virginia's economy. The primary source of English indentured servants were debtors and petty criminals, which spilled out of Britain's prison system. The problem was that there were not enough English men and women to cultivate the tobacco and cotton crops! In quasi-capitalist terms, the agricultural supply exceeded the human resource. Another source of labor was needed! Enter the **AFRICAN**! Africa represented a veritable inexhaustible source of labor! Africa was viewed as a human treasure trove!

English *law* first gave the **AFRICANS** the status of "indentured" servants. English *law* would later give the **AFRICANS** the status of slaves! Indentured status was *temporary*. The status of being a slave was *permanent*. This shift in status was done *legally*! It had the force of *law*! By the late 1600s, the **AFRICANS** in Virginia had been given the *legal* status of *slaves*. The following texts give evidence of how the **AFRICAN** left the ranks of indentured servitude and entered those of **SLAVERY**. This status would exist for the **AFRICAN** from the late 1600s through the end of the colonial period when the Americans, twelve other colonies in addition to Virginia, declared their independence form England in 1776. The political establishment that succeeded the English would continue the practice until it was ended during and immediately after the American Civil War (1861-1865).

If you notice in the following entries, the **AFRICAN'S** status erodes steadily and more importantly, by the year

1630, *legally!* His *skin color* becomes the basis of defining his humanity! This dynamic in the American mind exists even to this day!

The way the "law" worked was as follows: the English parliament, or local colonial assembly (in Virginia's case the House of Burgesses), would pass a law in the name of the king. It was the colonial governor's duty to make sure that the law was enforced. Local judges would preside over cases, and juries would render verdicts. The judge would then pronounce punishment. As it developed, even unto this day, this pattern remains.

It is the Jamestown decrees that set the stage for the **AFRICAN** to *Twist in the Wind!*

"How is it that we hear the loudest *yelps* for liberty among the [enslavers] of Negroes?"

*Samuel Johnson, 18$^{th}$ Century English Writer Commenting Upon American Hypocrisy*

**Twist! Twist! Twist!**

# The Jamestown Laws: The Legal Noose (1630-1699)

## *Sexual Relations Between AFRICANS and Englishmen and Women*

### September 17th, 1630

The following instance shows that one Hugh Davis, apparently white, was publicly flogged for having sexual intercourse with an **AFRICAN** woman. This shows that as early as 1630, a mere eleven years after the arrival of the twenty **AFRICANS** aboard the Dutch warship, that there was a concerted effort on the part of the English political establishment to define the human status of **AFRICANS** over against Englishmen and women.

### The Verdict and Punishment

Hugh Davis to be soundly whipped, before an assembly of Negroes and others for abusing himself to the dishonor of God and shame of Christians, by defiling his body in lying with a Negro; which fault he is to acknowledge next Sabbath day.

## The Legal Status of AFRICAN Children

**December 1662-Act XII.** Negro women's children to serve according to the condition of the mother.

**WHEREAS** some doubts have arrisen whether children got by any Englishman upon a Negro woman should be slave or ffree, Be it therefore enacted and declared by this present grand assembly, that all children borne in this country shalbe held bond or free only according to the condition of the mother, And that if any christian shall committ ffornication with a negro man or woman, hee or shee soe offending shall pay double the ffines imposed by the former act.

### *Baptized Slaves Could Not Be Automatically Freed*

**September 1667-ACT III.** An act declaring that baptisme of slaves doth not exempt them from bondage.

**WHEREAS** some doubts have risen whether children that are slaves by birth, and by the charity and piety of their owners made pertakers of the blessed sacrament of baptisme, should by vertue of their baptisme be made ffree; It is enacted and declared by this grand assembly, and the authority thereof, that the conferring of baptisme doth not alter the condition of the person as to his bondage or ffreedome; that diverse masters, ffreed from this doubt, may more carefully endeavour the propagation of christianity by permitting children, though slaves, or those of greater growth if capable to be admitted to that sacrament.

## There Will Be No Punishment For The Beating, Fatal Or Otherwise, Of An AFRICAN

**October 1669-ACT I.** An act about the casuall killing of slaves.

**WHEREAS** the only law in force for the punishment of refractory servants resisting their master, mistris or overseer cannot be inflicted upon negroes, nor the obstinacy of many of them by other then violent meanes supprest, Be it enacted and declared by this grand assembly, if any slave resist his master (or other by his masters order correcting him) and by the extremity of the correction should chance to die, that his death shall not be accompted ffelony, but the master (or that other person appointed by the master to punish him) be acquit from molestation, since it cannot be presumed that prepensed malice (which alone makes murther ffelony) should induce any man to destroy his owne estate.

## *It Is Now Legal To Kill Runaway White Indentured Servants, Enslaved AFRICANS And Native Americans*

**September 1672-ACT VIII**. An act for the apprehension and suppression of runawayes, negroes and slaves.

**FORASMUCH** as it hath beene manifested to this grand assembly that many negroes have lately beene, and now are out in rebellion in sundry parts of this country, and that noe meanes have yet beene found for the apprehension and suppression of them from whome many mischeifes of very dangerous consequence may arise to the country if either other negroes, Indians or servants should happen to fly forth and joyne with them; for the prevention of which, be it enacted by the governour, councell and burgesses of this grand assembly, and by the authority thereof, that if any negroe, molatto, Indian slave, or servant for life, runaway and shalbe persued by the warrant or hue and crye, it shall and may be lawfull for any person who shall endeavour to take them, upon the resistance of such negroe, molatto, Indian slave, or servant for life, to kill or wound him or them soe resisting; Provided alwayes, and it is the true intent and meaning hereof, that such negroe, molatto, Indian slave, or servant for life, be named and described in the hue and crye which is alsoe to be signed by the master or owner of the said runaway. And if it happen that such negroe, molatto, Indian slave, or servant for life doe dye of any wound in such their resistance received the master or owner of such shall receive satisfaction from the publique for his negroe, molatto, Indian slave, or servant for life, soe killed or dyeing of such wounds; and the person who shall kill or wound by virtue of any such hugh and crye any such soe resisting in manner as aforesaid shall not be questioned for the same, he forthwith giveing notice thereof and returning the hue and crye or warrant to the master or owner of him or them soe killed or wounded or to the next justice of peace. And it is further enacted by the authority aforesaid that all such negroes and slaves shalbe valued at ffowre thousand five hundred pounds of tobacco and caske a peece, and Indians at three thousand pounds of tobacco and caske a peice, And further if it shall happen that any negroe, molatto, Indians slave or servant for life, in such their resistance to receive any wound whereof they may not happen to dye, but shall lye any considerable tyme sick and disabled, then alsoe the master or owner of the same soe sick or disabled shall receive from the publique a reasonable satisfaction for such damages as they shall make appeare they have susteyned thereby at the county court, who shall thereupon grant the master or owner a certificate to the next assembly of what damages they shall make appeare; And it is further enacted that the neighbouring Indians doe and hereby are required and enjoyned to seize and apprehend all runawayes whatsoever that shall happen to come amongst them, and to bring them before some justice of the peace whoe upon the receipt of such servants, slave, or slaves, from the Indians, shall pay unto the said Indians for a recompence twenty armes length of Roanoake or the value thereof in goods as the Indians shall like of, for which the said justice of peace shall receive from the publique two hundred and fifty pounds of tobacco, and the said justice to proceed in conveying the runaway to his master according to the law in such cases already provided; This act to continue in force till the next assembly and noe longer unlesse it be thought fitt to continue.

## *Penalties For Resisting Arrest And Disrespecting A White Person*

**June 1680-ACT X**. An act for preventing Negroes Insurrections.

**WHEREAS** the frequent meeting of considerbale numbers of negroe slaves under pretence of feasts and burialls is judged of dangerous consequence; for prevention whereof for the future, Bee it enacted by the kings most excellent majestie by and with the consent of the generall assembly, and it is hereby enacted by the authority aforesaid, that from and after the publication of this law, it shall not be lawfull for any negroe or other slave to carry or arme himselfe with any club, staffe, gunn, sword or any other weapon of defence or offence, nor to goe or depart from of his masters ground without a certificate from his master, mistris or overseer and such permission not to be granted but upon perticuler and necessary occasions; and every negroe or slave soe offending not haveing a certificate as aforesaid shalbe sent to the next constable, who is hereby enjoyned and required to give the said negroe twenty lashes on his bare back well layd on, and soe sent home to his said master, mistris or overseer. And it is further enacted by the authority aforesaid that if any negroe or other slave shall presume to lift up his hand in opposition against any christian, shall for every such offence, upon due proofe made thereof by the oath of the party before a magistrate, have and receive thirty lashes on his bare back well laid on. And it is hereby further enacted by the authority aforesaid that if any negroe or other slave shall absent himself from his masters service and lye hid and lurking in obscure places, comitting injuries to the inhabitants, and shall resist any person or persons that shalby any lawfull authority by imployed to apprehend and take the said negroe, that then in case of such resistance, it shalbe lawfull for such person or persons to kill the said negroe or slave soe lying out and resisting, and that this law be once every six months published at the respective county courts and parish churches within this colony.

### A Law Restricting The Free Movement Of Slaves

**November 1682-ACT III.** An additional act for the better preventing insurrections by Negroes.

**WHEREAS** a certaine act of assembly held at James Citty the 8th day of June, in the yeare of our Lord 1680, intituled, an act preventing negroes insurrections hath not had its intended effect for want of due notice thereof being taken; it is enacted by the governour, councell and burgesses of this generall assembly, and by the authority thereof, that for the better putting the said act in due execution, the church wardens of each parish in this country at the charge of the parish by the first day of January next provide true coppies of this present and the aforesaid act, and make or cause entry thereof to be made in the register book of the said parish, and that the minister or reader of each parish shall twice every yeare vizt. some one Sunday or Lords day in each of the months of September and March in each parish church or chappell of ease in each parish in the time of divine service, after the reading of the second lesson, read and publish both this present and the aforerecited act under paine such churchwarden minister or reader makeing default, to forfeite each of them six hundred pounds of tobacco, one halfe to the informer and the other halfe to the use of the poore of the said parish. And for the further better preventing such insurrections by negroes or slaves, Bee it likewise enacted by the authority aforesaid, that noe master or overseer knowingly permitt or suffer, without the leave or licence of his or their master or overseer, any negroe or slave not properly belonging to him or them, to remaine or be upon his or their plantation above the space of four houres at any one time, contrary to the intent of the aforerecited act upon paine to forfeite, being thereof lawfully convicted, before some one justice of peace within the county where the fact shall be comitted, by the oath of two witnesses at the least, the summe of two hundred pounds of tobacco in cask for each time soe offending to him or them that will sue for the same, for which the said justice is hereby impowered to award judgment and execution.

## Severe Penalties For Theft Of The Master's Live Stock

**April 1699-ACT VI.** An act for the punishment of slaves for the first and second offence of Hog stealing.

**WHEREAS** the third act of assembly made at James Citty the 16th day of Aprill 1691, entituled an act for the more speedy prosecution of slaves commiting capitall crimes hath been found inconvenient by makeing the first offence of hog stealing felony, which is not so by the former laws of this his majestyes colony and dominion.

Be it therefore enacted by the Governour, Councell and Burgesses of this present Generall Assembly, and the authority thereof, and it is hereby enacted, That for the first offence of hog stealing commited by a negro or slave he shall be carried before a justice of the peace of the county where the fact was commited before whome being convicted of the said offence by one evidence or by his owne confession he shall by order of the said justice receive on his bare back thirty nine lashes well laid on, and for the second offence such negro or slave upon conviction before a court of record shall stand two hours in the pillory and have both his eares nailed thereto and at the expiration of the said two hours have his ears cutt off close by the nailes, any thing in the aforesaid act or in any other law to the contrary in any wise notwithstanding.

## *Children Born to AFRICAN Women to Be Considered Slaves For Life*

**December 1662-Act XII**. Negro womens children to serve according to the condition of the mother.

**WHEREAS** some doubts have arrisen whether children got by any Englishman upon a negro woman should be slave or ffree, Be it therefore enacted and declared by this present grand assembly, that all children borne in this country shalbe held bond or free only according to the condition of the mother, And that if any christian shall committ ffornication with a negro man or woman, hee or shee soe offending shall pay double the ffines imposed by the former act.

## *Becoming a Christian Will Not Be Grounds For Freeing an AFRICAN Slave*

**September 1667-ACT III**. An act declaring that baptisme of slaves doth not exempt them from bondage.

**WHEREAS** some doubts have risen whether children that are slaves by birth, and by the charity and piety of their owners made pertakers of the blessed sacrament of baptisme, should by vertue of their baptisme be made ffree; It is enacted and declared by this grand assembly, and the authority thereof, that the conferring of baptisme doth not alter the condition of the person as to his bondage or ffreedome; that diverse masters, ffreed from this doubt, may more carefully endeavour the propagation of christianity by permitting children, though slaves, or those of greater growth if capable to be admitted to that sacrament.

## *Killing An AFRICAN as A Matter of Punishment*

**October 1669-ACT I.** An act about the casuall killing of slaves.

**WHEREAS** the only law in force for the punishment of refractory servants resisting their master, mistris or overseer cannot be inflicted upon negroes, nor the obstinacy of many of them by other then violent meanes supprest, Be it enacted and declared by this grand assembly, if any slave resist his master (or other by his masters order correcting him) and by the extremity of the correction should chance to die, that his death shall not be accompted ffelony, but the master (or that other person appointed by the master to punish him) be acquit from molestation, since it cannot be presumed that prepensed malice (which alone makes murther ffelony) should induce any man to destroy his owne estate.

## *Dealing With Runaway AFRICANS*

**September 1672-ACT VIII.** An act for the apprehension and suppression of runawayes, negroes and slaves.

**FORASMUCH** as it hath beene manifested to this grand assembly that many negroes have lately beene, and now are out in rebellion in sundry parts of this country, and that noe meanes have yet beene found for the apprehension and suppression of them from whome many mischeifes of very dangerous consequence may arise to the country if either other negroes, Indians or servants should happen to fly forth and joyne with them; for the prevention of which, be it enacted by the governour, councell and burgesses of this grand assembly, and by the authority thereof, that if any negroe, molatto, Indian slave, or servant for life, runaway and shalbe persued by the warrant or hue and crye, it shall and may be lawfull for any person who shall endeavour to take them, upon the resistance of such negroe, molatto, Indian slave, or servant for life, to kill or wound him or them soe resisting; Provided alwayes, and it is the true intent and meaning hereof, that such negroe, molatto, Indian slave, or servant for life, be named and described in the hue and crye which is alsoe to be signed by the master or owner of the said runaway. And if it happen that such negroe, molatto, Indian slave, or servant for life doe dye of any wound in such their resistance received the master or owner of such shall receive satisfaction from the publique for his negroe, molatto, Indian slave, or servant for life, soe killed or dyeing of such wounds; and the person who shall kill or wound by virtue of any such hugh and crye any such soe resisting in manner as aforesaid shall not be questioned for the same, he forthwith giveing notice thereof and returning the hue and crye or warrant to the master or owner of him or them soe killed or wounded or to the next justice of peace. And it is further enacted by the authority aforesaid that all such negroes and slaves shalbe valued at ffowre thousand five hundred pounds of tobacco and caske a peece, and Indians at three thousand pounds of tobacco and caske a peice, And further if it shall happen that any negroe, molatto, Indians slave or servant for life, in such their resistance to receive any wound whereof they may not happen to dye, but shall lye any considerable tyme sick and disabled, then alsoe the master or owner of the same soe sick or disabled shall receive from the publique a reasonable satisfaction for such damages as they shall make appeare they have susteyned thereby at the county court, who shall thereupon grant the master or owner a certificate to the next assembly of what damages they shall make appeare; And it is further enacted that the neighbouring Indians doe and hereby are required and enjoyned to seize and apprehend all runawayes whatsoever that shall happen to come amongst them, and to bring them before some justice of the peace whoe upon the receipt of such servants, slave, or slaves, from the Indians, shall pay unto the said Indians for a recompence twenty armes length of Roanoake or the value thereof in goods as the Indians shall like of, for which the said justice of peace shall receive from the publique two hundred and fifty pounds of tobacco, and the said justice to proceed in conveying the runaway to his master according to the law in such cases already provided;

This act to continue in force till the next assembly and noe longer unlesse it be thought fitt to continue.

## *An Act Restricting the Free Movement of AFRICANS Pro-Active Suppression of Rebellions*

**June 1680-ACT X.** An act for preventing Negroes Insurrections.

**WHEREAS** the frequent meeting of considerbale numbers of negroe slaves under pretence of feasts and burialls is judged of dangerous consequence; for prevention whereof for the future, Bee it enacted by the kings most excellent majestie by and with the consent of the generall assembly, and it is hereby enacted by the authority aforesaid, that from and after the publication of this law, it shall not be lawfull for any negroe or other slave to carry or arme himselfe with any club, staffe, gunn, sword or any other weapon of defence or offence, nor to goe or depart from of his masters ground without a certificate from his master, mistris or overseer and such permission not to be granted but upon perticuler and necessary occasions; and every negroe or slave soe offending not haveing a certificate as aforesaid shalbe sent to the next constable, who is hereby enjoyned and required to give the said negroe twenty lashes on his bare back well layd on, and soe sent home to his said master, mistris or overseer. And it is further enacted by the authority aforesaid that if any negroe or other slave shall presume to lift up his hand in opposition against any christian, shall for every such offence, upon due proofe made thereof by the oath of the party before a magistrate, have and receive thirty lashes on his bare back well laid on. And it is hereby further enacted by the authority aforesaid that if any negroe or other slave shall absent himself from his masters service and lye hid and lurking in obscure places, comitting injuries to the inhabitants, and shall resist any person or persons that shalby any lawfull authority by imployed to apprehend and take the said negroe, that then in case of such resistance, it shalbe lawfull for such person or persons to kill the said negroe or slave soe lying out and resisting, and that this law be once every six months published at the respective county courts and parish churches within this colony.

### More Restrictions on Movement

**November 1682-ACT III.** An additional act for the better preventing insurrections by Negroes.

**WHEREAS** a certaine act of assembly held at James Citty the 8th day of June, in the yeare of our Lord 1680, intituled, an act preventing negroes insurrections hath not had its intended effect for want of due notice thereof being taken; it is enacted by the governour, councell and burgesses of this generall assembly, and by the authority thereof, that for the better putting the said act in due execution, the church wardens of each parish in this country at the charge of the parish by the first day of January next provide true coppies of this present and the aforesaid act, and make or cause entry thereof to be made in the register book of the said parish, and that the minister or reader of each parish shall twice every yeare vizt. some one Sunday or Lords day in each of the months of September and March in each parish church or chappell of ease in each parish in the time of divine service, after the reading of the second lesson, read and publish both this present and the aforerecited act under paine such churchwarden minister or reader makeing default, to forfeite each of them six hundred pounds of tobacco, one halfe to the informer and the other halfe to the use of the poore of the said parish. And for the further better preventing such insurrections by negroes or slaves, Bee it likewise enacted by the authority aforesaid, that nce master or overseer knowingly permitt or suffer, without the leave or licence of his or their master or overseer, any negroe or slave not properly belonging to him or them, to remaine or be upon his or their plantation above the space of four houres at any one time, contrary to the intent of the aforerecited act upon paine to forfeite, being thereof lawfully convicted, before some one justice of peace within the county where the fact shall be comitted, by the oath of two witnesses at the least, the summe of two hundred pounds of tobacco in cask for each time soe offending to him or them that will sue for the same, for which the said justice is hereby impowered to award judgment and execution.

## *Dealing With Theft of Live Stock by AFRICANS*

**April 1699-ACT VI.** An act for the punishment of slaves for the first and second offence of Hog stealing.

**WHEREAS** the third act of assembly made at James Citty the 16th day of Aprill 1691, entituled an act for the more speedy prosecution of slaves commiting capitall crimes hath been found inconvenient by makeing the first offence of hog stealing felony, which is not so by the former laws of this his majestyes colony and dominion.
Be it therefore enacted by the Governour, Councell and Burgesses of this present Generall Assembly, and the authority thereof, and it is hereby enacted, That for the first offence of hog stealing commited by a negro or slave he shall be carried before a justice of the peace of the county where the fact was commited before whome being convicted of the said offence by one evidence or by his owne confession he shall by order of the said justice receive on his bare back thirty nine lashes well laid on, and for the second offence such negro or slave upon conviction before a court of record shall stand two hours in the pillory and have both his eares nailed thereto and at the expiration of the said two hours have his ears cutt off close by the nailes, any thing in the aforesaid act or in any other law to the contrary in any wise notwithstanding.

## Benjamin Banneker's Appeal To Thomas Jefferson (1791)

Benjamin Banneker (1731-1806) was a true genius. Had he not been an **AFRICAN**, his talents would have taken him to the loftiest heights of America's scientific pantheon. Banneker was born in the Baltimore area of Maryland. His grandmother was an English woman that, for reasons unknown, broke social convention and married one of her slaves. Their daughter was Benjamin's mother.

He was raised in the Quaker/pacifist tradition. He was a self-taught scientist, agronomist, and astronomer. He had the distinction of building the first clock in the New World in 1753. It kept perfect time for forty years.

His agricultural genius helped him develop crops that kept the American Army from starving during the Revolutionary War. Perhaps his greatest achievement was to save the young American republic from embarrassment. Thomas Jefferson suggested that Banneker be placed on the commission tasked to design and construct the new capital located at what would be known as Washington, DC.

In 1791, the French Army officer in charge of the project, a certain Major L'Enfant, suddenly returned to France due to a pay dispute with the (George) Washington Administration. L'Enfant also took the plans for the city with him! Banneker literally saved the day. He had memorized the plans and reproduced them from memory in a matter of two days! The configuration of the nation's new capital was saved! In fact, to this day, Washington D.C. retains the basic configuration given it by Banneker.

One would think that this would have ingratiated him with the Government! He may have even thought of himself as an "insider!" Surely he could appeal to his fellow scientist, Secretary of State Thomas Jefferson! He had, by sheer force of mind, saved the new nation from embarrassment! He probably felt that his heroic deed would "prove" from a rational standpoint that the **AFRICAN** needed to have equal share in the fruits of the new nation. He knew that, by law, the **ANGLO-AMERICAN LEGAL TRADITION** condemned him! As an **AFRICAN**, he would *appeal* the **AFRICAN'S** sentence of death! He would appeal it and win! He would *appeal* the sentence to a fellow scientist! Thomas Jefferson! Surely a man of letters like Jefferson would understand what smaller minds could not! It is not known if Banneker knew of Jefferson's low opinion of **AFRICANS**[1]

In the summer of 1791, he wrote an appeal to Thomas Jefferson on behalf of **AFRICANS**. Jefferson's reply, which follows, is short patronizing and to the point! Judge for yourself! The, appeal filed in the court of reason, was

---

[1] Jefferson, like Washington, was a slave-holding Virginian. For a brief list and commentary on his writings, both public as well as private, see the following citations in *No Rights and No Respect*. The Declaration of Independence, 25-35, and most importantly his *Notes On The State Of Virginia*, (1781-1782), 37-39. He also played a major role in crafting the Constitution—which designated **AFRICANS** as 3/5 human, 48-62!

rejected! In fact, two years later the **Fugitive Slave Act of 1793** was signed into law by George Washington.[2] Washington signed the Act into law while presiding over the government in the city Banneker saved! *Twist! Twist! Twist!*

---

[2] Though we do not have a written record of Banneker's thoughts concerning Jefferson's patronizing rebuff, suffice it to say, this was not to be the last time **AFRICANS** would seek to "fit-in" relative to their perceived collegial relationship with the Federal Government! Harold L. Wallace wrote an extensive survey of the problems facing **AFRICANS** that try to make a career or just a living by being employed by the Federal Government! In a volume aptly entitled, *Federal Plantation: Affirmative In-Action Within our Federal Government*, he painfully relates the agony of **AFRICANS** that attempt to advance within the ranks of the **Federal Bureau of Investigation** and the **National Security Agency**! Wallace details how **AFRICAN** employees of these agencies, charged with seeking and neutralizing "evil doers, and spies," are constantly at war with their agencies by attempting to prove their worth to their employer! Harold L. Wallace, *Federal Plantation: Affirmative In-Action Within our Federal Government*, (Edgewood, MD: Duncan & Duncan, Publishers, 1996), 52-61. Wallace isn't the only African that attempts to chronicle the experiences of *Ne-grooooooooooows* that have crashed and burned in American Society due to their naïve belief that "doing a good job" would allow them an equal footing within their agency. Those writers are as follows, Paul M. Barrnett, *The Good Black: A True Story of Race in America*, (New York: E.P. Hutton, 1999), Joseph Jett, *Black and White on Wall Street: The Untold Story of the Man Wrongly Accused of Bringing Down Kidder Peabody* (New York: William Morrow and Company, 1999), Howard L. Wallace, *Federal Plantation: Affirmative (In) Action Within Our Federal Government* (Edgewood, MD: Duncan & Duncan Publishers, 1996) and Tyrone Power's *Eyes to My Soul: The Rise or Decline of a Black FBI Agent* (Dover, MA: The Majority Press). Bruce Wright, *Black Robes, White Justice: Why Our Legal System Doesn't Work for Blacks* (New York: Carol Publishing Group, 1994).

## A Letter from Benjamin Banneker to Thomas Jefferson

**SIR,**

I AM fully sensible of the greatness of that freedom, which I take with you on the present occasion; a liberty which seemed to me scarcely allowable, when I reflected on that distinguished and dignified station in which you stand, and the almost general prejudice and prepossession, which is so prevalent in the world against those of my complexion.

I suppose it is a truth too well attested to you, to need a proof here, that we are a race of beings, who have long labored under the abuse and censure of the world; that we have long been looked upon with an eye of contempt; and that we have long been considered rather as brutish than human, and scarcely capable of mental endowments.

Sir, I hope I may safely admit, in consequence of that report which hath reached me, that you are a man far less inflexible in sentiments of this nature, than many others; that you are measurably friendly, and well disposed towards us; and that you are willing and ready to lend your aid and assistance to our relief, from those many distresses, and numerous calamities, to which we are reduced. Now Sir, if this is founded in truth, I apprehend you will embrace every opportunity, to eradicate that train of absurd and false ideas and opinions, which so generally prevails with respect to us; and that your sentiments are concurrent with mine, which are, that one universal Father hath given being to us all; and that he hath not only made us all of one flesh, but that he hath also, without partiality, afforded us all the same sensations and endowed us all with the same faculties; and that however variable we may be in society or religion, however diversified in situation or color, we are all of the same family, and stand in the same relation to him.

Sir, if these are sentiments of which you are fully persuaded, I hope you cannot but acknowledge, that it is the indispensible duty of those, who maintain for themselves the rights of human nature, and who possess the obligations of Christianity, to extend their power and influence to the relief of every part of the human race, from whatever burden or oppression they may unjustly labor under; and this, I apprehend, a full conviction of the truth and obligation of these principles should lead all to. Sir, I have long been convinced, that if your love for yourselves, and for those inestimable laws, which preserved to you the rights of human nature, was founded on sincerity, you could not but be solicitous, that every individual, of whatever rank or distinction, might with you equally enjoy the blessings thereof; neither could you rest satisfied short of the most active effusion of your exertions, in order to their promotion from any state of degradation, to which the unjustifiable cruelty and barbarism of men may have reduced them.

Sir, I freely and cheerfully acknowledge, that I am of the **AFRICAN** race, and in that color which is natural to them of the deepest dye; and it is under a sense of the most profound gratitude to the **Supreme** Ruler of the Universe, that I now confess to you, that I am not under that state of tyrannical thraldom, and inhuman captivity, to which too many of my brethren are doomed, but that I have abundantly tasted of the fruition of those blessings, which proceed from that free and unequalled liberty with which you are favored ; and which, I hope, you will willingly allow you have mercifully received, from the immediate hand of that Being, from whom proceedeth every good and perfect Gift.

Sir, suffer me to recal to your mind that time, in which the arms and tyranny of the British crown were exerted, with every powerful effort, in order to reduce you to a state of servitude: look back, I entreat you, on the variety of dangers to which you were exposed; reflect on that time, in which every human aid appeared unavailable, and in which even hope and fortitude wore the aspect of inability to the conflict, and you cannot but be led to a serious and grateful sense of your miraculous and providential preservation ; you cannot but acknowledge, that the present freedom and tranquility which you enjoy you have mercifully received, and that it is the peculiar blessing of Heaven.

This, Sir, was a time when you cleary saw into the injustice of a state of **SLAVERY**, and in which you had just apprehensions of the horrors of its condition. It was now that your abhorrence thereof was so excited, that you publicly held forth this true and invaluable doctrine, which is worthy to be recorded and remembered in all succeeding ages: ``We hold these truths to be self-evident, that all men are created equal; that they are endowed by their Creator with certain unalienable rights, and that among these are, life, liberty, and the pursuit of happiness." Here was a time, in which your tender feelings for yourselves had engaged you thus to declare, you were then impressed with proper ideas of the great violation of liberty, and the free possession of those blessings, to which you were entitled by nature; but, Sir, how pitiable is it to reflect, that although you were so fully convinced of the benevolence of the Father of Mankind, and of his equal and impartial distribution of these rights and privileges, which he hath conferred upon them, that you should at the same time counteract his mercies, in detaining by fraud and violence so numerous a part of my brethren, under groaning captivity and cruel oppression, that you should at the same time be found guilty of that most criminal act, which you professedly detested in others, with respect to yourselves.

I suppose that your knowledge of the situation of my brethren, is too extensive to need a recital here; neither shall I presume to prescribe methods by which they may be relieved, otherwise than by recommending to you and all others, to wean yourselves from those narrow prejudices which you have imbibed with respect to them, and as Job proposed to his friends, ``put your soul in their souls' stead;'' thus shall your hearts be enlarged with kindness and benevolence towards them; and thus shall you need neither the direction of myself or others, in what manner to proceed herein. And now, Sir, although my sympathy and affection for my brethren hath caused my enlargement thus far, I ardently hope, that your candor and generosity will plead with you in my behalf, when I make known to you, that it was not originally my design; but having taken up my pen in order to direct to you, as a present, a copy of an Almanac, which I have calculated for the succeeding year, I was unexpectedly and unavoidably led thereto.

This calculation is the production of my arduous study, in this my advanced stage of life; for having long had unbounded desires to become acquainted with the secrets of nature, I have had to gratify my curiosity herein, through my own assiduous application to Astronomical Study, in which I need not recount to you the many difficulties and disadvantages, which I have had to encounter.

And although I had almost declined to make my calculation for the ensuing year, in consequence of that time which I had allotted therefor, being taken up at the Federal Territory, by the request of Mr. Andrew Ellicott, yet finding myself under several engagements to Printers of this state, to whom I had communicated my design, on my return to my place of residence, I industriously applied myself thereto, which I hope I have accomplished with correctness and accuracy; a copy of which I have taken the liberty to direct to you, and which I humbly request you will favorably receive ; and although you may have the opportunity of perusing it after its publication, yet I choose to send it to you in manuscript previous thereto, that thereby you might not only have an earlier inspection, but that you might also view it in my own hand writing.

And now, Sir, I shall conclude, and subscribe myself, with the most profound respect,

Your most obedient humble servant,

*BENJAMIN BANNEKER.*

### Thomas Jefferson's Reply to Banneker (1791)

## To Mr. BENJAMIN BANNEKER.
## Philadelphia, August 30, 1791.

*SIR,*

I THANK you, sincerely, for your letter of the 19th instant, and for the Almanac it contained. No body wishes more than I do, to see such proofs as you exhibit, that nature has given to our black brethren talents equal to those of the other colors of men; and that the appearance of the want of them, is owing merely to the degraded condition of their existence, both in Africa and America. I can add with truth, that no body wishes more ardently to see a good system commenced, for raising the condition, both of their body and mind, to what it ought to be, as far as the imbecility of their present existence, and other circumstances, which cannot be neglected, will admit.

I have taken the liberty of sending your Almanac to Monsieur de Condozett, Secretary of the Academy of Sciences at Paris, and Member of the Philanthropic Society, because I considered it as a document, to which your whole color had a right for their justification, against the doubts which have been entertained of them.

I am with great esteem, Sir, Your most obedient Humble Servant,

*THOMAS JEFFERSON.*

**Twist! Twist! Twist!**

**George Washington
1732-1799
Commander of the Colonial Rebel Army
Signed Fugitive Slave Act of 1793 into Law
First President of the United States 1789-1797**

### Guilty of Seeking Freedom: The Fugitive Slave Act of 1793

Unlike the better known **Fugitive Slave Act of 1850**,[1] this law was passed by the Second Congress in 1793 and signed into law by President George Washington. The **Fugitive Slave Act of 1793** gave unqualified legality to the Constitutional dictum first promulgated at the Constitutional Convention, eight years earlier in 1787 that explicitly declared that slaves were 3/5 human.[2] The escaped **AFRICAN** slave, declared a non-person by *law*, was to be hunted as any stray livestock. It was not as comprehensive as the **Fugitive Slave Act of 1850**. It contained no provision for disposition of the captured **AFRICAN**. Yet it proved that the **AFRICAN** was guilty, by *law*, of being less than human!

Although the Federal Government did not put its massive resources at the disposal of the Slave masters, the illegality of escape from **SLAVERY** was given Constitutional sanction. It was done legislatively by the Congress and by the Chief Executive's (George Washington) signature of approval. The Act was never challenged in the **Supreme Court**. If it were challenged, it would have been would have been upheld as the law of the land.

---

[1] Williams, *No Rights And No Respect*, 63-75.

[2] To get a better understanding of the Constitutional context of the 3/5 rule, I recommend you revisit pages 48-62 in *No Rights and No Respect*.

"Slavery is now no where more patiently endured, than in countries once inhabited by the zealots of liberty."

*Samuel Johnson on the Attitudes of the British Colonists in America (June 24, 1758)*

***Twist! Twist! Twist!***

## Fugitive Slave Act of 1793

For the better security of the peace and friendship now entered into by the contracting parties, against all infractions of the same, by the citizens of either party, to the prejudice of the other, neither party shall proceed to the infliction of punishments on the citizens of the other, otherwise than by securing the offender, or offenders, by imprisonment, or any other competent means, till a fair and impartial trial can be had by judges or juries of both parties, as near as can be, to the laws, customs, and usage's of the contracting parties, and natural justice: the mode of such trials to be hereafter fixed by the wise men of the **United States**, in congress assembled, with the assistance of such deputies of the Delaware nation, as may be appointed to act in concert with them in adjusting this matter to their mutual liking. And it is further agreed between the parties aforesaid, that neither shall entertain, or give countenance to, the enemies of the other, or protect, in their respective states, criminal fugitives, servants, or slaves, but the same to apprehend and secure, and deliver to the state or states, to which such enemies, criminals, servants, or slaves.

*Passed on February 12, 1793, by the Second Congress and signed into law by the nation's 1$^{st}$ President, George Washington.* **Twist! Twist! Twist!**

## An Appeal To Heaven: Nat Turner's Rebellion (1831)

Since the early days of America's slave experience, there was (and still is) a reasonable expectation that the "controlled" (**AFRICAN** Slaves) would rise up and violently attempt to disrupt the legally mandated status quo of **SLAVERY**. In so doing, their "controllers" (the slave masters) ran the risk of being drowned in their own blood. For good reason, the planter class feared an awful retribution at the hands of their **AFRICAN** slaves. The planters were not ignorant of the massacre of the French colonialists at the hands of their slaves in Haiti[1] in the late 18th and early 19th Centuries. The Southern planter class lived in sheer terror of bloody revolt fomented by **AFRICAN** preachers in the decades immediately preceding Nat Turner's rebellion in 1831.[2] The planters

---

[1] Word of the successful African revolt, under the brilliant military leadership of the African Toussaint L'Ouverture, spread like wildfire throughout the slave communities. The commanding officer of the Warwick County, Virginia Militia appealed to the governor in 1793 for additional arms after successfully suppressing an African revolt. He said, "since the melancholy affair [on the Island of Haiti]...the (white) inhabitants ...of this county have been repeatedly alarmed by some of their Slaves having attempted to raise an Insurrection, which was timely suppressed in this county by executing one of the principle leaders of the Insurrection. Herbert Aptheker, *American Slave Revolts*, 40th Anniversary Edition (New York: International Publishers, 1987), 96. One of the best treatments of the Haitian Revolution is Martin Ros' *Night of Fire, The Black Napoleon and the Battle for Haiti*, trans. Karen Ford-Treep, (New York: Sarpedon, 1994).

[2] Besides Turner, African preachers led two of the most famous **SLAVE** revolts in the early 1800s. These preachers *interpreted* the **Old**

didn't mind the **AFRICAN** being; however, whatever the slave learned about the Bible had to affirm the status quo. Obvious**ly, Nat** Turner disagreed.

Nat Turner, in his own words, felt called by the LORD to violently overthrow the slave regime in Virginia. Who was Nat Turner? What little we know of him is that he may have been born around 1800. He also is alleged to have been the son of an **AFRICAN** woman of royal blood. His mother is reputed to have traveled from East Africa to West Africa where, through an unfortunate set of circumstances,

---

**Testament** in such a way as to lead their followers to believe that God condemned their oppression as well as their oppressors. Those preachers were, Richmond, Virginia's Gabriel Prosser, (1802), Charleston, South Carolina's Denmark Vesey, (1822). However, unlike Turner, these rebellions were betrayed by insiders, and thereby aborted. Gayraud Wilmore, *Black Religion and Black Radicalism: An Interpretation of the Religious History of Afro-American People* (Maryknoll, NY, 1991), 53-73. Revelations have surfaced over the last two decades that suggest the **United States** Government sees the African preacher as a force to be feared and reckoned with. Since the First World War, African preachers deemed to be radical subversives or threats to national security have been placed under surveillance and harassed by the Federal Government. The denomination they represented was irrelevant. Federal agents, *agent provocateurs*, and informants monitored Baptist and Pentecostals. Ironically, their views on America's participation in the Great War were irrelevant. Bishop C.H. Mason, organizer of the Church of God in Christ, condemned America's participation in "the War to Make the *World* Safe for Democracy," because **AFRICANS** were not *safe* in America. Because of Bishop Mason's stand against the War, he was placed under observation. Robert M. Franklin, *Another Day's Journey: Black Churches Confront the American Crisis* (Minneapolis: Augsburg/Fortress Press, 1997), 50. Although the National Baptist Convention enthusiastically supported the War, its leadership was placed under surveillance. *The Commercial Appeal* (Memphis, TN), 31 March 1993.

she was enslaved and made her way to America by way of the infamous "Middle Passage."

Turner was born in Southampton County, Virginia. As his *Confession* suggests, he felt divinely appointed to rebel against Virginia's slave system. Turner's revolt should be viewed as an attempt on the part of an **AFRICAN** to address the slave's plight by disavowing the legitimacy of the **ANGLO-AMERICAN LEGAL TRADITION** and attempting to destroy those that benefited from the tradition. In the end, however, the American legal system destroyed him! In fact, the rebellion only served as a reason to pass more repressive legislation throughout the South restricting the movement of **AFRICANS**, both Slave and "Free"! On November 11, 1831, Turner was executed.

### *Turner's Appeal to Heaven*

The rebellion began August 21, 1831. Afterwards, by his own admission, he and his band of **AFRICAN** slave followers slew 50-55 whites. The revolt spread rapidly. However, within two months a combined force of Federal Troops and Virginia State Militia crushed Turner's revolt. In a pitched battle with the Federal Troops and State Militia, one hundred slaves were killed and thirteen free **AFRICANS** were summarily hanged.[2]

What follows are statements made to Mr. Thomas Gray by Turner while in prison. During his trial, Nat would plead

---

[2] John Hope Franklin, *From SLAVERY to Freedom: A History of Negro Americans* (New York: Alfred A. Knopf, 1974), 162.

*not guilty* because, by admission, he did *not feel guilty*. He also refused to testify in his own defense, believing his *Confession* spoke for him.

**Twist! Twist! Twist!**

### Nat Turner, 1800(?)-1831

# THE
# CONFESSIONS
# OF
# NAT TURNER, THE LEADER OF THE LATE INSURRECTION IN SOUTH HAMPTON, VA.

As fully and voluntarily made to **THOMAS R. GRAY**. In the prison where he was confined, and acknowledged b him to be such when read before the Court of Southampton; with the certificate, under seal of the Court convened at Jerusalem, Nov. 5, 1831, for his trial.

*Also, An Authentic Account Of The Whole Insurrection, With Lists Of The Whites Who Were Murdered, And Of The Negroes Brought Before The Court Of Southampton, And There Sentenced, &C.*

## *The Preamble*

## *Baltimore:*

### PUBLISHED BY THOMAS R. GRAY.
*Lucas & Deaver, print.*
### 1831

DISTRICT OF COLUMBIA, TO WIT:

*Be it remembered,* That on this tenth day of November, Anno Domini, eighteen hundred and thirty-one, **THOMAS R. GRAY** of the said District, deposited in this office the title of a book, which is in the words as following:

"*The Confessions of Nat Turner,* the leader of the late insurrection in Southampton, Virginia, as fully and voluntarily made to **THOMAS R. GRAY**, in the prison where he was confined, and acknowledged by him to be such when read before the Court of Southampton; with the certificate, under seal, of the Court convened at Jerusalem, November 5, 1831, for his trial. Also, an authentic account of the whole insurrection, with lists of the whites who were murdered, and of the negroes brought before the Court of Southampton, and there sentenced, &c. the right whereof he claims as proprietor, in conformity with an Act of Congress, entitled "An act to amend the several acts respecting Copy Rights."

**EDMUND J. LEE**, Clerk of the District.

*In testimony that the above is a true copy from the record of the District Court for the District of Columbia, I, Edmund I. Lee, the Clerk thereof, have hereunto set my hand and affixed the seal of my office, this 10th day of November, 1831.*
*EDMUND J. LEE, C. D. C.*
*(Seal.)*

## Thomas Gray's Introductory Material

The late insurrection in Southampton has greatly excited the public mind, and led to a thousand idle, exaggerated and mischievous reports. It is the first instance in our history of an open rebellion of the slaves, and attended with such atrocious circumstances of cruelty and destruction, as could not fail to leave a deep impression, not only upon the minds of the community where this fearful tragedy was wrought, but throughout every portion of our country, in which this population is to be found.

Public curiosity has been on the stretch to understand the origin and progress of this dreadful conspiracy, and the motives which influences its diabolical actors. The insurgent slaves had all been destroyed, or apprehended, tried and executed, (with the exception of the leader,) without revealing any thing at all satisfactory, as to the motives which governed them, or the means by which they expected to accomplish their object. Every thing connected with this sad affair was wrapt in mystery, until Nat Turner, the leader of this ferocious band, whose name has resounded throughout our widely extended empire, was captured.

This "great Bandit" was taken by a single individual, in a cave near the residence of his late owner, on Sunday, the thirtieth of October, without attempting to make the slightest resistance, and on the following day safely lodged in the jail of the County. His captor was Benjamin Phipps, armed with a shot gun well charged. Nat's only weapon was a small light sword which he immediately surrendered, and begged that his life might be spared.

Since his confinement, by permission of the Jailor, I have had ready access to him, and finding that he was willing to make a full and free confession of the origin, progress and consummation of the insurrectory movements of the slaves of which he was the contriver and head; I determined for the gratification of public curiosity to commit his statements to writing, and publish them, with little or no variation, from his own words. That this is a faithful record of his confessions, the annexed certificate of the County Court of Southampton, will attest. They certainly bear one stamp of truth and sincerity. He makes no attempt (as all the other insurgents who were examined did,) to exculpate himself, but frankly acknowledges his full participation in all the guilt of the transaction. He was not only the contriver of the conspiracy, but gave the first blow towards its execution.

It will thus appear, that whilst every thing upon the surface of society wore a calm and peaceful aspect; whilst not one note of preparation was heard to warn the devoted inhabitants of woe and death, a gloomy fanatic was revolving in the recesses of his own dark, bewildered, and overwrought mind, schemes of indiscriminate massacre to the whites.

Schemes too fearfully executed as far as his fiendish band proceeded in their desolating march. No cry for mercy penetrated their flinty bosoms. No acts of remembered kindness made the least impression upon these remorseless murderers. Men, women and children, from hoary age to helpless infancy were involved in the same cruel fate. Never did a band of savages do their work of death more unsparingly. Apprehension for their own personal safety seems to have been the only principle of restraint in the whole course of their bloody proceedings. And it is not the least remarkable feature in this horrid transaction, that a band actuated by such hellish purposes, should have resisted so feebly, when met by the whites in arms.

Desperation alone, one would think, might have led to greater efforts. More than twenty of them attacked Dr. Blunt's house on Tuesday morning, a little before daybreak, defended by two men and three boys. They fled precipitately at the first fire; and their future plans of mischief, were entirely disconcerted and broken up. Escaping thence, each individual sought his own safety either in concealment, or by returning home, with the hope that his participation might escape detection, and all were shot down in the course of a few days, or captured and brought to trial and punishment. Nat has survived all his followers, and the gallows will speedily close his career.

His own account of the conspiracy is submitted to the public, without comment. It reads an awful, and it is hoped, a useful lesson, as to the operations of a mind like his, endeavoring to grapple with things beyond its reach. How it first became bewildered and confounded, and finally corrupted and led to the conception and perpetration of the most atrocious and heart-rending deeds. It is calculated also to demonstrate the policy or our laws in restraint of this class of our population, and to induce all those entrusted with their execution, as well as our citizens generally, to see that they are strictly and rigidly enforced. Each particular community should look to its own safety, whilst the general guardians of the laws, keep a watchful eye over all. If Nat's statements can be relied on, the insurrection in this county was entirely local, and his designs confided but to a few, and these in his immediate vicinity. It was not instigated by motives of revenge or sudden anger, but the results of long deliberation, and a settled purpose of mind. The offspring of gloomy fanaticism, acting upon materials but too well prepared for such impressions. It will be long remembered in the annals of our country, and many a mother as she presses her infant darling to her bosom, will shudder at the recollection of Nat Turner, and his band of ferocious miscreants.

Believing the following narrative, by removing doubts and conjectures from the public mind which otherwise must have remained, would give general satisfaction, it is respectfully submitted to the public by their ob't serv't,

*T. R. GRAY.*
*Jerusalem, Southampton, Va. Nov. 5, 1831.*

## *The Acknowledgement By The Judicial Panel Of Receipt Of The Confession*

We the undersigned, members of the Court convened at Jerusalem, on Saturday, the 5th day of Nov. 1831, for the trial of Nat, *alias* Nat Turner, a negro slave, late the property of Putnam Moore, deceased, do hereby certify, that the confessions of Nat, to **THOMAS R. GRAY**, was read to him in our presence, and that Nat acknowledged the same to be full, free, and voluntary; and that furthermore, when called upon by the presiding Magistrate of the Court, to state if he had any thing to say, why sentence of death should not be passed upon him, replied he had nothing further than he had communicated to Mr. Gray. Given under our hands and seals at Jerusalem, this 5th day of November, 1831.

**JEREMIAH COBB,** [*Seal.*]
**THOMAS PRETLOW,** [*Seal.*]
**JAMES W. PARKER,** [*Seal.*]
**CARR BOWERS,** [*Seal.*]
**SAMUEL B. HINES,** [*Seal.*]
**ORRIS A. BROWNE,** [*Seal.*]

## *State of Virginia, Southampton County, to wit:*

I, James Rochelle, Clerk of the County Court of Southampton in the State of Virginia, do hereby certify, that Jeremiah Cobb, Thomas Pretlow, James W. Parker, Carr Bowers, Samuel B. Hines, and Orris A. Browne, esqr's are acting Justices of the Peace, in and for the County aforesaid, and were members of the Court which convened at Jerusalem, on Saturday the 5th day of November, 1831, for the trial of Nat *alias* Nat Turner, a negro slave, late the property of Putnam Moore, deceased, who was tried and convicted, as an insurgent in the late insurrection in the county of Southampton aforesaid, and that full faith and credit are due, and ought to be given to their acts as Justices of the peace aforesaid. In testimony whereof, I have hereunto set my hand and caused the seal of the Court aforesaid, to be affixed this 5th day of November, 1831.
JAMES ROCHELLE, C. S. C. C.
[Seal.]

## Introductory Note by Thomas Gray

Agreeable to his own appointment, on the evening he was committed to prison, with permission of the jailer, I visited NAT on Tuesday the 1st November, when, without being questioned at all, commenced his narrative in the following words:--

# The Confession

## *Introduction*

**Nat Turner**: You have asked me to give a history of the motives which induced me to undertake the late insurrection, as you call it--To do so I must go back to the days of my infancy, and even before I was born. I was thirty-one years of age the 2d of October last, and born the property of Benj. Turner, of this county. In my childhood a circumstance occurred which made an indelible impression on my mind, and laid the ground work of that enthusiasm, which has terminated so fatally to many, both white and black, and for which I am about to atone at the gallows.

## *Nat's Mission Ordained By God Prior TO His Birth*

It is here necessary to relate this circumstance--trifling as it may seem, it was the commencement of that belief which has grown with time, and even now, sir, in this dungeon, helpless and forsaken as I am, I cannot divest myself of. Being at play with other children, when three or four years old, I was telling them something, which my mother overhearing, said it had happened before I was I born--I stuck to my story, however, and related somethings which went, in her opinion, to confirm it--others being called on were greatly astonished, knowing that these things had happened, and caused them to say in my hearing, I surely would be a prophet, as the Lord had shewn me things that had happened before my birth. And my father and mother strengthened me in this my first impression, saying in my presence, I was intended for some great purpose, which they had always thought from certain marks on my head and breast--[a parcel of excrescences which I believe are not at all uncommon, particularly among negroes, as I have seen several with the same. In this case he has either cut them off or they have nearly disappeared]--My grand mother, who was very religious, and to whom I was much attached my master, who belonged to the church, and other religious persons who visited the house, and whom I often saw at prayers, noticing the singularity of my manners, I suppose, and my uncommon intelligence for a child, remarked I had too much sense to be raised, and if I was, I would never be of any service to any one as a slave--To a mind like mine, restless, inquisitive and observant of every thing that was passing, it is easy to suppose that religion was the subject to which it would be directed, and although this subject principally occupied my thoughts--there was nothing that I saw or heard of to which my attention was not directed.

The manner in which I learned to read and write, not only had great influence on my own mind, as I acquired it with the most perfect ease, so much so, that I have no recollection whatever of learning the alphabet--but to the astonishment of the family, one day, when a book was shewn me to keep me from crying, I began spelling the names of different objects--this was a source of wonder to all in the neighborhood, particularly the blacks--and this learning was constantly improved at all opportunities--when I got large enough to go to work, while employed, I was reflecting on many things that would present themselves to my imagination, and whenever an opportunity occurred of looking at a book, when the school children were getting their lessons, I would find many things that the fertility of my own imagination had depicted to me before; all my time, not devoted to my master's service, was spent either in prayer, or in making experiments in casting different things in moulds made of earth, in attempting to make paper, gunpowder, and many other experiments, that although I could not perfect, yet convinced me of its practicability if I had the means. \* I was not addicted to stealing in my youth, nor have ever been.

Yet such was the confidence of the negroes in the neighborhood, even at this early period of my life, in my superior judgment, that they would often carry me with them when they were going on any roguery, to plan for them. Growing up among them, with this confidence in my superior judgment, and when this, in their opinions, was perfected by Divine inspiration, from the circumstances already alluded to in my infancy, and which belief was ever afterwards zealously inculcated by the austerity of my life and manners, which became the subject of remark by white and black.-- Having soon discovered to be great, I must appear so, and therefore studiously avoided mixing in society, and wrapped.

When questioned as to the manner of manufacturing those different articles, he was found well informed on the subject myself in mystery, devoting my time to fasting and prayer--By this time, having arrived to man's estate, and hearing the scriptures commented on at meetings, I was struck with that particular passage which says: "Seek ye the kingdom of Heaven and all things shall be added unto you."

I reflected much on this passage, and prayed daily for light on this subject--As I was praying one day at my plough, the spirit spoke to me, saying "Seek ye the kingdom of Heaven and all things shall be added unto you."

**Thomas Gray:** what do you mean by the Spirit?

**Nat Turner**: The Spirit that spoke to the prophets in former days--and I was greatly astonished, and for two years prayed continually, whenever my duty would permit--and then again I had the same revelation, which fully confirmed me in the impression that I was ordained for some great purpose in the hands of the Almighty. Several years rolled round, in which many events occurred to strengthen me in this my belief. At this time I reverted in my mind to the remarks made of me in my childhood, and the things that had been shewn me--and as it had been said of me in my childhood by those by whom I had been taught to pray, both white and black, and in whom I had the greatest confidence, that I had too much sense to be raised, and if I was, I would never be of any use to any one as a slave.

Now finding I had arrived to man's estate, and was a slave, and these revelations being made known to me, I began to direct my attention to this great object, to fulfil the purpose for which, by this time, I felt assured I was intended. Knowing the influence I had obtained over the minds of my fellow servants, (not by the means of conjuring and such like tricks--for to them I always spoke of such things with contempt) but by the communion of the Spirit whose revelations I often communicated to them, and they believed and said my wisdom came from God. I now began to prepare them for my purpose, by telling them something was about to happen that would terminate in fulfilling the great promise that had been made to me--About this time I was placed under an overseer, from whom I ranaway - and after remaining in the woods thirty days, I returned, to the astonishment of the negroes on the plantation, who thought I had made my escape to some other part of the country, as my father had done before. But the reason of my return was, that the Spirit appeared to me and said I had my wishes directed to the things of this world, and not to the kingdom of Heaven, and that I should return to the service of my earthly master--"For he who knoweth his Master's will, and doeth it not, shall be beaten with many stripes, and thus, have I chastened you." And the negroes found fault, and murmured against me, saying that if they had my sense they would not serve any master in the world. And about this time I had a vision--and I saw white spirits and black spirits engaged in battle, and the sun was darkened--the thunder rolled in the Heavens, and blood flowed in streams--and I heard a voice saying, "Such is your luck, such you are called to see, and let it come rough or smooth, you must surely bare it." I now withdrew myself as much as my situation would permit, from the intercourse of my fellow servants, for the avowed purpose of serving the Spirit more fully--and it appeared to me, and reminded me of the things it had already shown me, and that it would then reveal to me the knowledge of the elements, the revolution of the planets, the operation of tides, and changes of the seasons. After this revelation in the year 1825, and the knowledge of the elements being made known to me, I sought more than ever to obtain true holiness before the great day of judgment should appear, and then I began to receive the true knowledge of faith. And from the first steps of righteousness until the last, was I made perfect; and the Holy Ghost was with me, and said, "Behold me as I stand in the Heavens"--and I looked and saw the forms of men in different attitudes--and there were lights in the sky to which the children of darkness gave other names than what they really were--for they were the lights of the Saviour's hands, stretched forth from east to west, even as they were extended on the cross on Calvary for the redemption of sinners. And I wondered greatly at these miracles, and prayed to be informed of a certainty of the meaning thereof--and shortly afterwards, while laboring in the field, I discovered drops of blood on the corn as though it were dew from heaven-- and I communicated it to many, both white and black, in the neighborhood--and I then found on the leaves in the woods hieroglyphic characters, and numbers, with the forms of men in different attitudes, portrayed in blood, and representing the figures I had seen before in the heavens. And now the Holy Ghost had revealed itself to me, and made plain the miracles it had shown me--For as the blood of Christ had been shed on this earth, and had ascended to heaven for the salvation of sinners, and was now returning to earth again in the form of dew--and as the leaves on the trees bore the impression of the figures I had seen in the heavens, it was plain to me that the Saviour was about to lay down the yoke he had borne for the sins of men, and the great day of judgment was at band. About this time I told these things to a white man, (Etheldred T. Brantley) on whom it had a wonderful effect--and he ceased from his wickedness, and was attacked immediately with a cutaneous eruption, and blood ozed from the pores of his skin, and after praying and fasting nine days, he was healed, and the Spirit appeared to me again, and said, as the Saviour had been baptised so should we be also--and when the white people would not let us be baptised by the church, we went down into the water together, in the sight of many who reviled us, and were baptised by the Spirit--After this I rejoiced greatly, and gave thanks to God. And on the 12th of May, 1828, I heard a loud noise in the heavens, and the Spirit instantly appeared to me and said the Serpent was loosened, and Christ had laid down the yoke he had borne for the sins of men, and that I should take it on and fight against the Serpent, for the time was fast approaching when the first should be last and the last should be first.

**Thomas Gray:** Do you not find yourself mistaken now?

**Nat Turner:** Was not Christ crucified. And by signs in the heavens that it would make known to me when I should commence the great work--and until the first sign appeared, I should conceal it from the knowledge of men--And on the appearance of the sign, (the eclipse of the sun last February) I should arise and prepare myself, and slay my enemies with their own weapons. And immediately on the sign appearing in the heavens, the seal was removed from my lips, and I communicated the great work laid out for me to do, to four in whom I had the greatest confidence, (Henry, Hark, Nelson, and Sam)--It was intended by us to have begun the work of death on the 4th July last--Many were the plans formed and rejected by us, and it affected my mind to such a degree, that I fell sick, and the time passed without our coming to any determination how to commence--Still forming new schemes and rejecting them, when the sign appeared again, which determined me not to wait longer.

Since the commencement of 1830, I had been living with Mr. Joseph Travis, who was to me a kind master, and placed the greatest confidence in me; in fact, I had no cause to complain of his treatment to me. On Saturday evening, the 20th of August, it was agreed between Henry, Hark and myself, to prepare a dinner the next day for the men we expected, and then to concert a plan, as we had not yet determined on any. Hark, on the following morning, brought a pig, and Henry brandy, and being joined by Sam, Nelson, Will and Jack, they prepared in the woods a dinner, where, about three o'clock, I joined them.

**Thomas Gray:** Why were you so backward in joining them?

**Nat Turner:** The same reason that had caused me not to mix with them for years before. I saluted them on coming up, and asked Will how came he there, he answered, his life was worth no more than others, and his liberty as dear to him. I asked him if he thought to obtain it? He said he would, or loose his life. This was enough to put him in full confidence. Jack, I knew, was only a tool in the hands of Hark, it was quickly agreed we should commence at home (Mr. J. Travis') on that night, and until we had armed and equipped ourselves, and gathered sufficient force, neither age nor sex was to be spared, (which was invariably adhered to.) We remained at the feast until about two hours in the night, when we went to the house and found Austin; they all went to the cider press and drank, except myself. On returning to the house, Hark went to the door with an axe, for the purpose of breaking it open, as we knew we were strong enough to murder the family, if they were awaked by the noise; but reflecting that it might create an alarm in the neighborhood, we determined to enter the house secretly, and murder them whilst sleeping. Hark got a ladder and set it against the chimney, on which I ascended, and hoisting a window, entered and came down stairs, unbarred the door, and removed the guns from their places. It was then observed that I must spill the first blood. On which, armed with a hatchet, and accompanied by Will, I entered my master's chamber, it being dark, I could not give a death blow, the hatchet glanced from his head, he sprang from the bed and called his wife, it was his last word, Will laid him dead, with a blow of his axe, and Mrs. Travis shared the same fate, as she lay in bed. The murder of this family, five in number, was the work of a moment, not one of them awoke; there was a little infant sleeping in a cradle, that was forgotten, until we had left the house and gone some distance, when Henry and Will returned and killed it; we got here, four guns that would shoot, and several old muskets, with a pound or two of powder. We remained some time at the barn, where we paraded; I formed them in a line as soldiers, and after carrying them through all the manoeuvres I was master of, marched them off to Mr. Salathul Francis', about six hundred yards distant. Sam and Will went to the door and knocked. Mr. Francis asked who was there, Sam replied, it was him, and he had a letter for him, on which he got up and came to the door, they immediately seized him, and dragging him out a little from the door, he was dispatched by repeated blows on the head; there was no other white person in the family. We started from there for Mrs. Reese's, maintaining the most perfect silence on our march, where finding the door unlocked, we entered, and murdered Mrs. Reese in her bed, while sleeping; her son awoke, but it was only to sleep the sleep of death, he had only time to say who is that, and he was no more. From Mrs. Reese's we went to Mrs. Turner's, a mile distant, which we reached about sunrise, on Monday morning. Henry, Austin, and Sam, went to the still, where, finding Mr. Peebles, Austin shot him, and the rest of us went to the house; as we approached, the family discovered us, and shut the door. Vain hope! Will, with one stroke of his axe, opened it, and we entered and found Mrs. Turner and Mrs. Newsome in the middle of a room, almost frightened to death. Will immediately killed Mrs. Turner, with one blow of his axe. I took Mrs. Newsome by the hand, and with the sword I had when I was apprehended, I struck her several blows over the head, but not being able to kill her, as the sword was dull. Will turning around and discovering it, despatched her also. A general destruction of property and search for money and ammunition, always succeeded the murders. By this time my company amounted to fifteen, and nine men mounted, who started for Mrs. Whitehead's, (the other six were to go through a by way to Mr. Bryant's and rejoin us at Mrs. Whitehead's,) as we approached the house we discovered Mr. Richard Whitehead standing in the cotton patch, near the lane fence; we called him over into the lane, and Will, the executioner, was near at hand, with his fatal axe, to send him to an untimely grave. As we pushed on to the house, I discovered some one run round the garden, and thinking it was some of the white family, I pursued them, but finding it was a servant girl belonging to the house, I returned to commence the work of death, but they whom I left, had not been idle; all the family were already murdered, but Mrs. Whitehead and her daughter Margaret. As I came round to the door I saw Will pulling Mrs. Whitehead out of the house, and at the step he nearly severed her head from her body, with his broad axe. Miss Margaret, when I discovered her, had concealed herself in the corner, formed by the projection of the cellar cap from the house; on my approach she fled, but was soon overtaken, and after repeated blows with a sword, I killed her by a blow on the head, with a fence rail. By this time, the six who had gone by Mr. Bryant's, rejoined us, and informed me they had done the work of death assigned them. We again divided, part going to Mr. Richard Porter's, and from thence to Nathaniel Francis', the others to Mr. Howell Harris', and Mr. T. Doyles. On my reaching Mr. Porter's, he had escaped with his family. I understood there, that the alarm had already spread, and I immediately returned to bring up those sent to Mr. Doyles, and Mr. Howell Harris'; the party I left going on to Mr. Francis', having told them I would join them in that neighborhood. I met these sent to Mr. Doyles' and Mr. Harris' returning, having met Mr. Doyle on the road and killed him; and learning from some who joined them, that Mr. Harris was from home, I immediately pursued the course taken by the party gone on before; but knowing they would complete the work of death and pillage, at Mr. Francis' before I could there, I went to Mr. Peter Edwards', expecting to find them there, but they had been here also. I then went to Mr. John T. Barrow's, they had been here and murdered him. I pursued on their track to Capt. Newit Harris', where I found the greater part mounted, and ready to start; the men now amounting to about forty, shouted and hurraed as I rode up, some were in the yard, loading their guns, others drinking. They said Captain Harris and his family had escaped, the property in the house they destroyed, robbing him of money and other valuables. I ordered them to mount and march instantly, this was about nine or ten o'clock, Monday morning. I proceeded to Mr. Levi Waller's, two or three miles distant. I took my station in the rear, and as it 'twas my object to carry terror and devastation wherever we went, I placed fifteen or twenty of the best armed and most to be relied on, in front, who generally approached the houses as fast as their horses could run; this was for two purposes, to prevent their escape and strike terror to the inhabitants--on this account I never got to the houses, after leaving Mrs. Whitehead's, until the murders were committed, except in one case. I sometimes got in sight in time to see the work of death completed, viewed the mangled bodies as they lay, in silent satisfaction, and immediately started in quest of other victims--Having murdered Mrs. Waller and ten children, we started for Mr.

William Williams' --having killed him and two little boys that were there; while engaged in this, Mrs. Williams fled and got some distance from the house, but she was pursued, overtaken, and compelled to get up behind one of the company, who brought her back, and after showing her the mangled body of her lifeless husband, she was told to get down and lay by his side, where she was shot dead. I then started for Mr. Jacob Williams, where the family were murdered--Here we found a young man named Drury, who had come on business with Mr. Williams--he was pursued, overtaken and shot. Mrs. Vaughan was the next place we visited--and after murdering the family here, I determined on starting for Jerusalem-- Our number amounted now to fifty or sixty, all mounted and armed with guns, axes, swords and clubs--On reaching Mr. James W. Parkers' gate, immediately on the road leading to Jerusalem, and about three miles distant, it was proposed to me to call there, but I objected, as I knew he was gone to Jerusalem, and my object was to reach there as soon as possible; but some of the men having relations at Mr. Parker's it was agreed that they might call and get his people. I remained at the gate on the road, with seven or eight; the others going across the field to the house, about half a mile off. After waiting some time for them, I became impatient, and started to the house for them, and on our return we were met by a party of white men, who had pursued our blood-stained track, and who had fired on those at the gate, and dispersed them, which I new nothing of, not having been at that time rejoined by any of them--Immediately on discovering the whites, I ordered my men to halt and form, as they appeared to be alarmed--The white men, eighteen in number, approached us in about one hundred yards, when one of them fired, (this was against the positive orders of Captain Alexander P. Peete, who commanded, and who had directed the men to reserve their fire until within thirty paces) And I discovered about half of them retreating, I then ordered my men to fire and rush on them; the few remaining stood their ground until we approached within fifty yards, when they fired and retreated. We pursued and overtook some of them who we thought we left dead; (they were not killed) after pursuing them about two hundred yards, and rising a little hill, I discovered they were met by another party, and had haulted, and were re-loading their guns, (this was a small party from Jerusalem who knew the negroes were in the field, and had just tied their horses to await their return to the road, knowing that Mr. Parker aad family were in Jerusalem, but knew nothing of the party that had gone in with Captain Peete; on hearing the firing they immediately rushed to the spot and arrived just in time to arrest the progress of these barbarous villians, and save the lives of their friends and fellow citizens.) Thinking that those who retreated first, and the party who fired on us at fifty or sixty yards distant, had all only fallen back to meet others with amunition. As I saw them re-loading their guns, and more coming up than I saw at first, and several of my bravest men being wounded, the others became panick struck and squandered over the field; the white men pursued and fired on us several times. Hark had his horse shot under him, and I caught another for him as it was running by me; five or six of my men were wounded, but none left on the field; finding myself defeated here I instantly determined to go through a private way, and cross the Nottoway river at the

Cypress Bridge, three miles below Jerusalem, and attack that place in the rear, as I expected they would look for me on the other road, and I had a great desire to get there to procure arms and amunition. After going a short distance in this private way, accompanied by about twenty men, I overtook two or three who told me the others were dispersed in every direction. After trying in vain to collect a sufficient force to proceed to Jerusalem, I determined to return, as I was sure they would make back to their old neighborhood, where they would rejoin me, make new recruits, and come down again. On my way back, I called at Mrs. Thomas's, Mrs. Spencer's, and several other places, the white families having fled, we found no more victims to gratify our thirst for blood, we stopped at Majr. Ridley's quarter for the night, and being joined by four of his men, with the recruits made since my defeat, we mustered now about forty strong. After placing out sentinels, I laid down to sleep, but was quickly roused by a great racket; starting up, I found some mounted, and others in great confusion; one of the sentinels having given the alarm that we were about to be attacked, I ordered some to ride round and reconnoitre, and on their return the others being more alarmed, not knowing who they were, fled in different ways, so that I was reduced to about twenty again; with this I determined to attempt to recruit, and proceed on to rally in the neighborhood, I had left. Dr. Blunt's was the nearest house, which we reached just before day; on riding up the yard, Hark fired a gun. We expected Dr. Blunt and his family were at Maj. Ridley's, as I knew there was a company of men there; the gun was fired to ascertain if any of the family were at home; we were immediately fired upon and retreated, leaving several of my men. I do not know what became of them, as I never saw them afterwards. Pursuing our course back and coming in sight of Captain Harris', where we had been the day before, we discovered a party of white men at the house, on which all deserted me but two, (Jacob and Nat,) we concealed ourselves in the woods until near night, when I sent them in search of Henry, Sam, Nelson, and Hark, and directed them to rally all they could, at the place we had had our dinner the Sunday before, where they would find me, and I accordingly returned there as soon as it was dark and remained until Wednesday evening, when discovering white men riding around the place as though they were looking for some one, and none of my men joining me, I concluded Jacob and Nat had been taken, and compelled to betray me. On this I gave up all hope for the present; and on Thursday night after having supplied myself with provisions from Mr. Travis's, I scratched a hole under a pile of fence rails in a field, where I concealed myself for six weeks, never leaving my hiding place but for a few minutes in the dead of night to get water which was very near; thinking by this time I could venture out, I began to go about in the night and eaves drop the houses in the neighborhood; pursuing this course for about a fortnight and gathering little or no intelligence, afraid of speaking to any human being, and returning every morning to my cave before the dawn of day. I know not how long I might have led this life, if accident had not betrayed me, a dog in the neighborhood passing by my hiding place one night while I was out, was attracted by some meat I had in my cave, and crawled in and stole it, and was coming out just as I returned. A few nights after, two negroes having started to go hunting with the same dog, and passed that way, the dog came again to the place, and having just gone out to walk about, discovered me and barked, on which thinking myself discovered, I spoke to them to beg concealment. On making myself known they fled from me. Knowing then they would betray me, I immediately left my hiding place, and was pursued almost incessantly until I was taken a fortnight afterwards by Mr. Benjamin Phipps, in a little hole I had dug out with my sword, for the purpose of concealment, under the top of a fallen tree. On Mr. Phipps' discovering the place of my concealment, he cocked his gun and aimed at me. I requested him not to shoot and I would give up, upon which he demanded my sword. I delivered it to him, and he brought me to prison. During the time I was pursued, I had many hair breadth escapes, which your time will not permit you to relate. I am here loaded with chains, and willing to suffer the fate that awaits me.

### *Final Points In Gray's Interrogation of Turner*

I here proceeded to make some inquiries of him after assuring him of the certain death that awaited him, and that concealment would only bring destruction on the innocent as well as guilty, of his own color, if he knew of any extensive or concerted plan. His answer was, I do not. When I questioned him as to the insurrection in North Carolina happening about the same time, he denied any knowledge of it; and when I looked him in the face as though I would search his inmost thoughts, he replied, "I see sir, you doubt my word; but can you not think the same ideas, and strange appearances about this time in the heaven's might prompt others, as well as myself, to this undertaking." I now had much conversation with and asked him many questions, having forborne to do so previously, except in the cases noted in parenthesis; but during his statement, I had, unnoticed by him, taken notes as to some particular circumstances, and having the advantage of his statement before me in writing, on the evening of the third day that I had been with him, I began a cross examination, and found his statement corroborated by every circumstance coming within my own knowledge or the confessions of others whom had been either killed or executed, and whom he had not seen nor had any knowledge since 22d of August last, he expressed himself fully satisfied as to the impracticability of his attempt. It has been said he was ignorant and cowardly, and that his object was to murder and rob for the purpose of obtaining money to make his escape. It is notorious, that he was never known to have a dollar in his life; to swear an oath, or drink a drop of spirits. As to his ignorance, he certainly never had the advantages of education, but he can read and write, (it was taught him by his parents,) and for natural intelligence and quickness of apprehension, is surpassed by few men I have ever seen. As to his being a coward, his reason as given for not resisting Mr. Phipps, shews the decision of his character. When he saw Mr. Phipps present his gun, he said he knew it was impossible for him to escape as the woods were full of men; he therefore thought it was better to surrender, and trust to fortune for his escape. He is a complete fanatic, or plays his part most admirably. On other subjects he possesses an uncommon share of intelligence, with a mind capable of attaining any thing; but warped and perverted by the influence of early impressions. He is below the ordinary stature, though strong and active, having the true negro face, every feature of which is strongly marked. I shall not attempt to describe the effect of his narrative, as told and commented on by himself, in the condemned hole of the prison. The calm, deliberate composure with which he spoke of his late deeds and intentions, the expression of his fiend-like face when excited by enthusiasm, still bearing the stains of the blood of helpless innocence about him; clothed with rags and covered with chains; yet daring to raise his manacled hands to heaven, with a spirit soaring above the attributes of man; I looked on him and my blood curdled in my veins.

## *Supplementary Details Of The Insurrection*

I will not shock the feelings of humanity, nor wound afresh the bosoms of the disconsolate sufferers in this unparalleled and inhuman massacre, by detailing the deeds of their fiend-like barbarity. There were two or three who were in the power of these wretches, had they known it, and who escaped in the most providential manner. There were two whom they thought they left dead on the field at Mr. Parker's, but who were only stunned by the blows of their guns, as they did not take time to re-load when they charged on them. The escape of a little girl who went to school at Mr Waller's, and where the children were collecting for that purpose. excited general sympathy. As their teacher had not arrived, they were at play in the yard, and seeing the negroes approach, ran up on a dirt chimney (such as are common to log houses,) and remained there unnoticed during the massacre of the eleven that were killed at this place. She remained on her hiding place till just before the arrival of a party, who were in pursuit of the murderers, when she came down and fled to a swamp, where, a mere child as she was, with the horrors of the late scene before her, she lay concealed until the next day, when seeing a party go up to the house, she came up, and on being asked how she escaped, replied with the utmost simplicity, "The Lord helped her." She was taken up behind a gentleman of the party, and returned to the arms of her weeping mother Miss Whitehead concealed herself between the bed and the mat that supported it, while they murdered her sister in the same room, without discovering her. She was afterwards carried off, and concealed for protection by a slave of the family, who gave evidence against several of them on their trial. Mrs. Nathaniel Francis, while concealed in a closet heard their blows, and the shrieks of the victims of these ruthless savages; they then entered the closet where she was concealed, and went out without discovering her. While in this hiding place, she heard two of her women in a quarrel about the division of her clothes. Mr. John T. Baron, discovering them approaching his house, told his wife to make her escape, and scorning to fly, fell fighting on his own threshold. After firing his rifle, he discharged his gun at them, and then broke it over the villain who first approached him, but he was overpowered, and slain. His bravery, however, saved from the hands of these monsters, his lovely and amiable wife, who will long lament a husband so deserving of her love. As directed by him, she attempted to escape through the garden, when she was caught and held by one of her servant girls, but another coming to her rescue, she fled to the woods, and concealed herself. Few indeed, were those who escaped their work of death. But fortunate for society, the hand of retributive justice has overtaken them; and not one that was known to be concerned has escaped.

### *The Court's Verdict*
### *The Commonwealth, of Virginia vs. Nat Turner.*

Charged with making insurrection, and plotting to take away the lives of divers free white persons, &c. on the 22d of August, 1831.

The court composed of - , having met for the trial of Nat Turner, the prisoner was brought in and arraigned, and upon his arraignment pleaded *Not guilty*; saying to his counsel, that he did not feel so.

On the part of the Commonwealth, Levi Waller was introduced, who being sworn, deposed as follows: (*agreeably to Nat's own Confession.*) Col. Trezvant[*] was then introduced, who being Sworn, narrated Nat's Confession to him, as follows: (*his Confession as given to Mr. Gray.*) The prisoner introduced no evidence, and the case was submitted without argument to the court, who having found him guilty, **Jeremiah Cobb, Esq. Chairman, pronounced the sentence of the court, in the following words:** "Nat Turner! Stand up. Have you any thing to say why sentence of death should not be pronounced against you?"

**Nat Turner:** I have not. I have made a full confession to Mr. Gray, and I have nothing more to say.

## The Sentence of the Court

*Attend then to the sentence of the Court. You have been arraigned and tried before this court, and convicted of one of the highest crimes in our criminal code. You have been convicted of plotting in cold blood, the indiscriminate destruction of men, of helpless women, and of infant children. The evidence before us leaves not a shadow of doubt, but that your hands were often imbrued in the blood of the innocent; and your own confession tells us that they were stained with the blood of a master; in your own language, "too indulgent." Could I stop here, your crime would be sufficiently aggravated. But the original contriver of a plan, deep and deadly, one that never can be effected, you managed so far to put it into execution, as to deprive us of many of our most valuable citizens; and this was done when they were asleep, and defenceless; under circumstances shocking to humanity. And while upon this part of the subject, I cannot but call your attention to the poor misguided wretches who have gone before you. They are not few in number--they were your bosom associates; and the blood of all cries aloud, and calls upon you, as the author of their misfortune. Yes! You forced them unprepared, from Time to Eternity. Borne down by this load of guilt, your only justification is, that you were led* *away by fanaticism. If this be true, from my soul I pity you; and while you have my sympathies, I am, nevertheless called upon to pass the sentence of the court. The time between this and your execution, will necessarily be very short; and your only hope must be in another world. The judgment of the court is, that you be taken hence to the jail from whence you came, thence to the place of execution, and on Friday next, between the hours of 10 A. M. and 2 P. M. be hung by the neck until you are **DEAD! DEAD! DEAD: AND MAY THE LORD HAVE MERCY UPON YOUR SOUL.***

## *A list of persons murdered in the Insurrection, on the 21st and 22nd of August,* **1831.**

- Joseph Travers and wife and three children,
- Mrs. Elizabeth Turner,
- Hartwell Prebles, Sarah Newsome,
- Mrs. P. Reese and son William,
- Trajan Doyle,
- Henry Bryant and wife and child, and wife's mother,
- Mrs. Catharine Whitehead,
- son Richard and four daughters and
- grand-child,
- Salathiel Francis,
- Nathaniel Francis' overseer and two children,
- John T. Barrow,
- George Vaughan,
- Mrs. Levi Waller and ten children,
- William Williams, wife and two boys,

- Mrs. Caswell Worrell and child,
- Mrs. Rebecca Vaughan,
- Ann Eliza Vaughan, and son Arthur,
- Mrs. John K. Williams and child,
- Mrs. Jacob Williams and three children, and
- Edwin Drury--amounting to fifty-five.

## *A List of Negroes brought before the Court of Southampton, with their owners' names, and sentence.*

- Daniel,-- -- -- -- Richard Porter, Convicted.
- Moses, -- -- -- -- -- J. T. Barrow, Do.
- Tom, -- -- -- -- Caty Whitehead, Discharged.
- Jack and Andrew, -- -- -- -- Caty Whitehead, Con. and transported.
- Jacob, -- -- -- -- Geo. H. Charlton, Disch'd without trial.
- Isaac, -- -- -- -- Ditto, Convi. and transported.
- Jack, -- -- -- -- Everett Bryant, Discharged.
- Nathan, -- -- -- -- Benj. Blunt's estate, Convicted.
- Nathan, Tom, and Davy, (boys,) -- -- -- -- Nathaniel Francis, Convicted and transported.
- Davy, -- -- -- -- Elizabeth Turner, Convicted.
- Curtis, -- -- -- -- Thomas Ridley, Do.
- Stephen, -- -- -- -- Do. Do.
- Hardy and Isham, -- -- -- -- Benjamin Edwards, Convicted and transp'd.
- Sam, -- -- -- -- Nathaniel Francis, Convicted.

- Hark, -- -- -- -- Joseph Travis' estate, Do.
- Moses, (a boy,) -- -- -- -- Do. Do. and transported.
- Davy, -- -- -- -- Levi Waller, Convicted.
- Nelson, -- -- -- -- Jacob Williams, Do.
- Nat, -- -- -- -- Edm'd Turner's estate. Do.
- Jack, -- -- -- -- Wm. Reese's estate, Do.
- Dred, -- -- -- -- Nathaniel Francis, Do.
- Arnold, Artist, (free,) -- -- -- -- Discharged.
- Sam, -- -- -- -- J. W. Parker, Acquitted.
- Ferry and Archer, -- -- -- -- J. W. Parker, Disch'd without trial.
- Jim, -- -- -- -- William Vaughan, Acquitted.
- Bob, -- -- -- -- Temperance Parker, Do.
- Davy, -- -- -- -- Joseph Parker,
- Daniel, -- -- -- -- Solomon D. Parker, Disch'd without trial.
- Thomas Haithcock, (free,) -- -- -- -- Sent on for further trial.
- Joe, -- -- -- -- John C. Turner, Convicted.
- Lucy, -- -- -- -- John T. Barrow, Do.
- Matt, -- -- -- -- Thomas Ridley, Acquitted.
- Jim, -- -- -- -- Richard Porter, Do.
- Exum Artes, (free,) Richard Porter, Sent on or further trial.
- Joe, -- -- -- -- Richard P. Briggs, Disch'd without trial.
- Bury Newsome, (free,) -- -- -- -- Sent on for further trial.
- Stephen, -- -- -- -- James Bell, Acquitted.

- Jim and Isaac, -- -- -- -- Samuel Champion, Convicted and trans'd.
- Preston, -- -- -- -- Hannah Williamson, Acquitted.
- Frank, -- -- -- -- Solomon D. Parker, Convi'd and transp'd.
- Jack and Shadrach, -- -- -- -- Nathaniel Simmons, Acquitted.
- Nelson, -- -- -- -- Benj. Blunt's estate, Do.
- Sam, -- -- -- -- Peter Edwards, Convicted.
- Archer, -- -- -- -- Arthur G. Reese, Acquitted.
- Isham Turner, (free,) -- -- -- -- Sent on for further trial.
- Nat Turner, -- -- -- --Putnam Moore, dec'd, Convicted.

### Henry Highland Garnett's Appeal To Open Revolt (1843)

Henry Highland Garnett was an outstanding Nineteenth Century Presbyterian preacher of **AFRICAN** descent. Born in the state of Delaware, he was the grandson of an **AFRICAN** from Kongo (Central Africa). His grandfather had been kidnapped and brought to America during the mid-18$^{th}$ Century. In 1825, he and his slave father George Garnett escaped from **SLAVERY** in Maryland and fled to the "free" state of New York.

Realizing that there were two types of **AFRICANS**, one directly enslaved and others with the rather dubious distinction of being "free," he realized that just being an **AFRICAN** was by law an offense! In fact, the **AFRICAN** was a convict of the highest order. Fifty years after the passage of the **Fugitive Slave Act of 1793**, twelve years after Nat Turner's unsuccessful appeal to violence, and while Dred Scott was preparing his eventually unsuccessful quest for freedom via the nation's court system, in 1843, Garnett delivered the following speech at an **AFRICAN** convention, held in Buffalo, New York. In his address, he made a plea for the slaves to rise up in revolt against their "masters."

It was a fiery well-crafted speech, but it did not cause the **AFRICANS** to rise up against their oppressors!

## Garnett's Call For Open Revolt

Brethren and fellow citizens: -- your brethren of the north, East, and West have been accustomed to meet together in National Conventions, to sympathize with each Other, and to weep over your unhappy condition. In these meetings we have addressed all classes of the free, but we have never until this time, sent a word of consolation and advice to you. We have been contented in sitting still and mourning over your sorrows, earnestly hoping that before this day your sacred liberty would have been restored. But, we have hoped in vain. Years have rolled on, and tens of thousands have been borne on streams of blood and tears, to the shores of eternity. While you have been oppressed, we have also been partakers with you; nor can we be free while you are enslaved. We, therefore, write to you as being bound with you.

Many of you are bound to us, not only by the ties of a common humanity, but we are connected by the more tender relations of parents, wives, husbands, children, brothers, and sisters, and friends. As such we most affectionately address you.

**SLAVERY** has fixed a deep gulf between you and us, and while it shuts out from you the relief and consolation which your friends would willingly render, it affects and persecutes you with a fierceness which we might not expect to see in the fiends of hell. But still the Almighty Father of mercies has left to us a glimmering ray of hope, which shines out like a lone star in a cloudy sky. Mankind are becoming wiser, and better -- the oppressor's power is fading, and you, every day, are becoming better informed, and more numerous. Your grievances, brethren, are many. We shall not attempt, in this short address, to present to the world all the dark catalogue of this nation's sins, which have been committed upon an innocent people. Nor is it indeed necessary, for you feel them from day to day, and all the civilized world look upon them with amazement.

Two hundred and twenty-seven years ago, the first of our injured race were brought to the shores of America. They came not with glad spirits to select their homes in the New World. They came not with their own consent, to find an unmolested enjoyment of the blessings of this fruitful soil. The first dealings they had with men calling themselves Christians, exhibited to them the worst features of corrupt and sordid hearts; and convinced them that no cruelty is too great, no villainy and no robbery too abhorrent for even enlightened men to perform, when influenced by avarice and lust.

Neither did they come flying upon the wings of Liberty, to a land of freedom. But they came with broken hearts, from their beloved native land, and were doomed to unrequited toil and deep degradation. Nor did the evil of their bondage end at their emancipation by death. Succeeding generations inherited their chains, and millions have come from eternity into time, and have returned again to the world of spirits, cursed and ruined by American **SLAVERY**.

The propagators of the system, or their immediate ancestors, very soon discovered its growing evil, and its tremendous wickedness, and secret promises were made to destroy it. The gross inconsistency of a people holding slaves, who had themselves "ferried o'er the wave" for freedom's sake, was too apparent to be entirely overlooked. The voice of Freedom cried, "Emancipate your slaves." Humanity supplicated with tears for the deliverance of the children of Africa. Wisdom urged her solemn plea. The bleeding captive plead his innocence, and pointed to Christianity who stood weeping at the cross. Jehovah frowned upon the nefarious institution, and thunderbolts, red with vengeance, struggled to leap forth to blast the guilty wretches who maintained it. But all was in vain. **SLAVERY** had stretched its dark wings of death over the land, the Church stood silently by -- the priests prophesied falsely, and the people loved to have it so. Its throne is established, and now it reigns triumphant.

Nearly three millions of your fellow-citizens are prohibited by law and public opinion, (which in this country is stronger than law,) from reading the Book of Life. Your intellect has been destroyed as much as possible, and every ray of light they have attempted to shut out from your minds. The oppressors themselves have become involved in the ruin. They have become weak, sensual, and rapacious- they have cursed you-they have cursed themselves-they have cursed the earth which they have trod.

The colonists threw the blame upon England. They said that the mother country entailed the evil upon them, and that they would rid themselves of it if they could. The world thought they were sincere, and the philanthropic pitied them. But time soon tested their sincerity.

In a few years the colonists grew strong, and severed themselves from the British Government. Their independence was declared, and they took their station among the sovereign powers of the earth. The declaration was a glorious document. Sages admired it, and the patriotic of every nation reverenced the God-like sentiments which it contained. When the power of Government returned to their hands, did they emancipate the slaves? No; they rather added new links to our chains. Were they ignorant of the principles of Liberty? Certainly they were not. The sentiments of their revolutionary orators fell in burning eloquence upon their hearts, and with one voice they cried, LIBERTY OR DEATH. Oh what a sentence was that! It ran from soul to soul like electric fire, and nerved the arm of thousands to fight in the holy cause of Freedom. Among the diversity of opinions that are entertained in regard to physical resistance, there are but a few found to gainsay that stern declaration. We are among those who do not.

**SLAVERY**! How much misery is comprehended in that single word? What mind is there that does not shrink from its direful effects? Unless the image of God be obliterated from the soul, all men cherish the love of Liberty. The nice discerning political economist does not regard the sacred right more than the untutored **AFRICAN** who roams in the wilds of Congo. Nor has the one more right to the full enjoyment of his freedom than the other. In every man's mind the good seeds of liberty are planted, and he who brings his fellow down so low, as to make him contented with a condition of **SLAVERY**, commits the highest crime against God and man. Brethren, your oppressors aim to do this. They endeavor to make you as much like brutes as possible. When they have blinded the eyes of your mind- when they have embittered the sweet waters of life-then, and not till then, has American **SLAVERY** done its perfect work.

TO SUCH DEGRADATION IT IS SINFUL IN THE EXTREME FOR YOU TO MAKE VOLUNTARY SUBMISSION. The divine commandments you are in duty bound to reverence and obey. If you do not obey them, you will surely meet with the displeasure of the Almighty. He requires you to love him **Supreme**ly, and your neighbor as yourself -- to keep the Sabbath day holy -- to search the Scriptures -- and bring up your children with respect for his laws, and to worship no other God but him. But **SLAVERY** sets all these at nought, and hurls defiance in the face of Jehovah. The forlorn condition in which you are placed, does not destroy your moral obligation to God. You'are not certain of heaven, because you suffer yourselves to remain in a state of **SLAVERY**, where you cannot obey the commandments of the Sovereign of the universe. If the ignorance of **SLAVERY** is a passport to heaven, then it is a blessing, and no curse, and you should rather desire its perpetuity than its abolition. God will not receive **SLAVERY**, nor ignorance, nor any other state of mind, for love and obedience to him. Your condition does not absolve you from your moral obligation. The diabolical injustice by which your liberties are cloven down, NEITHER GOD, NOR ANGELS, OR JUST MEN, COMMAND YOU TO SUFFER FOR A SINGLE MOMENT. THEREFORE IT IS YOUR SOLEMN AND IMPERATIVE DUTY TO USE EVERY MEANS, BOTH MORAL, INTELLECTUAL, AND PHYSICAL THAT PROMISES SUCCESS. If a band of heathen men should attempt to enslave a race of Christians, and to place their children under the influence of some false religion, surely Heaven would frown upon the men who would not resist such aggression, even to death. If, on the other hand, a band of Christians should attempt to enslave a race of heathen men, and to entail **SLAVERY** upon them, and to keep them in heathenism in the midst of Christianity, the God of heaven would smile upon every effort which the injured might make to disenthral themselves.

Brethren, it is as wrong for your lordly oppressors to keep you in **SLAVERY** as it was for the man thief to steal our ancestors from the coast of Africa. You should therefore now use the same manner of resistance, as would have been just in our ancestors when the bloody foot-prints of the first remorseless soul-thief was placed upon the shores of our fatherland. The humblest peasant is as free in the sight of God as the proudest monarch that ever swayed a sceptre. Liberty is a spirit sent out from God, and like its great Author, is no respecter of persons.

Brethren, the time has come when you must act for yourselves. It is an old and true saying that, "if hereditary bondmen would be free, they must themselves strike the blow." You can plead your own cause, and do the work of emancipation better than any others. The nations of the world are moving in the great cause of universal freedom, and some of them at least will, ere long, do you justice. The combined powers of Europe have placed their broad seal of disapprobation upon the **AFRICAN** slave-trade. But in the slaveholding parts of the **United States**, the trade is as brisk as ever. They buy and sell you as though you were brute beasts. The North has done much -- her opinion of **SLAVERY** in the abstract is known. But in regard to the South, we adopt the opinion of the *New York Evangelist* -- We have advanced so far, that the cause apparently waits for a more effectual door to be thrown open than has been yet. We are about to point out that more effectual door. Look around you, and behold the bosoms of your loving wives heaving with untold agonies! Hear the cries of your poor children!

Remember the stripes your fathers bore. Think of the torture and disgrace of your noble mothers. Think of your wretched sisters, loving virtue and purity, as they are driven into concubinage and are exposed to the unbridled lusts of incarnate devils. Think of the undying glory that hangs around the ancient name of Africa-and forget not that you are native born American citizens, and as such, you are justly entitled to all the rights that are granted to the freest. Think how many tears you have poured out upon the soil which you have cultivated with unrequited toil and enriched with your blood; and then go to your lordly enslavers and tell them plainly, that you *are determined to be free*. Appeal to their sense of justice, and tell them that they have no more right to oppress you, than you have to enslave them. Entreat them to remove the grievous burdens which they have imposed upon you, and to remunerate you for your labor. Promise them renewed diligence in the cultivation of the soil, if they will render to you an equivalent for your services. Point them to the increase of happiness and prosperity in the British West Indies since the Act of Emancipation. Tell them in language which they cannot misunderstand, of the exceeding sinfulness of **SLAVERY**, and of a future judgment, and of the righteous retributions of an indignant God. Inform them that all you desire is FREEDOM, and that nothing else will suffice. Do this, and for ever after cease to toil for the heartless tyrants, who give you no other reward but stripes and abuse. If they then commence the work of death, they, and not you, will be responsible for the consequences. You had better all die -- *die immediately*, than live slaves and entail your wretchedness upon your posterity. If you would be free in this generation, here is your only hope. However much you and all of us may desire it, there is not much hope of redemption without the shedding of blood. If you must bleed, let it all come at once rather *die freemen, than live to be slaves*. It is impossible like the children of Israel, to make a grand exodus from the land of bondage.

The Pharaohs are on both sides of the blood-red waters! You cannot move en masse, to the dominions of the British

Queen[1]-nor can you pass through Florida and overrun Texas, and at last find peace in Mexico. The propagators of American **SLAVERY** are spending their blood and treasure, that they may plant the black flag in the heart of Mexico and riot in the halls of the Montezumas.[2]

In the language of the Rev. Robert Hall, when addressing the volunteers of Bristol, who were rushing forth to repel the invasion of Napoleon, who threatened to lay waste the fair homes of England, "Religion is too much interested in your behalf, not to shed over you her most gracious influences."

You will not be compelled to spend much time in order to become inured to hardships. From the first moment that you breathed the air of heaven, you have been accustomed to nothing else but hardships. The heroes of the American

---

[1] He refers to Canada and the British West Indies.

[2] One of the greatest lies perpetrated by America was that the white settlers, such as Davy Crockett, Sam Houston, Jim Bowie, etc., were selfless freedom loving persons desiring to throw off the yoke of Mexican oppression in Texas. With Mexico's successful independence drive from Spain (1824), all formerly Spanish territory, California, New Mexico, parts of Utah, Arizona and Texas fell under the jurisdiction of Mexico. The Mexican Government refused to allow **SLAVERY** in its territories—Texas included. The White American settlers did. From 1836-1848, the **United States** in various military operations, the most (in) famous being the so-called Mexican-American War (1846-) seized the above named regions. With Mexico driven out of those regions, **SLAVERY** became a possibility! Texas became a slave state as soon as it was absorbed into the Federal Union. It remained so until the end of the Civil War. Garnetts' speech was made in 1843, had **AFRICANS** been able to make it Mexico, they would have been free.

Revolution were never put upon harder fare than a peck of corn and a few herrings per week. You have not become enervated by the luxuries of life. Your sternest energies have been beaten out upon the anvil of severe trial. **SLAVERY** has done this, to make you subservient, to its own purposes; but it has done more than this, it has prepared you for any emergency. If you receive good treatment, it is what you could hardly expect; if you meet with pain, sorrow, and even death, these are the common lot of slaves.

Fellow men! Patient sufferers! behold your dearest rights crushed to the earth! See your sons murdered, and your wives, mothers and sisters doomed to prostitution. In the name of the merciful God, and by all that life is worth, let it no longer be a debatable question whether it is better to choose *Liberty or death..*

## References To Past Slave Revolts

In 1822, Denmark Veazie, of South Carolina, formed a plan for the liberation of his fellow men. In the whole history of human efforts to overthrow **SLAVERY**, a more complicated and tremendous plan was never formed. He was betrayed by the treachery of his own people, and died a martyr to freedom. Many a brave hero fell, but history, faithful to her high trust, will transcribe his name on the same monument with Moses, Hampden, Tell, Bruce and Wallace, Toussaint L'Ouverture, Lafayette and Washington. That tremendous movement shook the whole empire of **SLAVERY**. The guilty soulthieves were overwhelmed with fear. It is a matter of fact, that at that time, and in consequence of the threatened revolution, the slave States talked strongly of emancipation. But they blew but one blast of the trumpet of freedom and then laid it aside. As these men became quiet, the slaveholders ceased to talk about emancipation; and now behold your condition today! Angels sigh over it, and humanity has long since exhausted her tears in weeping on your account!

The patriotic Nathaniel Turner followed Denmark Veazie. He was goaded to desperation by wrong and injustice. By despotism, his name has been recorded on the list of infamy, and future generations will remember him among the noble and brave.

Next arose the immortal Joseph Cinque, the hero of the Amistad. He was a native **AFRICAN**, and by the help of God he emancipated a whole shipload of his fellow men on the high seas. And he now sings of liberty on the sunny hills of Africa and beneath his native palm-trees, where he hears the lion roar and feels himself as free as that king of the forest.

Next arose Madison Washington that bright star of freedom, and took his station in the constellation of true heroism. He was a slave on board the brig Creole, of Richmond, bound to New Orleans, that great slave mart, with a hundred and four others. Nineteen struck for liberty or death. But one life was taken, and the whole were emancipated, and the vessel was carried into Nassau, New Providence.

Noble men! Those who have fallen in freedom's conflict, their memories will be cherished by the true-hearted and the God-fearing in all future generations; those who are living, their names are surrounded by a halo of glory.

Brethren, arise, arise! Strike for your lives and liberties. Now is the day and the hour. Let every slave throughout the land do this and the days of **SLAVERY** are numbered. You cannot be more oppressed than you have been -- you cannot suffer greater cruelties than you have already. *Rather die freemen than live to be slaves.* Remember that you are FOUR MILLIONS!

It is in your power so to torment the God-cursed slaveholders that they will be glad to let you go free. If the scale was turned, and black men were the masters and white men the slaves, every destructive agent and element would be employed to lay the oppressor low. Danger and death would hang over their heads day and night. Yes, the tyrants would meet with plagues more terrible than those of Pharaoh. But you are a patient people. You act as though, you were made for the special use of these devils. You act as though your daughters were born to pamper the lusts of your masters and overseers. And worse than all, you tamely submit while your lords tear your wives from your embraces and defile them before your eyes. In the name of God, we ask you, are you men? Where is the blood of your fathers? Has it all run out of your veins? Awake, awake; millions of voices are calling you! Your dead fathers speak to you from their graves. Heaven, as with a voice of thunder, calls on you to arise from the dust.

Let your motto be resistance! *resistance!* RESISTANCE! No oppressed people have ever secured their liberty without resistance. What kind of resistance you had better make, you must decide by the circumstances that surround you, and according to the suggestion of expediency. Brethren, adieu! Trust in the living God. Labor for the peace of the human race, and remember that you are FOUR MILLIONS.

August 21, 1843

*Twist! Twist! Twist!*

## Reconstruction's Collapse 1865-1877 And Southern "Redemption" (1877-1896)

The years 1860-1876 were heady ones indeed for the **AFRICAN**! In 1860, a man *perceived* to be friendly to **AFRICANS was elected** to the Federal Presidency, Abraham Lincoln. The Southern states threatened to secede from the Union if Lincoln was elected. He was and, in 1861, they did. Until recently, Lincoln was *perceived* to be a friend of the **AFRICAN**. Careful research on the part of Lerone Bennett[1] has proven this to be false. Lincoln's main objective was preservation of the Federal Union. **SLAVERY** was of little interest to him! Even his much-vaunted **Emancipation Proclamation** was a cynical political ploy! It "gave" **AFRICAN** slaves their "freedom" in areas where *he had no jurisdiction*. It was also designed to take the wind out of the sails of the British and French. The two powers occupied Canada to America's North and Mexico to America's South, respectivily.[2]

Even Lincoln's death by assassination in 1865 failed to dampen the general atmosphere of enthusiasm on the part of **AFRICANS**. In the wake of Lincoln's death, the South had been devastated and the old cotton-based, slave-

---
[1] Lerone Bennett, Jr., *Forced Into Glory: Abraham Lincoln's White Dream*, (Chicago: Johnson Publishing, 2000). Also see, Williams, *No Rights And No Respect*, 160-168.

[2] Ibid.

holding aristocracy's power had been broken by their loss on the battlefield in 1865. **AFRICANS** then began to participate in ways unthinkable in Southern life, prior to the Civil War. **AFRICANS** occupied judicial positions, juries, state legislatures, Federal Senate and Congressional seats, etc. They even had a hand in writing state constitutions!

A wave of Federal legislation, aimed at ***RECONSTRUCTING*** Southern society seemed to signal a new era in America for the **AFRICAN**. In 1865, the **Freedman's Bureau Act of 1865** was passed, in amended form, only to be vetoed by Lincoln's successor, Andrew Johnson.[3]

**Amendments 13-15** to the Federal Constitution were passed in quick succession.[4]

In addition, to insure the deliberate pacification of the former rebel states, as well as articulate Federal authority, the South was occupied by Federal Troops. Laws were laws—*mere ink on paper*, but Federal *bayonets* seemed to guarantee that any stirring of rebellion would be crushed without mercy. The presence of the Federal Army also provided a certain measure of protection for the **AFRICANS**.

---

[3] Ibid. 179-182.

[4] Ibid. 183-187.

## The South's Course Towards "Redemption"

This policy of Reconstruction did not go unnoticed by Southerners determined to reestablish their pre-Civil War power! In other words, they were determined to, if forced to remain in the Union, reestablish unilateral control over the region. In their words, they wanted to *Redeem* the South! It was the White Southerner's turn to "appeal" his Federal sentence. He would do this in three separate, but interconnected ways. All three methods would be under girded by terrorism. The Southerner, between the years 1865 and 1883, would successfully nullify the **Federal legislative process** (see the enactment and then virtual nullification of the **Enforcement Act of 1870 and Civil Rights Act of 1875**). Another method of Southern "Redemption" was taking advantage of **political cowardice** on the part of the Republican Party. The election of **Rutherford B. Hayes** to the presidency in 1876 was a prime example of Northern/Republican political cowardice in reference to the **Federal Presidential/Electoral process**. Manipulation of the **Federal Judicial Process** was accomplished by the **U.S. Supreme Court**'s *Cruikshank* ruling in 1875 and its 1883 declaration that the **Civil Rights Act of 1875 was unconstitutional.** This action, on the part of the **Supreme Court**, coupled with its infamous ruling in the matter of *Plessy v. Ferguson* in 1896, provided the judicial "coup d' grace," concerning the **AFRICAN'S** so-called "Civil Rights."

However, there would be a final, albeit weak appeal to Southern pragmatism, by Booker T. Washington.

## *Nullification of the Enforcement Act of 1875 By Terrorist Means*

Terrorism was a threat to the physical safety of **AFRICANS**. Terrorism was also a direct challenge to the authority of the Federal Government! Groups of demobilized Confederate soldiers organized themselves into para-military groups in a successful attempt to terrorize the newly freed **AFRICANS** back into a semi-slave state. The formation of these groups caused the Government to pass the **Enforcement Act of 1870.** The Act was an attempt to give the Federal authorities occupying the South the legal wherewithal to combat terrorist groups. The problems with such groups was that they were tightly organized and secretive. They had the ability to wage guerrilla warfare against the **AFRICANS** and Federal Troops.[5]

---

[5] The best known of these groups is the Ku Klux Klan, organized in Pulaski Tennessee in the winter of 1865. However, careful research on the part of John Brinson reveals a plethora of Klan type groups organized throughout the South, he lists the following groups: the Original Southern Klans, (Georgia), the Knights of the Ku Klux Klan, of Florida, The Federated Klans of Alabama, The Knights of the Kavaliers, (Virginia), American Keystone Society, (Pennsylvania), United Sons of Dixie, (Tennessee), American Shores Patrol, (Virginia), the Christian American, (Texas), The Fact Finders, (Georgia), The Fight For Free Enterprise (Texas), The Mason-Dixon Society, (Kentucky), Free White Americans, (Tennessee), We The People (Georgia), The Vigilantes (Georgia), The Veterans & Patriots Federation of Labor,(Tennessee) The Order of American Patriots

As you read further, you will find a copy of the doomed **Enforcement Act of 1875** for your inspection. A likewise doomed piece of legislation, the **Civil Rights Act of 1875** is included.

## *Southern "Redemption" And Political Cowardice In The Presidential Election of 1876*

On the Federal electoral level, in a deal that would forever alter the destiny of **AFRICANS** in America, Reconstruction collapsed with the promise made to the South by the Republican nominee for the presidency, **Rutherford B. Hayes**. In a not so secret deal, Hayes vowed to withdraw Federal Troops from the South *if* white Southerners would assist in swinging the 1876 presidential election his way. The Southerners did and soon after he was sworn in as president, he withdrew all Federal Troops from the South. This left the **AFRICANS** at the mercy of their former masters. Thus, an unprecedented reign of terror engulfed the South, as once again the **AFRICAN** *twisted* in the wind with American Society pronouncing him guilty and sentencing him to a living death.

---

(Texas), The Southern Committee to Uphold the Constitution, (Texas), The Patrick Henrys (Georgia), The Southern States Industrial Council (Texas), The National Small Businessmen's Association (Michigan), John D. Brinson, *Reparations! We Must Demand What Is Due Us!* (Richmond, CA: CD Publisher, 1999), 16.

## *The Federal Judicial Process and the African*

At the judicial level, in the case of the ***United States** v. Cruikshank, the **Supreme Court*** indirectly upheld a massacre of freed men at the hands of an armed force of former Confederate soldiers in Grant Parish, Louisiana in 1872. In a dispute over the state election, **AFRICANS** cordoned off the county seat of Colfax and held the whites off for three weeks. Finally the **AFRICANS** were overwhelmed and slaughtered. Federal charges were brought against the whites. However, using the appeals process, the whites took the case all the way to the **Supreme Court**. The court basically gutted the convictions in its *Cruikshank* ruling.

Two other pieces of Federal judicial craft are included. The first is the **U.S. Supreme Court**'s 1883 ruling declaring the **Civil Rights Act of 1875** unconstitutional. The last is the **Supreme Court**'s infamous ruling in the case of *Plessy v. Ferguson*.

As you will see, the South's three-pronged attack was successful. Namely, **nullification of anti-terrorism laws** such as the **Enforcement Act of 1870**, taking advantage of the North's **political cowardice** as in the case of Rutherford Hayes' ascension to the Federal Presidency, and the **US Supreme Court**'s adverse rulings such as in its decision in the matter of the **Civil Rights Act of 1875's** constitutionality and in *Plessy v. Ferguson* (1896) were resounding successes.

**Ulysses S. Grant
1822-1885
Commanding General Union Army
1864-1865
President of the United States
1868-1877
Signed into Law the Enforcement Act of 1870
And
The Civil Rights Act of 1875**

*The negro slaves of the South are the happiest, and, in some sense, the freest people in the world. The children and the aged and infirm work not at all, and yet have all the comforts and necessaries of life provided for them. They enjoy liberty, because they are oppressed neither by care nor labor. The women do little hard work, and are protected from the despotism of their husbands by their masters. The negro men and stout boys work, on the average, in good weather, not more than nine hours a day. The balance of their time is spent in perfect abandon. Besides' they have their Sabbaths and holidays. White men, with so much of license and liberty, would die of ennui; but negroes luxuriate in corporeal and mental repose. With their faces upturned to the sun, they can sleep at any hour; and quiet sleep is the greatest of human enjoyments. "Blessed be the man who invented sleep." 'Tis happiness in itself--and results from contentment with the present, and confident assurance of the future.*

## *George Fitzhugh 19$^{th}$ Century Pro Slavery Advocate*

## *Twist! Twist! Twist!*

## Enforcement Act of 1870

An Act to enforce the Right of Citizens of the **United States** to vote in the several States of this Union, and for other Purposes.

Be it enacted by the Senate and House of Representatives of the **United States** of America in Congress assembled, That all citizens of the **United States** who are or shall be otherwise qualified by law to vote at any election by the people in any State, Territory, district, county, city, parish, township, school district, municipality, or other territorial subdivision, shall be entitled and allowed to vote at all such elections, without distinction of race, color, or previous condition of servitude; any constitution, law, custom, usage, or regulation of any State or Territory, or by or under its authority, to the contrary not withstanding.

SEC. 2. *And be it further enacted*, That if by or under the authority of the constitution or laws of any State, or the laws of any Territory, any act is or shall be required to be done as a prerequisite or qualification for voting, and by such constitution or laws persons or officers are or shall be charged with the performance of duties in furnishing to citizens an opportunity to perform such prerequisite, or to become qualified to vote, it shall be the duty of every such person and officer to give to all citizens of the **United States** the same and equal opportunity to perform such prerequisite, and to become qualified to vote without distinction of race, color, or previous condition of servitude; and if any such person or officer shall refuse or knowingly omit to give full effect to this section, he shall, for every such offence, forfeit and pay the sum of five hundred dollars to the person aggrieved thereby, to be recovered by an action on the case, with full costs, and such allowance for counsel fees as the court shall deem just, and shall also, for every such offence, be deemed guilty of a misdemeanor, and shall, on conviction thereof, be fined not less than five hundred dollars, or be imprisoned not less than one month and not more than one year, or both, at the discretion of the court.

SEC. 3. *And be it further enacted*, That whenever, by or under the authority of the constitution or laws of any State, or the laws of any Territory, any act is or shall be required to [be] done by any citizen as a prerequisite to qualify or entitle him to vote, the offer of any such citizen to perform the act required to be done as aforesaid shall, if it fail to be carried into execution by reason of the wrongful act or omission aforesaid of the person or officer charged with the duty of receiving or permitting such performance or offer to perform, or acting thereon, be deemed and held as a performance in law of such act; and the person so offering and failing as aforesaid, and being otherwise qualified, shall be entitled to vote in the same manner and to the same extent as if he had in fact performed such act; and any judge, inspector, or other officer of election whose duty it is or shall be to receive, count, certify, register, report, or give effect tot he vote of any such citizen who shall wrongfully refuse or omit to receive, count, certify, register, report, or give effect to the vote of such citizen upon the presentation by him of his affidavit stating such offer and the time and place thereof, and the name of the officer or person whose duty it was to act thereon, and that such act, shall for every such offence forfeit and pay the sum of five hundred dollars to the person aggrieved thereby, to be recovered by an action on the case, with full costs, and such allowance for counsel fees as the court shall deem just, and shall also for every such offence by guilty of a misdemeanor, and shall, on conviction thereof, be fined not less than five hundred dollars, or be imprisoned not less than one month and not more than one year, or both, at the discretion of the court.

SEC. 4. *And be it further enacted*, That if any person, by force, bribery, threats, intimidation, or other unlawful means, shall hinder, delay, prevent, or obstruct, or shall combine and confederate with others to hinder, delay, prevent, or obstruct, any citizen from doing any act required to be done to qualify him to vote or from voting at any election as aforesaid, such person shall for every such offence forfeit and pay the sum of five hundred dollars to the person aggrieved thereby, to be recovered by an action on the case, with full costs, and such allowance for counsel fees as the court shall deem just, and shall also for every such offence be guilty of a misdemeanor, and shall, on conviction thereof, be fined not less than five hundred dollars, or be imprisoned not less than one month and not more than one year, or both, at the discretion of the court.

SEC. 5. *And be it further enacted*, That if any person shall prevent, hinder, control, or intimidate, or shall attempt to prevent, hinder, control or intimidate, any person from exercising or in exercising the right of suffrage, to whom the right of suffrage is secured or guaranteed by the fifteenth amendment to the Constitution of the **United States**, by means of bribery, threats, or threats of depriving such person of employment or occupation, or of ejecting such person from rented house, lands, or other property, or by threats of refusing to renew leases or contracts for labor, or by threats of violence to himself or family, such person so offending shall be deemed guilty of a misdemeanor, and shall, on conviction thereof, be fined not less than five hundred dollars, or be imprisoned not less than one month and not more than one year, or both, at the discretion of the court.

SEC. 6. *And be it further enacted*, That if two or more persons shall band or conspire together, or go in disguise upon the public highway, or upon the premises of another, with intent to violate any provision of this act, or to injure, oppress, threaten, or intimidate any citizen with intent to prevent or hinder his free exercise and enjoyment of any right or privilege granted or secured to him by the Constitution or laws of the **United States**, or because of his having exercised the same, such persons shall be held guilty of felony, and, on conviction thereof, shall be fined or imprisoned, or both, at the discretion of the court, --the fine not to exceed five thousand dollars, and the imprisonment not to exceed ten years, --and shall, moreover, be thereafter ineligible to, and disabled from holding, any office or place of honor, profit, or trust created by the Constitution or laws of the **United States**.

SEC. 7. *And be it further enacted,* That if the act of violating any provision in either of the two preceding sections, any other felony, crime, or misdemeanor shall be committed, the offender, on conviction of such violation of said sections, shall be punished for the same with such punishments as are attached to the said felonies, crimes, and misdemeanors by the laws of the State in which the offence may be committed.

SEC. 8. *And be it further enacted,* That the district courts of the **United States**, within their respective districts, shall have, exclusively of the courts of the several States, cognizance of all crimes and offences committed against the provisions of this act, and also, concurrently with the circuit courts of the **United States**, of all causes, civil and criminal, arising under this act, except as herein otherwise provided and the jurisdiction hereby conferred shall be exercised in conformity with the laws and practice governing **United States** courts; and all crimes and offences committed against the provisions of this act may be prosecuted by the indictment of a grand jury, or, in cases of crimes and offences not infamous, the prosection may be either by indictment or information filed by the district attorney in a court having jurisdiction.

SEC. 9. *And be it further enacted,* That the district attorneys, marshals, and deputy marshals of the **United States**, the commissioners appointed by the circuit and territorial courts of the **United States**, with powers of arresting, imprisoning, or bailing offenders against the laws of the **United States**, and every other officer who may be specially empowered by the President of the **United States**, shall be, and they are hereby, specially authorized and required, at the expense of the **United States**, to institute proceedings against all and every person who shall violate the provisions of this act, and cause him or them to be arrested and imprisoned, or bailed, as the case may be, for trial before such court of the **United States** or territorial court as has cognizance of the offense. And with a view to afford reasonable protection to all persons in their constitutional right to vote without distinction of race, color, or previous condition of servitude, and to prompt discharge of the duties of this act, it shall be the duty of the circuit courts of the **United States**, and the superior courts of the Territories of the **United States**, form time to time, to increase the number of commissioners, so as to afford a speedy and convenient means for the arrest and examination of persons charged with a violation of this act; and such commissioners are hereby authorized and required to exercise and discharge all the powers and duties conferred on them by this act, and the same duties with regard to offences created by this act as they are authorized by law to exercise with regard to other offences against the laws of the **United States**.

SEC. 10. *And be it further enacted,* That it shall be the duty of all marshals and deputy marshals to obey and execute all warrants and precepts issued under the provisions of this act, when to them directed; and should any marshal or deputy marshal refuse to receive such warrant or other process when tendered, or to use all proper means diligently to execute the same, he shall, on conviction thereof, be fined in the sum of one thousand dollars, to the use of the person deprived of the rights conferred by this act. And the better to enable the said commissioners to execute their duties faithfully and efficiently, in conformity with the Constitution of the **United States** and the requirements of this act, they are hereby authorized and empowered, within their districts respectively, to appoint, in writing, under their hands, any one or more suitable persons, from time to time, to execute all such warrants and other process as may be issued by them in the lawful performance of their respective duties, and the persons so appointed to execute any warrant or process as aforesaid shall have authority to summon and call to their aid the bystanders or posse comitatus of the proper county, or such portion of the land or naval forces of the **United States**, or of the militia, as may be necessary to the performance of the duty with which they are charged, and to insure a faithful observance of the fifteenth amendment tot he constitution of the **United States**; and such warrants shall run and be executed by said officers anywhere in the State or Territory within which they are issued.

SEC. 11. *And be it further enacted,* That any person who shall knowingly and wilfully obstruct, hinder, or prevent any officer or other person charged with the execution of any warrant to process issued under the provisions of this act, or any person or persons lawfully assisting him or them from arresting any person for whose apprehension such warrant or process may have been issued, or shall rescue or attempt to rescue such person from the custody of the officer or other person or persons, or those lawfully assisting as aforesaid, when so arrested pursuant to the authority herein given and declared, or shall aid, abet, or assist any person so arrested as aforesaid, directly or indirectly, to escape from the custody of the officer or other person legally authorized as aforesaid, or shall harbor or conceal any person for whose arrest a warrant or process shall have been issued as aforesaid, so as to prevent his discovery and arrest after notice or knowledge of the fact that a warrant has been issued for the apprehension of such person, shall, for either of said offences, be subject to a fine not exceeding one thousand dollars, or imprisonment not exceeding six months, or both, at the discretion of the court, on conviction before the district or circuit court of the **United States** for the district or circuit in which said offence may have been committed, or before the proper court of criminal jurisdiction, if committed within any one of the organized Territories of the **United States**.

SEC. 12. *And be it further enacted*, That the commissioners, district attorneys, the marshals, their deputies, and the clerks of the said district, circuit, and territorial courts shall be paid for their services the like fees as may be allowed to them for similar services in other cases. The person or persons authorized to execute the process to be issued by such commissioners for the arrest of offenders against the provisions of this act shall be entitled to the usual fees allowed to the marshal for an arrest for each person he or they may arrest and take before any such commissioner as aforesaid, with such other fees as may be deemed reasonable by such commissioner for such other additional services as may be necessarily performed by him or them, such as attending at the examination, keeping the prisoner in custody, and providing him with food and lodging during his detention and until the final determination of such commissioner, and in general for performing such other duties as may be required in the premises; such fees to be made up in conformity with the fees usually charged by the officers of the courts of justice within the proper district or county as near as may be practicable, and paid out of the treasury of the **United States** on the certificate of the judge of the district within which the arrest is made, and to be recoverable from the defendant as part of the judgment in case of conviction.

SEC. 13. *And be it further enacted,* That it shall be lawful for the President of the **United States** to employ such part of the land or naval forces of the **United States**, or of the militia, as shall be necessary to aid in the execution of judicial process issued under this act.

SEC. 14. *And be it further enacted*, That whenever any person shall hold office, except as a member of Congress or of some State legislature, contrary to the provisions of the third section of the fourteenth article of the amendment of the Constitution of the **United States**, it shall be the duty of the district attorney of the **United States** for the district in which such person shall hold office, as aforesaid, to proceed against such person, by writ of quo warranto, returnable to the circuit or district court of the **United States** in such district, and to prosecute the same to the removal of such person from office; and any writ of quo warranto so brought, as aforesaid, shall take precedence of all other cases on the docket of the court to which it is made returnable, and shall not be continued unless for cause proved to the satisfaction of the court.

SEC. 15. *And be it further enacted,* That any person who shall hereafter knowingly accept or hold any office under the **United States**, or nay State to which he is ineligible under the third section of the fourteenth article of amendment of the constitution of the **United States**, or who shall attempt to hold or e exercise the duties of any such office, shall be deemed guilty of a misdemeanor against the **United States**, and, upon conviction thereof before the circuit or district court of the **United States**, shall be imprisoned not more than one year, or fined not exceeding one thousand dollars, or both, at the discretion of the court.

SEC. 16. *And be it further enacted,* That all persons within the jurisdiction of the **United States** shall have the same right in every State and Territory in the **United States** to make and enforce contracts, to sue, be parties, give evidence, and to the full and equal benefit of all laws and proceedings for the security of person and property as is enjoyed by white citizens, and shall be subject to like punishment, pains, penalties, taxes, licenses, and exactions of every kind, and none other, any law, statute, ordinance, regulation, or custom to the contrary notwithstanding. NO tax or charge shall be imposed or enforced by any State upon any person immigrating thereto from a foreign country which is not equally imposed and enforced upon every person immigrating to such State from any other foreign country; and any law of any State in conflict with this provision is hereby declared null and void.

SEC. 17. *And be it further enacted,* That any person who, under color of any law, statute, ordinance, regulation, or custom shall subject, or cause to be subjected, any inhabitant of any State or Territory to the deprivation of any right secured or protected by the last preceding section of this act, or to different punishment , pains, or penalties on account of such person being an alien, or by reason of his color or Race, than is prescribed fro the punishment of citizens, shall be deemed guilty of a misdemeanor, and, on conviction, shall be punished by fine not exceeding one thousand dollars, or imprisonment not exceeding on year, or both, in the discretion of the court.

SEC. 18. *And be it further enacted,* That the act to protect all persons in the **United States** in their civil rights, and furnish the means of their vindication, passed April nine, eighteen hundred and sixty-six, is hereby re-enacted; and sections sixteen and seventeen hereof shall be enforced according to the provisions of said act.

SEC. 19. *And be it further enacted,* That if at any election for representative or delegate in the Congress of the **United States** any person shall knowingly personate and vote, or attempt to vote, in the name of any other person, whether living, dead, or fictitious; or vote more than once at the same election for any candidate for the same office; or vote at a place where he may not be lawfully entitled to vote; or vote without having a lawful right to vote; or do any unlawful act to secure a right or an opportunity to vote for himself or any other person; or by force, threat, menace, intimidation, bribery, reward, or offer, or promise thereof, or otherwise unlawfully prevent any qualified voter of any State of the **United States** of America, or of any Territory thereof, from freely exercising the right of suffrage, or by any such means induce any voter to refuse to exercise such right; or compel or induce by any such means, or otherwise, any officer of an election in any such State or Territory to receive a vote from a person not legally qualified or entitled to vote; or interfere in any manner with any officer of said elections in the discharge of his duties; or by any of such means, or other unlawful means, induce any officer of an election, or officer whose duty it is to ascertain, announce, or declare the result of any such election, or give or make any certificate document, or evidence in relation thereto, to violate or refuse to comply with his duty, or any law regulating the same; or knowingly and wilfully receive the vote of any person entitled to vote; or aid, counsel, procure, or advise any such voter, person, or officer to do any act hereby made a crime, or to omit to do any duty the omission of which is hereby made a crime, or attempt to do so, every such person shall be deemed guilty of a crime, and shall for such crime be liable to prosection in any court of the **United States** of competent jurisdiction, and, on conviction thereof, shall be punished by a fine not exceeding five hundred dollars, or by imprisonment for a term not exceeding three years, or both, in the discretion of the court, and shall pay the costs of prosection.

SEC. 20. *And be it further enacted,* That if, at any registration of voters for an election for representative or delegate in the Congress of the **United States**, any person shall knowingly personate and register, or attempt to register, in the name of any other person, whether living dead, or fictitious, or fraudulently register, or fraudulently attempt to register, not having a lawful right so to do; or do any unlawful act to secure registration for himself or any other person; or by force, threat, menace, intimidation, bribery, reward, or offer, or promise thereof, or other unlawful means, prevent or hinder any person having a lawful right to register form duly exercising such right; or compel or induce, by any of such means, or other unlawful means, any officer of registration to admit to registration any person not legally entitled thereto, or interfere in any manner with any officer of registration in the discharge of his duties, or by any such means, or other unlawful means,. Induce any officer of registration to violate or refuse to comply with his duty, or any law regulating the same; or knowingly and wilfully receive the vote of any person not entitled to vote, or refuse to receive the vote of any person entitled to vote, or aid, counsel, procure, or advise any such voter, person, or officer to do any act hereby made a crime, or to omit any act, the omission of which is hereby made a crime, every such person shall be deemed guilty of a crime, and shall be liable to prosecution and punishment therefore, as provided in section nineteen of this act for persons guilty of any of the crimes therein specified: *Provided*, That every registration made under the laws of any State or Territory, for any State or other election at which such representative or delegate in Congress shall be chosen, shall be deemed to be a registration within the meaning of this act, notwithstanding the same shall also be made for the purposes of any State, territorial, or municipal election.

SEC. 21. *And be it further enacted*, That whenever, by the laws of any State or Territory, the name of any candidate or person to be voted for as representative or delegate in Congress shall be required to be printed, written, or contained in any ticket or ballot with other candidates or persons to be voted for at the same election for State, territorial, municipal, or local officers, it shall be sufficient prima facie evidence, either for the purpose of indicting or convicting any person charged with voting, or attempting or offering to vote, unlawfully under the provisions of the preceding sections, or for committing either of the offenses thereby created, to prove that the person so charged or indicted, voted, or attempted or offered to vote, such ballot or ticket, or committed either of the offenses named in the preceding sections of this act with reference to such ballot. And the proof and establishment of such facts shall be taken, held, and deemed to be presumptive evidence that such person voted, or attempted or offered to vote, for such representative or delegate, as the case may be, or that such offense was committed with reference to the election of such representative or delegate, and shall be sufficient to warrant his conviction, unless it shall be shown that any such ballot, when cast, or attempted or offered to be cast, by him, did not contain the name of any candidate for the office of representative or delegate in the Congress of the **United States**, or that such offense was not committed with reference to the election of such representative or delegate.

SEC. 22. *And be it further enacted,* That any officer of any election at which any representative or delegate in the Congress of the **United States** shall be voted for, whether such officer of election be appointed or created by or under any law or authority of the **United States**, or by or under any State, territorial, district, or municipal law or authority, who shall neglect or refuse to perform any duty in regard to such election required of him by any law of the **United States**, or of any State or Territory thereof; or violate any duty so imposed, or knowingly do any act thereby unauthorized, with intent to affect any such election, or the result thereof; or fraudulently make any false certificate of the result of such election in regard to such representative or delegate; or withhold, conceal, or destroy any certificate of record so required by law respecting, concerning, or pertaining to the election of any such representative or delegate; or neglect or refuse to make and return the same as so required by law; or aid, counsel, procure, or advise any voter, person, or officer to do any act by this or any of the preceding sections made a crime; or to omit to do any duty the omission of which is by this or any of said sections made a crime, or attempt to do so, shall be deemed guilty of a crime and shall be liable to prosecution and punishment therefor, as provided in the nineteenth section of this act for persons guilty of any of the crimes therein specified.

SEC. 23. *And be it further enacted,* That whenever any person shall be defeated or deprived of his election to any office, except elector of President or Vice-President, representative or delegate in Congress, or member of a State legislature, by reason of the denial to any citizen or citizens who shall offer to vote, of the right to vote, on account of race, color, or previous condition of servitude, his right to hold and enjoy such office, and the emoluments thereof, shall not be impaired by such denial; and such person may bring any appropriate suit or proceeding to recover possession of such office, and in cases where it shall appear that the sole question touching the title to such office arises out of the denial of the right to vote to citizens who so offered to vote, on account of race, color, or previous condition of servitude, such suit or proceeding may be instituted in the circuit or district court of the **United States** of the circuit or district in which such person resides. And said circuit or district court shall have, concurrently with the State courts, jurisdiction thereof so far as to determine the rights of the parties to such office by reason of the denial of the right guaranteed by the fifteenth article of amendment to the Constitution of the **United States**, and secured by this act.

*APPROVED, May 31, 1870.*

*Twist! Twist! Twist!*

## The Cruikshank Ruling (1875)

## U S v. Cruikshank 1875
## U.S. Supreme Court
## U S v. CRUIKSHANK, 92 U.S. 542 (1875)
## 92 U.S. 542
## UNITED STATES
## v.
## CRUIKSHANK ET AL.

### October Term, 1875

### U S v. Cruikshank 92 U.S. 542 (1875)

This was an indictment for conspiracy under the sixth section of the act of May 30, 1870, known as the Enforcement Act (16 Stat. 140), and consisted of thirty-two counts.

The first count was for banding together, with intent 'unlawfully and feloniously to injure, oppress, threaten, and intimidate' two citizens of the **United States**, 'of **AFRICAN** descent and persons of color,' 'with the unlawful and felonious intent thereby' them 'to hinder and prevent in their respective free [92 U.S. 542, 545] exercise and enjoyment of their lawful right and privilege to peaceably assemble together with each other and with other citizens of the said **United States** for a peaceable and lawful purpose.'

The second avers an intent to hinder and prevent the exercise by the same persons of the 'right to keep and bear arms for a lawful purpose.'

The third avers an intent to deprive the same persons 'of their respective several lives and liberty of person, without due process of law.'

The fourth avers an intent to deprive the same persons of the 'free exercise and enjoyment of the right and privilege to the full and equal benefit of all laws and proceedings for the security of persons and property' enjoyed by white citizens.

The fifth avers an intent to hinder and prevent the same persons 'in the exercise and enjoyment of the rights, privileges, immunities, and protection granted and secured to them respectively as citizens of the said **United States**, and as citizens of the said State of Louisiana, by reason of and for and on account of the race and color' of the said persons.

The sixth avers an intent to hinder and prevent the same persons in 'the free exercise and enjoyment of the several and respective right and privilege to vote at any election to be thereafter by law had and held by the people in and of the said State of Louisiana.'
The seventh avers an intent 'to put in great fear of bodily harm, injure, and oppress' the same persons, 'because and for the reason' that, having the right to vote, they had voted.

The eighth avers an intent 'to prevent and hinder' the same persons 'in their several and respective free exercise and enjoyment of every, each, all, and singular and several rights and privileges granted and secured' to them 'by the constitution and laws of the **United States**.'

*The next eight counts are a repetition of the first eight, except that, instead of the words 'band together,' the words 'combine, conspire, and confederate together' are used. Three of the defendants were found guilty under the first sixteen counts, and not guilty under the remaining counts. [92 U.S. 542, 546] The parties thus convicted moved in arrest of judgment on the following grounds:--*

1. Because the matters and things set forth and charged in the several counts, one to sixteen inclusive, do not constitute offences against the laws of the **United States**, and do not come within the purview, true intent, and meaning of the act of Congress, approved 31st May, 1870, entitled 'An Act to enforce the right of citizens of the **United States**,' & c.

2. Because the matters and things in the said indictment set forth and charged do not constitute offences cognizable in teh Circuit Court, and do not come within its power and jurisdiction.

3. Because the offences created by the sixth section of the act of Congress referred to, and upon which section the aforesaid sixteen courts are based, are not constitutionally within the jurisdiction of the courts of the **United States**, and because the matters and things therein referred to are

judicially cognizable by State tribunals only, and legislative action thereon is among the constitutionally reserved rights of the several States.

4. Because the said act, in so far as it creates offences and imposes penalties, is in violation of the Constitution of the **United States**, and an infringement of the rights of the several States and the people.

5. Because the eighth and sixteenth counts of the indictment are too vague, general, insufficient, and uncertain, to afford the accused proper notice to plead and prepare their defence, and set forth no specific offence under the law.

6. Because the verdict of the jury against the defendants is not warranted or supported by law. On this motion the opinions of the judges were divided, that of the presiding judge being that the several counts in question are not sufficient in law, and do not contain charges of criminal matter indictable under the laws of the **United States**; and that the motion in arrest of judgment should be granted. The case comes up at the instance of the **United States**, on certificate of this division of opinion.

Sect. 1 of the Enforcement Act declares, that all citizens of the **United States**, otherwise qualified, shall be allowed to vote at all elections, without distinction of race, color, or previous servitude. [92 U.S. 542, 547] Sect. 2 provides, that, if by the law of any State or Territory a prerequisite to voting is necessary, equal opportunity for it shall be given to all, without distinction, &c.; and any person charged with the duty of furnishing the prerequisite, who refuses or knowingly omits to give full effect to this section, shall be guilty of misdemeanor.

Sect. 3 provides, that an offer of performance, in respect to the prerequisite, when proved by affidavit of the claimant, shall be equivalent to performance; and any judge or inspector of election who refuses to accept it shall be guilty, &c.

Sect. 4 provides, that any person who, by force, bribery, threats, intimidation, or other unlawful means, hinders, delays, prevents, or obstructs any citizen from qualifying himself to vote, or combines with others to do so, shall be guilty, &c.

Sect. 5 provides, that any person who prevents, hinders, controls, or intimidates any person from exercising the right of suffrage, to whom it is secured by the fifteenth amendment, or attempts to do so, by bribery or threats of violence, or deprivation of property or employment, shall be guilty, &c.

The sixth section is as follows:--
> 'That if two or more persons shall band or conspire together, or go in disguise upon the public highway, or upon the premises of another, with intent to violate any provisions of this act, or to injure, oppress, threaten, or intimidate any citizen with intent to prevent or hinder his free exercise and enjoyment of any right or privilege granted or secured to him by the constitution or laws of

the **United States**, or because of his having exercised the same, such persons shall be held guilty of felony, and, on conviction thereof, shall be fined or imprisoned, or both, at the discretion of the court,-the fine not to exceed $5,000, and the imprisonment not to exceed ten years; and shall, moreover, be thereafter ineligible to, and disabled from holding, any office or place of honor, profit, or trust created by the constitution or laws of the **United States**.'

This case was argued at the October Term, 1874, by Mr. Attorney- General Williams and Mr. Solicitor-General Phillips for the plaintiff in error; and by Mr. Reverdy Johnson, Mr. David Dudley Field, Mr. Philip Phillips, and Mr. R. H. Marr for the defendants in error. [92 U.S. 542, 548]

MR. CHIEF JUSTICE WAITE delivered the opinion of the court.

This case comes here with a certificate by the judges of the Circuit Court for the District of Louisiana that they were divided in opinion upon a question which occurred at the hearing. It presents for our consideration an indictment containing sixteen counts, divided into two series of eight counts each, based upon sect. 6 of the Enforcement Act of May 31, 1870. That section is as follows:--

'That if two or more persons shall band or conspire together, or go in disguise upon the public highway, or upon the premises of another, with intent to violate any provision of this act, or to injure, oppress, threaten, or intimidate any citizen, with intent to prevent or hinder his free exercise and enjoyment of any right or privilege granted or secured to him by the constitution or laws of the **United States**, or because of his having exercised the same, such persons shall be held guilty of felony, and, on conviction thereof, shall be fined or imprisoned, or both, at the discretion of the court,-the fine not to exceed $5,000, and the imprisonment not to exceed ten years, and shall, moreover, be thereafter ineligible to, and disabled from holding, any office or place of honor, profit, or trust created by the constitution or laws of the **United States**.' 16 Stat. 141.

The question certified arose upon a motion in arrest of judgment after a verdict of guilty generally upon the whole sixteen counts, and is stated to be, whether 'the said sixteen counts of said indictment are severally good and sufficient in law, and contain charges of criminal matter indictable under the laws of the **United States**.'

The general charge in the first eight counts is that of 'banding,' and in the second eight, that of 'conspiring' together to injure, oppress, threaten, and intimidate Levi Nelson and Alexander Tillman, citizens of the **United States**, of **AFRICAN** descent and persons of color, with the intent thereby to hinder and prevent them in their free exercise and enjoyment of rights and privileges 'granted and secured' to them 'in common with all other good citizens of the **United States** by the constitution and laws of the **United States**.'

The offences provided for by the statute in question do not consist in the mere 'banding' or 'conspiring' of two or [92 U.S. 542, 549] more persons together, but in their banding or conspiring with the intent, or for any of the purposes, specified. To bring this case under the operation of the statute, therefore, it must appear that the right, the enjoyment of which the conspirators intended to hinder or prevent, was one granted or secured by the constitution or laws of the **United States**. If it does not so appear, the criminal matter charged has not been made indictable by any act of Congress.

We have in our political system a government of the **United States** and a government of each of the several States. Each one of these governments is distinct from the others, and each has citizens of its own who owe it allegiance, and whose rights, within its jurisdiction, it must protect. The same person may be at the same time a citizen of the **United States** and a citizen of a State, but his rights of citizenship under one of these governments will be different from those he has under the other. Slaughter-House Cases, 16 Wall. 74.

Citizens are the members of the political community to which they belong. They are the people who compose the community, and who, in their associated capacity, have established or submitted themselves to the dominion of a government for the promotion of their general welfare and the protection of their individual as well as their collective rights. In the formation of a government, the people may confer upon it such powers as they choose. The government, when so formed, may, and when called upon should, exercise all the powers it has for the protection of the rights of its citizens and the people within its jurisdiction; but it can exercise no other. The duty of a government to afford protection is limited always by the power it possesses for that purpose.

Experience made the fact known to the people of the **United States** that they required a national government for national purposes. The separate governments of the separate States, bound together by the articles of confederation alone, were not sufficient for the promotion of the general welfare of the people in respect to foreign nations, or for their complete protection as citizens of the confederated States. For this reason, the people of the **United States**, 'in order to form a more perfect union, establish justice, insure domestic tranquillity, provide for [92 U.S. 542, 550] the common defence, promote the general welfare, and secure the blessings of liberty' to themselves and their posterity (Const. Preamble), ordained and established the government of the **United States**, and defined its powers by a constitution, which they adopted as its fundamental law, and made its rule of action.

The government thus established and defined is to some extent a government of the States in their political capacity. It is also, for certain purposes, a government of the pepole. Its powers are limited in number, but not in degree. Within the scope of its powers, as enumerated and defined, it is

**Supreme** and above the States; but beyond, it has no existence. It was erected for special purposes, and endowed with all the powers necessary for its own preservation and the accomplishment of the ends its people had in view. It can neither grant nor secure to its citizens any right or privilege not expressly or by implication placed under its jurisdiction.

The people of the **United States** resident within any State are subject to two governments: one State, and the other National; but there need be no conflict between the two. The powers which one possesses, the other does not. They are established for different purposes, and have separate jurisdictions. Together they make one whole, and furnish the people of the **United States** with a complete government, ample for the protection of all their rights at home and abroad. True, it may sometimes happen that a person is amenable to both jurisdictions for one and the same act. Thus, if a marshal of the **United States** is unlawfully resisted while executing the process of the courts within a State, and the resistance is accompanied by an assault on the officer, the sovereignty of the **United States** is violated by the resistance, and that of the State by the breach of peace, in the assault. So, too, if one passes counterfeited coin of the **United States** within a State, it may be an offence against the **United States** and the State: the **United States**, because it discredits the coin; and the State, because of the fraud upon him to whom it is passed. This does not, however, necessarily imply that the two governments possess powers in common, or bring them into conflict with each other. It is the natural consequence of a citizenship [92 U.S. 542, 551] which owes allegiance to two sovereignties, and claims protection from both. The citizen cannot complain, because he has voluntarily submitted himself to such a form of government. He owes allegiance to the two departments, so to speak, and within their respective spheres must pay the penalties which each exacts for disobedience to its laws. In return, he can demand protection from each within its own jurisdiction.

The government of the **United States** is one of delegated powers alone. Its authority is defined and limited by the Constitution. All powers not granted to it by that instrument are reserved to the States or the people. No rights can be acquired under the constitution or laws of the **United States**, except such as the government of the **United States** has the authority to grant or secure. All that cannot be so granted or secured are left under the protection of the States.

We now proceed to an examination of the indictment, to ascertain whether the several rights, which it is alleged the defendants intended to interfere with, are such as had been in law and in fact granted or secured by the constitution or laws of the **United States**.

The first and ninth counts state the intent of the defendants to have been to hinder and prevent the citizens named in the free exercise and enjoyment of their 'lawful right and privilege to peaceably assemble together with each other and with other citizens of the **United States** for a peaceful and lawful purpose.' The right of the people peaceably to assemble for lawful purposes existed long before the adoption of the Constitution of the **United States**. In fact, it is, and always has been, one of the attributes of citizenship under a free government. It 'derives its source,' to use the language of Chief Justice Marshall, in Gibbons v. Ogden, 9 Wheat. 211, 'from those laws whose authority is acknowledged by civilized man throughout the world.' It is found wherever civilization exists. It was not, therefore, a right granted to the people by the Constitution. The government of the **United States** when established found it in existence, with the obligation on the part of the States to afford it protection. As no direct power over it was granted to Congress, it remains, according to the ruling in Gibbons v. Ogden, id. 203, subject to State jurisdiction. [92 U.S. 542, 552] Only such existing rights were committed by the people to the protection of Congress as came within the general scope of the authority granted to the national government.

The first amendment to the Constitution prohibits Congress from abridging 'the right of the people to assemble and to petition the government for a redress of grievances.' This, like the other amendments proposed and adopted at the same time, was not intended to limit the powers of the State governments in respect to their own citizens, but to operate upon the National government alone. Barron v. The City of Baltimore, 7 Pet. 250; Lessee of Livingston v. Moore, id. 551; Fox v. Ohio, 5 How. 434; Smith v. Maryland, 18 id. 76; Withers v. Buckley, 20 id. 90; Pervear v. The Commonwealth, 5 Wall. 479; Twitchell v. The Commonwealth, 7 id. 321; Edwards v. Elliott, 21 id. 557. It is now too late to question the correctness of this construction. As was said by the late Chief Justice, in Twitchell v. The Commonwealth, 7 Wall. 325, 'the scope and application of these amendments are no longer subjects of discussion here.' They left the authority of the States just where they found it, and added nothing to the already existing powers of the **United States**.

The particular amendment now under consideration assumes the existence of the right of the people to assemble for lawful purposes, and protects it against encroachment by Congress. The right was not created by the amendment; neither was its continuance guaranteed, except as against congressional interference. For their protection in its enjoyment, therefore, the people must look to the States. The power for that purpose was originally placed there, and it has never been surrendered to the **United States**.

The right of the people peaceably to assemble for the purpose of petitioning Congress for a redress of grievances, or for any thing else connected with the powers or the duties of the national government, is an attribute of national citizenship, and, as such, under the protection of, and guaranteed by, the **United States**. The very idea of a government, republican in form, implies a right on the part of its citizens to meet peaceably for consultation in respect to public affairs and to petition for a redress of grievances. If it had been alleged in [92 U.S. 542, 553] these counts that the object of the defendants was to prevent a meeting for such a purpose, the case would have been within the statute, and within the scope of the sovereignty of the

**United States**. Such, however, is not the case. The offence, as stated in the indictment, will be made out, if it be shown that the object of the conspiracy was to prevent a meeting for any lawful purpose whatever.

The second and tenth counts are equally defective. The right there specified is that of 'bearing arms for a lawful purpose.' This is not a right granted by the Constitution. Neither is it in any manner dependent upon that instrument for its existence. The second amendment declares that it shall not be infringed; but this, as has been seen, means no more than that it shall not be infringed by Congress. This is one of the amendments that has no other effect than to restrict the powers of the national government, leaving the people to look for their protection against any violation by their fellow-citizens of the rights it recognizes, to what is called, in The City of New York v. Miln, 11 Pet. 139, the 'powers which relate to merely municipal legislation, or what was, perhaps, more properly called internal police,' 'not surrendered or restrained' by the Constituton of the **United States**.

The third and eleventh counts are even more objectionable. They charge the intent to have been to deprive the citizens named, they being in Louisiana, 'of their respective several lives and liberty of person without due process of law.' This is nothing else than alleging a conspiracy to falsely imprison or murder citizens of the **United States**, being within the territorial jurisdiction of the State of Louisiana. The rights of life and personal liberty are natural rights of man. 'To secure these rights,' says the Declaration of

Independence, 'governments are instituted among men, deriving their just powers from the consent of the governed.' The very highest duty of the States, when they entered into the Union under the Constitution, was to protect all persons within their boundaries in the enjoyment of these 'unalienable rights with which they were endowed by their Creator.' Sovereignty, for this purpose, rests alone with the States. It is no more the duty or within the power of the **United States** to punish for a conspiracy [92 U.S. 542, 554] to falsely imprison or murder within a State, than it would be to punish for false imprisonment or murder itself.

The fourteenth amendment prohibits a State from depriving any person of life, liberty, or property, without due process of law; but this adds nothing to the rights of one citizen as against another. It simply furnishes an additional guaranty against any encroachment by the States upon the fundamental rights which belong to every citizen as a member of society. As was said by Mr. Justice Johnson, in Bank of Columbia v. Okely, 4 Wheat. 244, it secures 'the individual from the arbitrary exercise of the powers of government, unrestrained by the established principles of private rights and distributive justice.' These counts in the indictment do not call for the exercise of any of the powers conferred by this provision in the amendment.

The fourth and twelfth counts charge the intent to have been to prevent and hinder the citizens named, who were of **AFRICAN** descent and persons of color, in 'the free exercise and enjoyment of their several right and privilege to the full and equal benefit of all laws and proceedings, then and there, before that time, enacted or ordained by the said State of Louisiana and by the **United States**; and then and there, at that time, being in force in the said State and District of Louisiana aforesaid, for the security of their respective persons and property, then and there, at that time enjoyed at and within said State and District of Louisiana by white persons, being citizens of said State of Louisiana and the **United States**, for the protection of the persons and property of said white citizens.' There is no allegation that this was done because of the race or color of the persons conspired against. When stripped of its verbiage, the case as presented amounts to nothing more than that the defendants conspired to prevent certain citizens of the **United States**, being within the State of Louisiana, from enjoying the equal protection of the laws of the State and of the **United States**.

The fourteenth amendment prohibits a State from denying to any person within its jurisdiction the equal protection of the laws; but this provision does not, any more than the one which precedes it, and which we have just considered, add any thing [92 U.S. 542, 555] to the rights which one citizen has under the Constitution against another. The equality of the rights of citizens is a principle of republicanism. Every republican government is in duty bound to protect all its citizens in the enjoyment of this principle, if within its power. That duty was originally assumed by the States; and it still remains there. The only obligation resting upon the **United States** is to see that the States do not deny the right. This the amendment guarantees, but no more. The power of the national government is limited to the enforcement of this guaranty.

No question arises under the Civil Rights Act of April 9, 1866 (14 Stat. 27), which is intended for the protection of citizens of the **United States** in the enjoyment of certain rights, without discrimination on account of race, color, or previous condition of servitude, because, as has already been stated, it is nowhere alleged in these counts that the wrong contemplated against the rights of these citizens was on account of their race or color.

Another objection is made to these counts, that they are too vague and uncertain. This will be considered hereafter, in connection with the same objection to other counts.

The sixth and fourteenth counts state the intent of the defendants to have been to hinder and prevent the citizens named, being of **AFRICAN** descent, and colored, 'in the free exercise and enjoyment of their several and respective right and privilege to vote at any election to be thereafter by law had and held by the people in and of the said State of Louisiana, or by the people of and in the parish of Grant aforesaid.' In Minor v. Happersett, 21 Wall. 178, we decided that the Constitution of the **United States** has not conferred the right of suffrage upon any one, and that the **United States** have no voters of their own creation in the States. In **United States** v. Reese et al., supra, p. 214, we hold that the fifteenth amendment has invested the citizens of the **United States** with a new constitutional right, which is, exemption from discrimination in the exercise of the elective franchise on account of race, color, or previous condition of servitude. From this it appears that the right of suffrage is not a necessary attribute of national citizenship; but that exemption from discrimination in the exercise of that right on [92 U.S. 542, 556] account of race, &c., is. The right to vote in the States comes from the States; but the right of exemption from the prohibited discrimination comes from the **United States**. The first has not been granted or secured by the Constitution of the **United States**; but the lat has been.

Inasmuch, therefore, as it does not appear in these counts that the intent of the defendants was to prevent these parties from exercising their right to vote on account of their race, &c., it does not appear that it was their intent to interfere with any right granted or secured by the constitution or laws of the **United States**. We may suspect that race was the cause of the hostility; but it is not so averred. This is material to a description of the substance of the offence, and cannot be supplied by implication. Every thing essential must be charged positively, and not inferentially. The defect here is not in form, but in substance.

The seventh and fifteenth counts are no better than the sixth and fourteenth. The intent here charged is to put the parties named in great fear of bodily harm, and to injure and oppress them, because, being and having been in all things qualified, they had voted 'at an election before that time had and held according to law by the people of the said State of Louisiana, in said State, to wit, on the fourth day of November, A.D. 1872, and at divers other elections by the people of the State, also before that time had and held according to law.' There is nothing to show that the elections voted at were any other than State elections, or that the conspiracy was formed on account of the race of the parties against whom the conspirators were to act. The charge as made is really of nothing more than a conspiracy to commit a breach of the peace within a State. Certainly it will not be claimed that the **United States** have the power or are required to do mere police duly in the States. If a State cannot protect itself against domestic violence, the **United States** may, upon the call of the executive, when the legislature cannot be convened, lend their assistance for that purpose. This is a guaranty of the Constitution (art. 4, sect. 4); but it applies to no case like this.

We are, therefore, of the opinion that the first, second, third, fourth, sixth, seventh, ninth, tenth, eleventh, twelfth, fourteenth, [92 U.S. 542, 557] and fifteenth counts do not contain charges of a criminal nature made indictable under the laws of the **United States**, and that consequently they are not good and sufficient in law. They do not show that it was the intent of the defendants, by their conspiracy, to hinder or prevent the enjoyment of any right granted or secured by the Constitution.

We come now to consider the fifth and thirteenth and the eighth and sixteenth counts, which may be brought together for that purpose. The intent charged in the fifth and thirteenth is 'to hinder and prevent the parties in their respective free exercise and enjoyment of the rights, privileges, immunities, and protection granted and secured to them respectively as citizens of the **United States**, and as citizens of said State of Louisiana,' 'for the reason that they, . . . being then and there citizens of said State and of the **United States**, were persons of **AFRICAN** descent and race, and persons of color, and not white citizens thereof;' and in the eighth and sixteenth, to hinder and prevent them 'in their several and respective free exercise and enjoyment of every, each, all, and singular the several rights and privileges granted and secured to them by the constitution and laws of the **United States**.' The same general statement of the rights to be interfered with is found in the fifth and thirteenth counts.

According to the view we take of these counts, the question is not whether it is enough, in general, to describe a statutory offence in the language of the statute, but whether the offence has here been described at all. The statute provides for the punishment of those who conspire 'to injure, oppress, threaten, or intimidate any citizen, with intent to prevent or hinder his free exercise and enjoyment of any right or privilege granted or secured to him by the constitution or laws of the **United States**.' These counts in the indictment charge, in substance, that the intent in this case was to hinder and prevent these citizens in the free exercise and enjoyment of 'every, each, all, and singular' the rights granted them by the Constitution, &c. There is no specification of any particular right. The language is broad enough to cover all.

In criminal cases, prosecuted under the laws of the **United States**, the accused has the constitutional right 'to be informed [92 U.S. 542, 558] of the nature and cause of the accusation.' Amend. VI. In **United States** v. Mills, 7 Pet. 142, this was construed to mean, that the indictment must set forth the offence 'with clearness and all necessary certainty, to apprise the accused of the crime with which he stands charged;' and in **United States** v. Cook, 17 Wall. 174, that 'every ingredient of which the offence is composed must be accurately and clearly alleged.' It is an elementary principle of criminal pleading, that where the definition of an offence, whether it be at common law or by statute, 'includes generic terms, it is not sufficient that the indictment shall charge the offence in the same generic terms as in the definition; but it must state the species,-it must descend to particulars. 1 Arch. Cr. Pr. and Pl., 291. The object of the indictment is, first, to furnish the accused with such a description of the charge against him as will enable him to make his defence, and avail himself of his conviction or acquittal for protection against a further prosecution for the same cause; and, second, to inform the court of the facts alleged, so that it may decide whether they are sufficient in law to support a conviction, if one should be had. For this, facts are to be stated, not conclusions of law alone. A crime is made up of acts and intent; and these must be set forth in the indictment, with reasonable particularity of time, place, and circumstances.

It is a crime to steal goods and chattels; but an indictment would be bad that did not specify with some degree of certainty the articles stolen. This, because the accused must be advised of the essential particulars of the charge against him, and the court must be able to decide whether the property taken was such as was the subject of larceny. So, too, it is in some States a crime for two or more persons to conspire to cheat and defraud another out of his property; but it has been held that an indictment for such an offence must contain allegations setting forth the means proposed to be used to accomplish the purpose. This, because, to make such a purpose criminal, the conspiracy must be to cheat and defraud in a mode made criminal by statute; and as all cheating and defrauding has not been made criminal, it is necessary for the indictment to state the means proposed, in order that the court [92 U.S. 542, 559] may see that they are in fact illegal. State v. Parker, 43 N. H. 83; State v. Keach, 40 Vt. 118; Alderman v. The People, 4 Mich. 414; State v. Roberts, 34 Me. 32. In Maine, it is an offence for two or more to conspire with the intent unlawfully and wickedly to commit any crime punishable by imprisonment in the State prison (State v. Roberts); but we think it will hardly be claimed that an indictment would be good under this statute, which charges the object of the conspiracy to have been 'unlawfully and wickedly to commit each, every, all, and singular the crimes punishable by imprisonment in the State prison.' All crimes are not so punishable. Whether a particular crime be such a one or not, is a question of law. The accused has, therefore, the right to have a specification of the charge against him in this respect, in order that he may decide whether he should present his defence by motion to quash, demurrer, or plea; and the court, that it may determine whether the facts will sustain the indictment. So here, the crime is made to consist in the unlawful combination with an intent to prevent the enjoyment of any right granted or secured by the

Constitution, &c. All rights are not so granted or secured. Whether one is so or not is a question of law, to be decided by the court, not the prosecutor. Therefore, the indictment should state the particulars, to inform the court as well as the accused. It must be made to appear-that is to say, appears from the indictment, without going further-that the acts charged will, if proved, support a conviction for the offence alleged.

But it is needless to pursue the argument further. The conclusion is irresistible, that these counts are too vague and general. They lack the certainty and precision required by the established rules of criminal pleading. It follows that they are not good and sufficient in law. They are so defective that no judgment of conviction should be pronounced upon them.

The order of the Circuit Court arresting the judgment upon the verdict is, therefore, affirmed; and the cause remanded, with instructions to discharge the defendants.

MR. JUSTICE CLIFFORD dissenting.

I concur that the judgment in this case should be arrested, but for reasons quite different from those given by the court. [92 U.S. 542, 560] Power is vested in Congress to enforce by appropriate legislation the prohibition contained in the fourteenth amendment of the Constitution; and the fifth section of the Enforcement Act provides to the effect, that persons who prevent, hinder, control, or intimidate, or who attempt to prevent, hinder, control, or intimidate, any person to whom the right of suffrage is secured or guaranteed by that amendment, from exercising, or in exercising such right, by means of bribery or threats; of depriving such person of employment or occupation; or of ejecting such person from rented house, lands, or other property; or by threats of refusing to renew leases or contracts for labor; or by threats of violence to himself or family,-such person so offending shall be deemed guilty of a misdemeanor, and, on conviction thereof, shall be fined or imprisoned, or both, as therein provided. 16 Stat. 141.

Provision is also made, by sect. 6 of the same act, that, if two or more persons shall band or conspire together, or go in disguise, upon the public highway, or upon the premises of another, with intent to violate any provision of that act, or to injure, oppress, threaten, or intimidate any citizen with intent to prevent or hinder his free exercise and enjoyment of any right or privilege granted or secured to him by the constitution and laws of the **United States**, or because of his having exercised the same, such persons shall be deemed guilty of felony, and, on conviction thereof, shall be fined or imprisoned, or both, and be further punished as therein provided.

More than one hundred persons were jointly indicted at the April Term, 1873, of the Circuit Court of the **United States** for the District of Louisiana, charged with offences in violation of the provisions of the Enforcement Act. By the record, it appears that the indictment contained thirty-two counts, in two series of sixteen counts each: that the first series were drawn under the fifth and sixth sections of the act; and that the second series were drawn under the seventh section of the same act; and that the latter series charged that the prisoners are guilty of murder committed by them in the act of violating some of the provisions of the two preceding sections of that act.

Eight of the persons named in the indictment appeared on [92 U.S. 542, 561] the 10th of June, 1874, and went to trial under the plea of not guilty, previously entered at the time of their arraignment. Three of those who went to trial-to wit, the three defendants named in the transcript-were found guilty by the jury on the first series of the counts of the indictment, and not guilty on the second series of the counts in the same indictment.

Subsequently the convicted defendants filed a motion for a new trial, which motion being overruled they filed a motion in arrest of judgment. Hearing was had upon that motion; and the opinions of the judges of the Circuit Court being opposed, the matter in difference was duly certified to this court, the question being whether the motion in arrest of judgment ought to be granted or denied.

Two only of the causes of arrest assigned in the motion will be considered in answering the questions certified: (1.) Because the matters and things set forth and charged in the several counts in question do not constitute offences against the laws of the **United States**, and do not come within the purview, true intent, and meaning of the Enforcement Act. (2.) Because the several counts of the indictment in question are too vague, insufficient, and uncertain to afford the accused proper notice to plead and prepare their defence, and do not set forth any offence defined by the Enforcement Act.

Four other causes of arrest were assigned; but, in the view taken of the case, it will be sufficient to examine the two causes above set forth.

Since the questions were certified into this court, the parties have been fully heard in respect to all the questions presented for decision in the transcript. Questions not pressed at the argument will not be considered; and, inasmuch as the counsel in behalf of the **United States** confined their arguments entirely to the thirteenth, fourteenth, and sixteenth counts of the first series in the indictment, the answers may well be limited to these counts, the others being virtually abandoned. Mere introductory allegations will be omitted as unimportant, for the reason that the questions to be answered relate to the allegations of the respective counts describing the offence.

As described in the thirteenth count, the charge is, that the [92 U.S. 542, 562] defendants did, at the time and place mentioned, combine, conspire, and confederated together, between and among themselves, for and with the unlawful and felonious intent and purpose one Levi Nelson and one Alexander Tillman, each of whom being then and there a citizen of the **United States**, of **AFRICAN** descent, and a person of color, unlawfully and feloniously to injure, oppress, threaten, and intimidate, with the unlawful and felonious intent thereby the said persons of color, respectively, then and there to hinder and prevent in their respective and several free exercise and enjoyment of the rights, privileges, and immunities, and protection, granted and secured to them respectively as citizens of the **United States** and citizens of the State, by reason of their race and color; and because that they, the said persons of color, being then and there citizens of the State and of the **United States**, were then and there persons of **AFRICAN** descent and race, and persons of color, and not white citizens thereof; the same being a right or privilege granted or secured to the said persons of color respectively, in common with all other good citizens of the **United States**, by the Federal Constitution and the laws of Congress.

Matters of law conceded, in the opinion of the court, may be assumed to be correct without argument; and, if so, then discussion is not necessary to show that every ingredient of which an offence is composed must be accurately and clearly alleged in the indictment, or the indictment will be bad, and may be quashed on motion, or the judgment may be arrested before sentence, or be reversed on a writ of error. **United States** v. Cook, 17 Wall. 174.

Offences created by statute, as well as offences at common law, must be accurately and clearly described in an indictment; and, if the offence cannot be so described without expanding the allegations beyond the mere words of the statute, then it is clear that the allegations of the indictment must be expanded to that extent, as it is universally true that no indictment is sufficient which does not accurately and clearly allege all the ingredients of which the offence is composed, so as to bring the accused within the true intent and meaning of the statute defining the offence. Authorities of great weight, besides those referred to by me, in the dissenting opinion just read, [92 U.S. 542, 563] may be found in support of that proposition. 2 East, P. C. 1124; Dord v. People, 9 Barb. 675; Ike v. State, 23 Miss. 525; State v. Eldridge, 7 Eng. 608.

Every offence consists of certain acts done or omitted under certain circumstances; and, in the indictment for the offence, it is not sufficient to charge the accused generally with having committed the offence, but all the circumstances constituting the offence must be specially set forth. Arch. Cr. Pl., 15th ed., 43.

Persons born on naturalized in the **United States**, and subject to the jurisdiction thereof, are citizens thereof; and the fourteenth amendment also provides, that no State shall make or enforce any law which shall abridge the privileges or immunities of citizens of the **United States**. Congress may, doubtless, prohibit any violation of that provision, and may provide that any person convicted of violating the same shall be guilty of an offence, and be subject to such reasonable punishment as Congress may prescribe.

Conspiracies of the kind described in the introductory clause of the sixth section of the Enforcement Act are explicitly forbidden by the subsequent clauses of the same section; and it may be that if the indictment was for a conspiracy at common law, and was pending in a tribunal having jurisdiction of common-law offences, the indictment in its present form might be sufficient, even though it contains no definite allegation whatever of any particular overt act committed by the defendants in pursuance of the alleged conspiracy. Decided cases may doubtless be found in which it is held that an indictment for a conspiracy, at common law, may be sustained where there is an unlawful agreement between two or more persons to do an unlawful act, or to do a lawful act by unlawful means; and authorities may be referred to which support the proposition, that the indictment, if the conspiracy is well pleaded, is sufficient, even though it be not alleged that any overt act had been done in pursuance of the unlawful combination.

Suffice it to say, however, that the authorities to that effect are opposed by another class of authorities equally respectable, and even more numerous, which decide that the indictment is [92 U.S. 542, 564] bad unless it is alleged that some overt act was committed in pursuance of the intent and purpose of the alleged conspiracy; and in all the latter class of cases it is held, that the overt act, as well as the unlawful combination, must be clearly and accurately alleged.

Two reasons of a conclusive nature, however, may be assigned which show, beyond all doubt, that it is not necessary to enter into the inquiry which class of those decisions is correct.

1. Because the common law is not a source of jurisdiction in the circuit courts, nor in any other Federal court.

Circuit Courts have no common-law jurisdiction of offences of any grade or description; and it is equally clear that the appellate jurisdiction of the **Supreme Court** does not extend to any case or any question, in a case not within the jurisdiction of the subordinate Federal courts. State v. Wheeling Bridge Co., 13 How. 503; **United States** v. Hudson et al., 7 Cranch, 32.

2. Because it is conceded that the offence described in the indictment is an offence created and defined by an act of Congress.

Indictments for offences created and defined by statute must in all cases follow the words of the statute: and, where there is no departure from that rule, the indictment is in general sufficient, except in cases where the statute is elliptical, or where, by necessary implication, other constituents are component parts of the offence; as where the words of the statute defining the offence have a compound signification, or are enlarged by what immediately precedes or follows the words describing the offence, and in the same connection. Cases of the kind do arise, as where, in the dissenting opinion in **United States** v. Reese et al., supra, p. 222, it was held, that the words offer to pay a capitation tax were so expanded by a succeeding clause of the same sentence that the word 'offer' necessarily included readiness to perform what was offered, the provision being that the offer should be equivalent to actual performance if the offer failed to be carried into execution by the wrongful act or omission of the party to whom the offer was made.

Two offences are in fact created and defined by the sixth section of the Enforcement Act, both of which consist of a [92 U.S. 542, 565] conspiracy with an intent to perpetrate a forbidden act. They are alike in respect to the conspiracy;

but differ very widely in respect to the act embraced in the prohibition.

1. Persons, two or more, are forbidden to band or conspire together, or go in disguise upon the public highway, or on the premises of another, with intent to violate any provision of the Enforcement Act, which is an act of twenty-three sections.

Much discussion of that clause is certainly unnecessary, as no one of the counts under consideration is founded on it, or contains any allegations describing such an offence. Such a conspiracy with intent to injure, oppress, threaten, or intimidate any person, is also forbidden by the succeeding clause of that section, if it be done with intent to prevent or hinder his free exercise and enjoyment of any right or privilege granted or secured to him by the constitution or laws of the **United States**, or because of having exercised the same. Sufficient appears in the thirteenth count to warrant the conclusion, that the grand jury intended to charge the defendants with the second offence created and defined in the sixth section of the Enforcement Act.

Indefinite and vague as the description of the offence there defined, is, it is obvious that it is greatly more so as described in the allegations of the thirteenth count. By the act of Congress, the prohibition is extended to any right or privilege granted or secured by the constitution or laws of Congress; leaving it to the pleader to specify the particular right or privilege which had been invaded, in order to give the accusation that certainty which the rules of criminal pleading everywhere require in an indictment; but the pleader in this case, overlooking any necessity for any such specification, and making no attempt to comply with the rules of criminal pleading in that regard, describes the supposed offence in terms much more vague and indefinite than those employed in the act of Congress.

Instead of specifying the particular right or privilege which had been invaded, the pleader proceeds to allege that the defendants, with all the others named in the indictment, did combine, conspire, and confederate together, with the unlawful intent and purpose the said persons of **AFRICAN** descent and [92 U.S. 542, 566] persons of color then and there to injure, oppress, threaten, and intimidate, and thereby then and there to hinder and prevent them in the free exercise and enjoyment of the rights, privileges, and immunities and protection granted and secured to them as citizens of the **United States** and citizens of the State, without any other specification of the rights, privileges, immunities, and protection which had been violated or invaded, or which were threatened, except what follows; to wit, the same being a right or privilege granted or secured in common with all other good citizens by the constitution and laws of the **United States**.

Vague and indefinite allegations of the kind are not sufficient to inform the accused in a criminal prosecution of the nature and cause of the accusation against him, within the meaning of the sixth amendment of the Constitution.

Valuable rights and privileges, almost without number, are granted and secured to citizens by the constitution and laws of Congress; none of which may be, with impunity, invaded in violation of the prohibition contained in that section. Congress intended by that provision to protect citizens in the enjoyment of all such rights and privileges; but in affording such protection in the mode there provided Congress never intended to open the door to the invasion of the rule requiring certainty in criminal pleading, which for ages has been regarded as one of the great safeguards of the citizen against oppressive and groundless prosecutions.

Judge Story says the indictment must charge the time and place and nature and circumstances of the offence with clearness and certainty, so that the party may have full notice of the charge, and be able to make his defence with all reasonable knowledge and ability. 2 Story, Const., sect. 1785

Nothing need be added to show that the fourteenth count is founded upon the same clause in the sixth section of the Enforcement Act as the thirteenth court, which will supersede the necessity of any extended remarks to explain the nature and character of the offence there created and defined. Enough has already been remarked to show that that particular clause of the section was passed to protect citizens in the free exercise and enjoyment of every right or privilege granted [92 U.S. 542, 567] or secured to them by the constitution and laws of Congress, and to provide for the punishment of those who band or conspire together, in the manner described, to injure, oppress, or intimidate any citizen, to prevent or hinder him from the free exercise and enjoyment of all such rights or privileges, or because of his having exercised any such right or privilege so granted or secured.

What is charged in the fourteenth count is, that the defendants did combine, conspire, and confederate the said citizens of **AFRICAN** descent and persons of color to injure, oppress, threaten, and intimidate, with intent the said citizens thereby to prevent and hinder in the free exercise and enjoyment of the right and privilege to vote at any election to be thereafter had and held according to law by the people of the State, or by the people of the parish; they, the defendants, well knowing that the said citizens were lawfully qualified to vote at any such election thereafter to be had and held.

Confessedly, some of the defects existing in the preceding count are avoided in the count in question; as, for example, the description of the particular right or privilege of the said citizens which it was the intent of the defendants to invade is clearly alleged; but the difficulty in the count is, that it does not allege for what purpose the election or elections were to be ordered, nor when or where the elections were to be had and held. All that is alleged upon the subject is, that it was the intent of the defendants to prevent and hinder the said citizens of **AFRICAN** descent and persons of color in the free exercise and enjoyment of the right and privilege to vote at any election thereafter to be had and held, according to law, by the people of the State, or by the people of the parish, without any other allegation whatever as to the purpose of the election, or any allegation as to the time and place when and where the election was to be had and held.
Elections thereafter to be held must mean something different from pending elections; but whether the pleader means to charge that the intent and purpose of the alleged

conspiracy extended only to the next succeeding elections to be held in the State or parish, or to all future elections to be held in the State or parish during the lifetime of the parties, may admit of [92 U.S. 542, 568] a serious question, which cannot be easily solved by any thing contained in the allegations of the count.

Reasonable certainty, all will agree, is required in criminal pleading; and if so it must be conceded, we think, that the allegation in question fails to comply with that requirement. Accused persons, as matter of common justice, ought to have the charge against them set forth in such terms that they may readily understand the nature and character of the accusation, in order that they, when arraigned, may know what answer to make to it, and that they may not be embarrassed in conducting their defence; and the charge ought also to be laid in such terms that, if the party accused is put to trial, the verdict and judgment may be pleaded in bar of a second accusation for the same offence.
Tested by these considerations, it is quite clear that the fourteenth count is not sufficient to warrant the conviction and sentence of the accused.

Defects and imperfections of the same kind as those pointed out in the thirteenth count also exist in the sixteenth count, and of a more decided character in the latter count than in the former; conclusive proof of which will appear by a brief examination of a few of the most material allegations of the charge against the defendants. Suffice it to say, without entering into details, that the introductory allegations of the count are in all respects the same as in the thirteenth and fourteenth counts. None of the introductory allegations allege that any overt act was perpetrated in pursuance of the alleged conspiracy; but the jurors proceed to present that the unlawful and felonious intent and purpose of the defendants were to prevent and hinder the said citizens of **AFRICAN** descent and persons of color, by the means therein described, in the free exercise and enjoyment of each, every, all, and singular the several rights and privileges granted and secured to them by the constitution and laws of the **United States** in common with all other good citizens, without any attempt to describe or designate any particular right or privilege which it was the purpose and intent of the defendants to invade, abridge, or deny.

Descriptive allegations in criminal pleading are required to be reasonably definite and certain, as a necessary safeguard [92 U.S. 542, 569] to the accused against surprise, misconception, and error in conducting his defence, and in order that the judgment in the case may be a bar to a second accusation for the same charge. Considerations of the kind are entitled to respect; but it is obvious, that, if such a description of the ingredient of an offence created and defined by an act of Congress is held to be sufficient, the indictment must become a snare to the accused; as it is scarcely possible that an allegation can be framed which would be less certain, or more at variance with the universal rule that every ingredient of the offence must be clearly and accurately described so as to bring the defendant within the true intent and meaning of the provision defining the offence. Such a vague and indefinite description of a material ingredient of the offence is not a compliance with the rules of pleading in framing an indictment. On the contrary, such an indictment is insufficient, and must be held bad on demurrer or in arrest of judgment.

Certain other causes for arresting the judgment are assigned in the record, which deny the constitutionality of the Enforcement Act; but, having come to the conclusion that the indictment is insufficient, it is not necessary to consider that question.

**Rutherford B. Hayes**

**1822-1893**

**Ordered Federal Troops To Evacuate The South In 1877
Thereby Ushering In The Collapse Of Reconstruction And A Reign Of Terror Upon Africans In The American South**

**President of the United States
1877-1881**

## The Civil Rights Act of 1875

The following Act was a valiant effort on the part of the Grant Administration to ensure the rights of **AFRICAN** Freedmen in the South. Like so many pieces of Reconstruction legislation, it would soon become a causality of the South's Redemption beginning in 1877 with the assumption of **Rutherford B. Hayes** to the Presidency. It would later be declared *unconstitutional by the Supreme Court in 1883*.

## Civil Rights Act of 1875
## March 1, 1875

Chap. 114.—An act to protect all citizens in their civil and legal rights.
**WHEREAS**, it is essential to just government we recognize the equality of all men before the law, and hold that it is the duty of government in its dealings with the people to mete out equal and exact justice to all, of whatever nativity, race, color, or persuasion, religious or political; and it being the appropriate object of legislation to enact great fundamental principles into law:

Therefore:

Be it enacted by the Senate and House of Representatives of the **United States** of American in Congress assembled, That all persons within the jurisdiction of the **United States** shall be entitled to the full and equal and enjoyment of the accommodations, advantages, facilities, and privileges of inns, public conveyances on land or water, theaters, and other places of public amusement; subject only to the conditions and limitations established by law, and applicable alike to citizens of every race and color, regardless of any previous condition of servitude.

Sec. 2. That any person who shall violate the foregoing section by denying to any citizen, except for reasons by law applicable to citizens of every race and color, and regardless of any previous condition of servitude, the full enjoyment of any of the accommodations, advantages, facilities, or privileges in said section enumerated, or by aiding or luciting such denial, shall, for every offence, forfeit and pay the sum of five hundred dollars to the person aggrieved thereby, to be recovered in an action of debt, with full costs; and shall also, for every such offense, be deemed guilty of a misdemeanor, and, upon conviction thereof, shall be fined not less than five hundred nor more than one thousand dollars, or shall be imprisoned not less than thirty days nor more than one year: Provided, that all persons may elect to sue for the State under their rights at common law and by State statutes; and having so elected to proceed in the one mode or the other, their right to proceed in the other jurisdiction shall be barred. But this proviso shall not apply to criminal proceedings, either under this act or the criminal law of any State: And provided further, That a judgment for the penalty in favor of the party aggrieved, or a judgment upon an indictment, shall be a bar to either prosecution respectively.

Sec. 3. That the district and circuit courts of the **United States** shall have, exclusively of the courts of the several States, cognizance of all crimes and offenses against, and violations of, the provisions of this act; and actions for the penalty given by the preceding section may be prosecuted in the territorial, district, or circuit courts of the **United States** wherever the defendant may be found, without regard to the other party; and the district attorneys, marshals, and deputy marshals of the **United States**, and commissioners appointed by the circuit and territorial courts of the **United States**, with powers of arresting and imprisoning or bailing offenders against the laws of the **United States**, are hereby specially authorized and required to institute proceedings against every person who shall violate the provisions of this act, and cause him to be arrested and imprisoned or bailed, as the case may be, for trial before such court of the **United States**, or territorial court, as by law has cognizance of the offense, except in respect of the right of action accruing to the person aggrieved; and such district attorneys shall cause such proceedings to be prosecuted to their termination as in other cases: Provided, That nothing contained in this section shall be construed to deny or defeat any right of civil action accruing to any person, whether by reason of this act or otherwise; and any district attorney who shall willfully fail to institute and prosecute the proceedings herein required, shall, for every such offense, forfeit and pay the sum of five hundred dollars to the person aggrieved thereby, to be recovered by an action of debt, with full costs, and shall, on conviction thereof, be deemed guilty of a misdemeanor, and be fined not less than one thousand nor more than five thousand dollars: And provided further, That a judgment for the penalty in favor of the party aggrieved against any such district attorney, or a judgment upon an indictment against any such district attorney, shall be a bar to either prosecution respectively.

Sec. 4. That no citizen possessing all other qualification which are or may be prescribed by law shall be disqualified for service as grand or petit juror in any court of the **United States**, or of any State, on account of race, color, or previous condition of servitude; and any officer or other person charged with any duty in the selection or summoning of jurors who shall exclude or fail to summon any citizen for the cause aforesaid shall, on conviction thereof, be deemed guilty of a misdemeanor, and be fined not more than five thousand dollars.

Sec. 5. That all cases arising under the provisions of this act in the courts of the **United States** shall be reviewable by the **Supreme Court** of the **United States**, without regard to the sum in controversy, under the same provisions and regulations as are now provided by law for the review of other causes in said court.

Approved, March 1, 1875.

## The Civil Rights Act of 1875 Declared Unconstitutional (1883)

Submitted October Term, 1882
October 16th, 1883

109 U.S. 3
ON CERTIFICATE OF DIVISION FROM THE CIRCUIT COURT OF THE **UNITED STATES** FOR THE DISTRICT OF KANSAS

**Syllabus**

1. The 1st and 2d sections of the Civil Rights Act passed March 1st, 1876, are unconstitutional enactments as applied to the several States, not being authorized either by the XIIIth or XIVth Amendments of the Constitution

2. The XIVth Amendment is prohibitory upon the States only, and the legislation authorized to be adopted by Congress for enforcing it is not direct legislation on the matters respecting which the States are prohibited from making or enforcing certain laws, or doing certain acts, but is corrective legislation such as may be necessary or proper for counteracting and redressing the effect of such laws or acts. [p*4]

The XIIIth Amendment relates only to **SLAVERY** and involuntary servitude (which it abolishes), and, although, by its reflex action, it establishes universal freedom in the **United States**, and Congress may probably pass laws directly enforcing its provisions, yet such legislative power extends only to the subject of **SLAVERY** and its incidents, and the denial of equal accommodations in inns, public conveyances, and places of public amusement (which is forbidden by the sections in question), imposes no badge of **SLAVERY** or involuntary servitude upon the party but at most, infringes rights which are protected from State aggression by the XIVth Amendment.

4. Whether the accommodations and privileges sought to be protected by the 1st and 2d sections of the Civil Rights Act are or are not rights constitutionally demandable, and if they are, in what form they are to be protected, is not now decided.

5. Nor is it decided whether the law, as it stands, is operative in the Territories and District of Columbia, the decision only relating to its validity as applied to the States.

6. Nor is it decided whether Congress, under the commercial power, may or may not pass a law securing to all persons equal accommodations on lines of public conveyance between two or more States.

These cases were all founded on the first and second sections of the Act of Congress known as the Civil Rights Act, passed March 1st, 1875, entitled "An Act to protect all citizens in their civil and legal rights." 18 Stat. 335. Two of the cases, those against Stanley and Nichols, were indictments for denying to persons of color the accommodations and privileges of an inn or hotel; two of them, those against Ryan and Singleton, were, one on information, the other an indictment, for denying to individuals the privileges and accommodations of a theatre, the information against Ryan being for refusing a colored person a seat in the dress circle of Maguire's theatre in San Francisco, and the indictment against Singleton was for denying to another person, whose color was not stated, the full enjoyment of the accommodations of the theatre known as the Grand Opera House in New York,

said denial not being made for any reasons by law applicable to citizens of every race and color, and regardless of any previous condition of servitude.

The case of Robinson and wife against the Memphis & Charleston R.R. Company was an action brought in the Circuit Court of the **United States** for the Western District of Tennessee to recover the penalty of five hundred dollars [p*5] given by the second section of the act, and the gravamen was the refusal by the conductor of the railroad company to allow the wife to ride in the ladies' car, for the reason, as stated in one of the counts, that she was a person of **AFRICAN** descent. The jury rendered a verdict for the defendants in this case upon the merits, under a charge of the court to which a bill of exceptions was taken by the plaintiffs. The case was tried on the assumption by both parties of the validity of the act of Congress, and the principal point made by the exceptions was that the judge allowed evidence to go to the jury tending to show that the conductor had reason to suspect that the plaintiff, the wife, was an improper person because she was in company with a young man whom he supposed to be a white man, and, on that account, inferred that there was some improper connection between them, and the judge charged the jury, in substance, that, if this was the conductor's *bona fide* reason for excluding the woman from the car, they might take it into consideration on the question of the liability of the company. The case was brought here by writ of error at the suit of the plaintiffs. The cases of Stanley, Nichols, and

Singleton came up on certificates of division of opinion between the judges below as to the constitutionality of the first and second sections of the act referred to, and the case of Ryan on a writ of error to the judgment of the Circuit Court for the District of California sustaining a demurrer to the information.

The Stanley, Ryan, Nichols, and Singleton cases were submitted together by the solicitor general at the last term of court, on the 7th day of November, 1882. There were no appearances, and no briefs filed for the defendants.

The Robinson case was submitted on the briefs at the last term, on the 9th day of arch, 1883. [p*8]

**Opinions**

**BRADLEY, J., Opinion of the Court**

MR. JUSTICE BRADLEY delivered the opinion of the court. After stating the facts in the above language, he continued:

It is obvious that the primary and important question in all [p*9] the cases is the constitutionality of the law, for if the law is unconstitutional, none of the prosecutions can stand.

The sections of the law referred to provide as follows:

SEC. 1. That all persons within the jurisdiction of the **United States** shall be entitled to the full and equal enjoyment of the accommodations, advantages, facilities, and privileges of inns, public conveyances on land or water, theatres, and other places of public amusement, subject only to the conditions and limitations established by law and applicable alike to citizens of every race and color, regardless of any previous condition of servitude.

SEC. 2. That any person who shall violate the foregoing section by denying to any citizen, except for reasons by law applicable to citizens of every race and color, and regardless of any previous condition of servitude, the full enjoyment of any of the accommodations, advantages, facilities, or privileges in said section enumerated, or by aiding or inciting such denial, shall for every such offence, forfeit and pay the sum of five hundred dollars to the person aggrieved thereby, to be recovered in an action of debt, with full costs, and shall also, for every such offence, be deemed guilty of a misdemeanor, and, upon conviction thereof, shall be fined not less than five hundred nor more than one thousand dollars, or shall be imprisoned not less than thirty days nor more than one year, *Provided,* That all persons may elect to sue for the penalty aforesaid, or to proceed under their rights at common law and by State statutes, and having so elected to proceed in the one mode or the other, their right to proceed in the other jurisdiction shall be barred. But this provision shall not apply to criminal proceedings, either under this act or the criminal law of any State; *and provided further,* that a judgment for the penalty in favor of the party aggrieved, or a judgment upon an indictment, shall be a bar to either prosecution respectively.

Are these sections constitutional? The first section, which is the principal one, cannot be fairly understood without attending to the last clause, which qualifies the preceding part.

The essence of the law is not to declare broadly that all persons shall be entitled to the full and equal enjoyment of the accommodations, advantages, facilities, and privileges of inns, [p*10] public conveyances, and theatres, but that such enjoyment shall not be subject to any conditions applicable only to citizens of a particular race or color, or who had been in a previous condition of servitude. In other words, it is the purpose of the law to declare that, in the enjoyment of the accommodations and privileges of inns, public conveyances, theatres, and other places of public amusement, no distinction shall be made between citizens of different race or color or between those who have, and those who have not, been slaves. Its effect is to declare that, in all inns, public conveyances, and places of amusement, colored citizens, whether formerly slaves or not, and citizens of other races, shall have the same accommodations and privileges in all inns, public conveyances, and places of amusement as are enjoyed by white citizens, and vice versa. The second section makes it a penal offence in any person to deny to any citizen of any race or color, regardless of previous servitude, any of the accommodations or privileges mentioned in the first section.

Has Congress constitutional power to make such a law? Of course, no one will contend that the power to pass it was contained in the Constitution before the adoption of the last three amendments. The power is sought, first, in the Fourteenth Amendment, and the views and arguments of distinguished Senators, advanced whilst the law was under consideration, claiming authority to pass it by virtue of that amendment, are the principal arguments adduced in favor of the power. We have carefully considered those arguments, as was due to the eminent ability of those who put them forward, and have felt, in all its force, the weight of authority which always invests a law that Congress deems itself competent to pass. But the responsibility of an independent judgment is now thrown upon this court, and we are bound to exercise it according to the best lights we have.

The first section of the Fourteenth Amendment (which is the one relied on), after declaring who shall be citizens of the **United States**, and of the several States, is prohibitory in its character, and prohibitory upon the States. It declares that: [p*11]

No State shall make or enforce any law which shall abridge the privileges or immunities of citizens of the **United States**; nor shall any State deprive any person of life, liberty, or property without due process of law; nor deny to any person within its jurisdiction the equal protection of the laws.

It is State action of a particular character that is prohibited. Individual invasion of individual rights is not the subject matter of the amendment. It has a deeper and broader scope. It nullifies and makes void all State legislation, and State action of every kind, which impairs the privileges and immunities of citizens of the **United States** or which injures them in life, liberty or property without due process of law, or which denies to any of them the equal protection of the laws. It not only does this, but, in order that the national will, thus declared, may not be a mere *brutum fulmen,* the last section of the amendment invests Congress with power to enforce it by appropriate legislation. To enforce what? To enforce the prohibition. To adopt appropriate legislation for correcting the effects of such prohibited State laws and State acts, and thus to render them effectually null, void, and innocuous. This is the legislative power conferred upon Congress, and this is the whole of it. It does not invest Congress with power to legislate upon subjects which are within the domain of State legislation, but to provide modes of relief against State legislation, or State action, of the kind referred to. It does not authorize Congress to create a code of municipal law for the regulation of private rights, but to provide modes of redress against the operation of State laws and the action of State officers executive or judicial when these are subversive of the fundamental rights specified in the amendment. Positive rights and privileges are undoubtedly secured by the Fourteenth Amendment, but they are secured by way of prohibition against State laws and State proceedings affecting those rights and privileges, and by power given to Congress to legislate for the purpose of carrying such prohibition into effect, and such legislation must necessarily be predicated upon such supposed State laws or State proceedings, and be directed to the correction [p*12] of their operation and effect. A quite full discussion of this aspect of the amendment may be found in *United Sates v. Cruikshank,* 92 U.S. 542; *Virginia v. Rives,* 100 U.S. 313, and *Ex parte Virginia,* 100 U.S. 339.

An apt illustration of this distinction may be found in some of the provisions of the original Constitution. Take the subject of contracts, for example. The Constitution prohibited the States from passing any law impairing the obligation of contracts. This did not give to Congress power to provide laws for the general enforcement of contracts, nor power to invest the courts of the **United States** with jurisdiction over contracts, so as to enable parties to sue upon them in those courts. It did, however, give the power to provide remedies by which the impairment of contracts by State legislation might be counteracted and corrected, and this power was exercised. The remedy which Congress actually provided was that contained in the 25th section of the Judiciary Act of 1789, 1 Stat. 8, giving to the **Supreme Court** of the **United States** jurisdiction by writ of error to review the final decisions of State courts whenever they should sustain the validity of a State statute or authority alleged to be repugnant to the Constitution or laws of the **United States**. By this means, if a State law was passed impairing the obligation of a contract and the State tribunals sustained the validity of the law, the mischief could be corrected in this court. The legislation of Congress, and the proceedings provided for under it, were corrective in their character. No attempt was made to draw into the **United States** courts the litigation of contracts generally, and no such attempt would have been sustained. We do not say that the remedy provided was the only one that might have been provided in that case. Probably Congress had power to pass a law giving to the courts of the **United States** direct jurisdiction over contracts alleged to be impaired by a State law, and under the broad provisions of the act of March 3d 1875, ch. 137, 18 Stat. 470, giving to the circuit courts jurisdiction of all cases arising under the Constitution and laws of the **United States**, it is possible that such jurisdiction now exists. But under that, or any other law, it must appear as [p*13] well by allegation, as proof at the trial, that the Constitution had been violated by the action of the State legislature. Some obnoxious State law passed, or that might be passed, is necessary to be assumed in order to lay the foundation of any federal remedy in the case, and for the very sufficient reason that the constitutional prohibition is against *State laws* impairing the obligation of contracts.

And so, in the present case, until some State law has been passed, or some State action through its officers or agents has been taken, adverse to the rights of citizens sought to be protected by the Fourteenth Amendment, no legislation of the **United States** under said amendment, nor any proceeding under such legislation, can be called into activity, for the prohibitions of the amendment are against State laws and acts done under State authority. Of course, legislation may, and should, be provided in advance to meet the exigency when it arises, but it should be adapted to the mischief and wrong which the amendment was intended to provide against, and that is State laws, or State action of some kind, adverse to the rights of the citizen secured by the amendment. Such legislation cannot properly cover the whole domain of rights appertaining to life, liberty and property, defining them and providing for their vindication. That would be to establish a code of municipal law regulative of all private rights between man and man in society. It would be to make Congress take the place of the State legislatures and to supersede them. It is absurd to affirm that, because the rights of life, liberty, and property (which include all civil rights that men have) are, by the amendment, sought to be protected against invasion on the part of the State without due process of law, Congress may therefore provide due process of law for their vindication in every case, and that, because the denial by a State to any persons of the equal protection of the laws is prohibited by the amendment, therefore Congress may establish laws for their equal protection. In fine, the legislation which Congress is authorized to adopt in this behalf is not general legislation upon the rights of the citizen, but corrective legislation, that is, such as may be necessary and proper for counteracting such laws as the States may [p*14] adopt or enforce, and which, by the amendment, they are prohibited from making or enforcing, or such acts and proceedings as the States may commit or take, and which, by the amendment, they are prohibited from committing or taking. It is not necessary for us to state, if we could, what legislation would be proper for Congress to adopt. It is sufficient for us to examine whether the law in question is of that character.

An inspection of the law shows that it makes no reference whatever to any supposed or apprehended violation of the Fourteenth Amendment on the part of the States. It is not predicated on any such view. It proceeds *ex directo* to declare that certain acts committed by individuals shall be deemed offences, and shall be prosecuted and punished by proceedings in the courts of the **United States**. It does not profess to be corrective of any constitutional wrong committed by the States; it does not make its operation to depend upon any such wrong committed. It applies equally to cases arising in States which have the justest laws respecting the personal rights of citizens, and whose authorities are ever ready to enforce such laws, as to those which arise in States that may have violated the prohibition of the amendment. In other words, it steps into the domain of local jurisprudence, and lays down rules for the conduct of individuals in society towards each other, and imposes sanctions for the enforcement of those rules, without referring in any manner to any supposed action of the State or its authorities.

If this legislation is appropriate for enforcing the prohibitions of the amendment, it is difficult to see where it is to stop. Why may not Congress, with equal show of authority, enact a code of laws for the enforcement and vindication of all rights of life, liberty, and property? If it is supposable that the States may deprive persons of life, liberty, and property without due process of law (and the amendment itself does suppose this), why should not Congress proceed at once to prescribe due process of law for the protection of every one of these fundamental rights, in every possible case, as well as to prescribe equal privileges in inns, public conveyances, and theatres? The truth is that the implication of a power to legislate in this manner is based [p*15] upon the assumption that, if the States are forbidden to legislate or act in a particular way on a particular subject, and power is conferred upon Congress to enforce the prohibition, this gives Congress power to legislate generally upon that subject, and not merely power to provide modes of redress against such State legislation or action. The assumption is certainly unsound. It is repugnant to the Tenth Amendment of the Constitution, which declares that powers not delegated to the **United States** by the Constitution, nor prohibited by it to the States, are reserved to the States respectively or to the people.

We have not overlooked the fact that the fourth section of the act now under consideration has been held by this court to be constitutional. That section declares that no citizen, possessing all other qualifications which are or may be prescribed by law, shall be disqualified for service as grand or petit juror in any court of the **United States**, or of any State, on account of race, color, or previous condition of servitude, and any officer or other person charged with any duty in the selection or summoning of jurors who shall exclude or fail to summon any citizen for the cause aforesaid, shall, on conviction thereof, be deemed guilty of a misdemeanor, and be fined not more than five thousand dollars.

In *Ex parte Virginia,* 100 U.S. 339, it was held that an indictment against a State officer under this section for excluding persons of color from the jury list is sustainable. But a moment's attention to its terms will show that the section is entirely corrective in its character. Disqualifications for service on juries are only created by the law, and the first part of the section is aimed at certain disqualifying laws, namely, those which make mere race or color a disqualification, and the second clause is directed against those who, assuming to use the authority of the State government, carry into effect such a rule of disqualification. In the Virginia case, the State, through its officer, enforced a rule of disqualification which the law was intended to abrogate and counteract. Whether the statute book of the State actually laid down any such rule of disqualification or not, the State, through its officer, enforced such a rule, and it is against such State action, through its officers and agents, that the last clause of the section is directed. [p*16] This aspect of the law was deemed sufficient to divest it of any unconstitutional character, and makes it differ widely from the first and second sections of the same act which we are now considering.

These sections, in the objectionable features before referred to, are different also from the law ordinarily called the "Civil Rights Bill," originally passed April 9th, 1866, 14 Stat. 27, ch. 31, and reenacted with some modifications in sections 16, 17, 18, of the Enforcement Act, passed ay 31st, 1870, 16 Stat. 140, ch. 114. That law, as reenacted, after declaring that all persons within the jurisdiction of the **United States** shall have the same right in every State and Territory to make and enforce contracts, to sue, be parties, give evidence, and to the full and equal benefit of all laws and proceedings for the security of persons and property as is enjoyed by white citizens, and shall be subject to like punishment, pains, penalties, taxes, licenses and exactions of every kind, and none other, any law, statute, ordinance, regulation or custom to the contrary notwithstanding, proceeds to enact that any person who, under color of any law, statute, ordinance, regulation or custom, shall subject, or cause to be subjected, any inhabitant of any State or Territory to the deprivation of any rights secured or protected by the preceding section (above quoted), or to different punishment, pains, or penalties, on account of such person's being an alien, or by reason of his color or race, than is prescribed for the punishment of citizens, shall be deemed guilty of a misdemeanor, and subject to fine and imprisonment as specified in the act. This law is clearly corrective in its character, intended to counteract and furnish redress against State laws and proceedings, and customs having the force of law, which sanction the wrongful acts specified. In the Revised Statutes, it is true, a very important clause, to-wit, the words "any law, statute, ordinance, regulation or custom to the contrary notwithstanding," which gave the declaratory section its point and effect, are omitted; but the penal part, by which the declaration is enforced, and which is really the effective part of the law, retains the reference to State laws by making the penalty apply only to those who should subject [p*17] parties to a deprivation of their rights under color of any statute, ordinance, custom, etc., of any State or Territory, thus preserving the corrective character of the legislation. Rev. St. §§ 177, 1978, 1979, 5510. The Civil Rights Bill here referred to is analogous in its character to what a law would have been under the original Constitution, declaring that the validity of contracts should not be impaired, and that, if any person bound by a contract should refuse to comply with it, under color or pretence that it had been rendered void or invalid by a State law, he should be liable to an action upon it in the courts of the **United States**, with the addition of a penalty for setting up such an unjust and unconstitutional defence.

In this connection, it is proper to state that civil rights, such as are guaranteed by the Constitution against State aggression, cannot be impaired by the wrongful acts of individuals, unsupported by State authority in the shape of laws, customs, or judicial or executive proceedings. The wrongful act of an individual, unsupported by any such authority, is simply a private wrong, or a crime of that individual; an invasion of the rights of the injured party, it is true, whether they affect his person, his property, or his reputation; but if not sanctioned in some way by the State, or not done under State authority, his rights remain in full force, and may presumably be vindicated by resort to the laws of the State for redress. An individual cannot deprive a man of his right to vote, to hold property, to buy and sell, to sue in the courts, or to be a witness or a juror; he may, by force or fraud, interfere with the enjoyment of the right in a particular case; he may commit an assault against the person, or commit murder, or use ruffian violence at the polls, or slander the good name of a fellow citizen; but, unless protected in these wrongful acts by some shield of State law or State authority, he cannot destroy or injure the right; he will only render himself amenable to satisfaction or punishment, and amenable therefor to the laws of the State where the wrongful acts are committed. Hence, in all those cases where the Constitution seeks to protect the rights of the citizen against discriminative and unjust laws of the State by prohibiting such laws, it is not individual offences, but abrogation and [p*18] denial of rights, which it denounces and for which it clothes the Congress with power to provide a remedy. This abrogation and denial of rights for which the States alone were or could be responsible was the great seminal and fundamental wrong which was intended to be remedied. And the remedy to be provided must necessarily be predicated upon that wrong. It must assume that, in the cases provided for, the evil or wrong actually committed rests upon some State law or State authority for its excuse and perpetration.

Of course, these remarks do not apply to those cases in which Congress is clothed with direct and plenary powers of legislation over the whole subject, accompanied with an express or implied denial of such power to the States, as in the regulation of commerce with foreign nations, among the several States, and with the Indian tribes, the coining of money, the establishment of post offices and post roads, the declaring of war, etc. In these cases, Congress has power to pass laws for regulating the subjects specified in every detail, and the conduct and transactions of individuals in respect thereof. But where a subject is not submitted to the general legislative power of Congress, but is only submitted thereto for the purpose of rendering effective some prohibition against particular State legislation or State action in reference to that subject, the power given is limited by its object, and any legislation by Congress in the matter must necessarily be corrective in its character, adapted to counteract and redress the operation of such prohibited State laws or proceedings of State officers.

If the principles of interpretation which we have laid down are correct, as we deem them to be (and they are in accord with the principles laid down in the cases before referred to, as well as in the recent case of ***United States*** v. *Harris*, 106 U.S. 629), it is clear that the law in question cannot be sustained by any grant of legislative power made to Congress by the Fourteenth Amendment. That amendment prohibits the States from denying to any person the equal protection of the laws, and declares that Congress shall have power to enforce, by appropriate legislation, the provisions of the amendment. The law in question, without any reference to adverse State legislation on the subject, [p*19] declares that all persons shall be entitled to equal accommodations and privileges of inns, public conveyances, and places of public amusement, and imposes a penalty upon any individual who shall deny to any citizen such equal accommodations and privileges. This is not corrective legislation; it is primary and direct; it takes immediate and absolute possession of the subject of the right of admission to inns, public conveyances, and places of amusement. It supersedes and displaces State legislation on the same subject, or only allows it permissive force. It ignores such legislation, and assumes that the matter is one that belongs to the domain of national regulation. Whether it would not have been a more effective protection of the rights of citizens to have clothed Congress with plenary power over the whole subject is not now the question. What we have to decide is whether such plenary power has been conferred upon Congress by the Fourteenth Amendment; and, in our judgment, it has not.

We have discussed the question presented by the law on the assumption that a right to enjoy equal accommodation and privileges in all inns, public conveyances, and places of public amusement is one of the essential rights of the citizen which no State can abridge or interfere with. Whether it is such a right or not is a different question which, in the view we have taken of the validity of the law on the ground already stated, it is not necessary to examine. We have also discussed the validity of the law in reference to cases arising in the States only, and not in reference to cases arising in the Territories or the District of Columbia, which are subject to the plenary legislation of Congress in every branch of municipal regulation. Whether the law would be a valid one as applied to the Territories and the District is not a question for consideration in the cases before us, they all being cases arising within the limits of States. And whether Congress, in the exercise of its power to regulate commerce amongst the several States, might or might not pass a law regulating rights in public conveyances passing from one State to another is also a question which is not now before us, as the sections in question are not conceived in any such view. [p*20]

But the power of Congress to adopt direct and primary, as distinguished from corrective, legislation on the subject in hand is sought, in the second place, from the Thirteenth Amendment, which abolishes **SLAVERY**. This amendment declares

that neither **SLAVERY**, nor involuntary servitude, except as a punishment for crime, whereof the party shall have been duly convicted, shall exist within the **United States**, or any place subject to their jurisdiction,

and it gives Congress power to enforce the amendment by appropriate legislation.

This amendment, as well as the Fourteenth, is undoubtedly self-executing, without any ancillary legislation, so far as its terms are applicable to any existing state of circumstances. By its own unaided force and effect, it abolished **SLAVERY** and established universal freedom. Still, legislation may be necessary and proper to meet all the various cases and circumstances to be affected by it, and to prescribe proper modes of redress for its violation in letter or spirit. And such legislation may be primary and direct in its character, for the amendment is not a mere prohibition of State laws establishing or upholding **SLAVERY**, but an absolute declaration that **SLAVERY** or involuntary servitude shall not exist in any part of the **United States**.

It is true that **SLAVERY** cannot exist without law, any more than property in lands and goods can exist without law, and, therefore, the Thirteenth Amendment may be regarded as nullifying all State laws which establish or uphold **SLAVERY**. But it has a reflex character also, establishing and decreeing universal civil and political freedom throughout the **United States**, and it is assumed that the power vested in Congress to enforce the article by appropriate legislation clothes Congress with power to pass all laws necessary and proper for abolishing all badges and incidents of **SLAVERY** in the **United States**, and, upon this assumption ,it is claimed that this is sufficient authority for declaring by law that all persons shall have equal accommodations and privileges in all inns, public conveyances, and places of amusement, the argument being that the denial of such equal accommodations and privileges is, in itself, a subjection to a species of servitude within the meaning of the amendment. Conceding the major proposition to be true, that [p*21] Congress has a right to enact all necessary and proper laws for the obliteration and prevention of **SLAVERY** with all its badges and incidents, is the minor proposition also true, that the denial to any person of admission to the accommodations and privileges of an inn, a public conveyance, or a theatre does subject that person to any form of servitude, or tend to fasten upon him any badge of **SLAVERY**? If it does not, then power to pass the law is not found in the Thirteenth Amendment.

In a very able and learned presentation of the cognate question as to the extent of the rights, privileges and immunities of citizens which cannot rightfully be abridged by state laws under the Fourteenth Amendment, made in a former case, a long list of burdens and disabilities of a servile character, incident to feudal vassalage in France, and which were abolished by the decrees of the National Assembly, was presented for the purpose of showing that all inequalities and observances exacted by one man from another were servitudes or badges of **SLAVERY** which a great nation, in its effort to establish universal liberty, made haste to wipe out and destroy. But these were servitudes imposed by the old law, or by long custom, which had the force of law, and exacted by one man from another without the latter's consent. Should any such servitudes be imposed by a state law, there can be no doubt that the law would be repugnant to the Fourteenth, no less than to the Thirteenth, Amendment, nor any greater doubt that Congress has adequate power to forbid any such servitude from being exacted.

But is there any similarity between such servitudes and a denial by the owner of an inn, a public conveyance, or a theatre of its accommodations and privileges to an individual, even though the denial be founded on the race or color of that individual? Where does any **SLAVERY** or servitude, or badge of either, arise from such an act of denial? Whether it might not be a denial of a right which, if sanctioned by the state law, would be obnoxious to the prohibitions of the Fourteenth Amendment is another question. But what has it to do with the question of **SLAVERY**?

It may be that, by the Black Code (as it was called), in the times when **SLAVERY** prevailed, the proprietors of inns and public [p*22] conveyances were forbidden to receive persons of the **AFRICAN** race because it might assist slaves to escape from the control of their masters. This was merely a means of preventing such escapes, and was no part of the servitude itself. A law of that kind could not have any such object now, however justly it might be deemed an invasion of the party's legal right as a citizen, and amenable to the prohibitions of the Fourteenth Amendment.

The long existence of **AFRICAN SLAVERY** in this country gave us very distinct notions of what it was and what were its necessary incidents. Compulsory service of the slave for the benefit of the master, restraint of his movements except by the master's will, disability to hold property, to make contracts, to have a standing in court, to be a witness against a white person, and such like burdens and incapacities were the inseparable incidents of the institution. Severer punishments for crimes were imposed on the slave than on free persons guilty of the same offences. Congress, as we have seen, by the Civil Rights Bill of 1866, passed in view of the Thirteenth Amendment before the Fourteenth was adopted, undertook to wipe out these burdens and disabilities, the necessary incidents of **SLAVERY** constituting its substance and visible form, and to secure to all citizens of every race and color, and without regard to previous servitude, those fundamental rights which are the essence of civil freedom, namely, the same right to make and enforce contracts, to sue, be parties, give evidence, and to inherit, purchase, lease, sell and convey property as is enjoyed by white citizens. Whether this legislation was fully authorized by the Thirteenth Amendment alone, without the support which it afterward received from the Fourteenth Amendment, after the adoption of which it was reenacted with some additions, it is not necessary to inquire. It is referred to for the purpose of showing that, at that time (in 1866), Congress did not assume, under the authority given by the Thirteenth Amendment, to adjust what may be called the social rights of men and races in the community, but only to declare and vindicate those fundamental rights which appertain to the essence of citizenship, and the enjoyment or deprivation of which constitutes the essential distinction between freedom and **SLAVERY**. [p*23]

We must not forget that the province and scope of the Thirteenth and Fourteenth amendments are different: the former simply abolished **SLAVERY**; the latter prohibited the States from abridging the privileges or immunities of citizens of the **United States**, from depriving them of life, liberty, or property without due process of law, and from denying to any the equal protection of the laws. The amendments are different, and the powers of Congress under them are different. What Congress has power to do under one it may not have power to do under the other. Under the Thirteenth Amendment, it has only to do with **SLAVERY** and its incidents. Under the Fourteenth Amendment, it has power to counteract and render nugatory all State laws and proceedings which have the effect to abridge any of the privileges or immunities of citizens of the **United States**, or to deprive them of life, liberty or property without due process of law, or to deny to any of them the equal protection of the laws. Under the Thirteenth Amendment, the legislation, so far as necessary or proper to eradicate all forms and incidents of **SLAVERY** and involuntary servitude, may be direct and primary, operating upon the acts of individuals, whether sanctioned by State legislation or not; under the Fourteenth, as we have already shown, it must necessarily be, and can only be, corrective in its character, addressed to counteract and afford relief against State regulations or proceedings.

The only question under the present head, therefore, is whether the refusal to any persons of the accommodations of an inn or a public conveyance or a place of public amusement by an individual, and without any sanction or support from any State law or regulation, does inflict upon such persons any manner of servitude or form of **SLAVERY** as those terms are understood in this country? Many wrongs may be obnoxious to the prohibitions of the Fourteenth Amendment which are not, in any just sense, incidents or elements of **SLAVERY**. Such, for example, would be the taking of private property without due process of law, or allowing persons who have committed certain crimes (horse stealing, for example) to be seized and hung by the *posse comitatus* without regular trial, or denying to any person, or class of persons, the right to pursue any peaceful [p*24] avocations allowed to others. What is called class legislation would belong to this category, and would be obnoxious to the prohibitions of the Fourteenth Amendment, but would not necessarily be so to the Thirteenth, when not involving the idea of any subjection of one man to another. The Thirteenth Amendment has respect not to distinctions of race or class or color, but to **SLAVERY**. The Fourteenth Amendment extends its protection to races and classes, and prohibits any State legislation which has the effect of denying to any race or class, or to any individual, the equal protection of the laws.

Now, conceding for the sake of the argument that the admission to an inn, a public conveyance, or a place of public amusement on equal terms with all other citizens is the right of every man and all classes of men, is it any more than one of those rights which the states, by the Fourteenth Amendment, are forbidden to deny to any person? And is the Constitution violated until the denial of the right has some State sanction or authority? Can the act of a mere individual, the owner of the inn, the public conveyance or place of amusement, refusing the accommodation, be justly regarded as imposing any badge of **SLAVERY** or servitude upon the applicant, or only as inflicting an ordinary civil injury, properly cognizable by the laws of the State and presumably subject to redress by those laws until the contrary appears?

After giving to these questions all the consideration which their importance demands, we are forced to the conclusion that such an act of refusal has nothing to do with **SLAVERY** or involuntary servitude, and that, if it is violative of any right of the party, his redress is to be sought under the laws of the State, or, if those laws are adverse to his rights and do not protect him, his remedy will be found in the corrective legislation which Congress has adopted, or may adopt, for counteracting the effect of State laws or State action prohibited by the Fourteenth Amendment. It would be running the **SLAVERY** argument into the ground to make it apply to every act of discrimination which a person may see fit to make as to the guests he will entertain, or as to the people he will take into his coach or cab or car, or admit to his concert or theatre, or deal with in [p*25] other matters of intercourse or business.

Innkeepers and public carriers, by the laws of all the States, so far as we are aware, are bound, to the extent of their facilities, to furnish proper accommodation to all unobjectionable persons who in good faith apply for them. If the laws themselves make any unjust discrimination amenable to the prohibitions of the Fourteenth Amendment, Congress has full power to afford a remedy under that amendment and in accordance with it.

When a man has emerged from **SLAVERY**, and, by the aid of beneficent legislation, has shaken off the inseparable concomitants of that state, there must be some stage in the progress of his elevation when he takes the rank of a mere citizen and ceases to be the special favorite of the laws, and when his rights as a citizen or a man are to be protected in the ordinary modes by which other men's rights are protected. There were thousands of free colored people in this country before the abolition of **SLAVERY**, enjoying all the essential rights of life, liberty and property the same as white citizens, yet no one at that time thought that it was any invasion of his personal status as a freeman because he was not admitted to all the privileges enjoyed by white citizens, or because he was subjected to discriminations in the enjoyment of accommodations in inns, public conveyances and places of amusement. Mere discriminations on account of race or color were not regarded as badges of **SLAVERY**. If, since that time, the enjoyment of equal rights in all these respects has become established by constitutional enactment, it is not by force of the Thirteenth Amendment (which merely abolishes **SLAVERY**), but by force of the Thirteenth and Fifteenth Amendments.

On the whole, we are of opinion that no countenance of authority for the passage of the law in question can be found in either the Thirteenth or Fourteenth Amendment of the Constitution, and no other ground of authority for its passage being suggested, it must necessarily be declared void, at least so far as its operation in the several States is concerned.

This conclusion disposes of the cases now under consideration. In the cases of the ***United States*** v. *Michael Ryan,* and of *Richard A. Robinson and Wife v. The Memphis & Charleston* [p*26] *Railroad Company,* the judgments must be affirmed. In the other cases, the answer to be given will be that the first and second sections of the act of Congress of March 1st, 1875, entitled "An Act to protect all citizens in their civil and legal rights," are unconstitutional and void, and that judgment should be rendered upon the several indictments in those cases accordingly.

*And it is so ordered.*

### HARLAN, J., Dissenting Opinion

MR. JUSTICE HARLAN dissenting.

The opinion in these cases proceeds, it seems to me, upon grounds entirely too narrow and artificial. I cannot resist the conclusion that the substance and spirit of the recent amendments of the Constitution have been sacrificed by a subtle and ingenious verbal criticism.

It is not the words of the law, but the internal sense of it that makes the law; the letter of the law is the body; the sense and reason of the law is the soul.

Constitutional provisions, adopted in the interest of liberty and for the purpose of securing, through national legislation, if need be, rights inhering in a state of freedom and belonging to American citizenship have been so construed as to defeat the ends the people desired to accomplish, which they attempted to accomplish, and which they supposed they had accomplished by changes in their fundamental law. By this I do not mean that the determination of these cases should have been materially controlled by considerations of mere expediency or policy. I mean only, in this form, to express an earnest conviction that the court has departed from the familiar rule requiring, in the interpretation of constitutional provisions, that full effect be given to the intent with which they were adopted.

The purpose of the first section of the act of Congress of March 1, 1875, was to prevent race discrimination in respect of the accommodations and facilities of inns, public conveyances, and places of public amusement. It does not assume to define the general conditions and limitations under which inns, public conveyances, and places of public amusement may be conducted, but only declares that such conditions and limitations, whatever they may be, shall not be applied so as to work a [p*27] discrimination solely because of race, color, or previous condition of servitude. The second section provides a penalty against anyone denying, or aiding or inciting the denial, of any citizen, of that equality of right given by the first section except for reasons by law applicable to citizens of every race or color and regardless of any previous condition of servitude.

There seems to be no substantial difference between my brethren and myself as to the purpose of Congress, for they say that the essence of the law is not to declare broadly that all persons shall be entitled to the full and equal enjoyment of the accommodations, advantages, facilities, and privileges of inns, public conveyances, and theatres, but that such enjoyment shall not be subject to conditions applicable only to citizens of a particular race or color, or who had been in a previous condition of servitude. The effect of the statute, the court says, is that colored citizens, whether formerly slaves or not, and citizens of other races shall have the same accommodations and privileges in all inns, public conveyances, and places of amusement as are enjoyed by white persons, and vice versa.

The court adjudges, I think erroneously, that Congress is without power, under either the Thirteenth or Fourteenth Amendment, to establish such regulations, and that the first and second sections of the statute are, in all their parts, unconstitutional and void.

Whether the legislative department of the government has transcended the limits of its constitutional powers, "is at all times," said this court in *Fletcher v. Peck,* 6 Cr. 128,

a question of much delicacy which ought seldom, if ever, to be decided in the affirmative in a doubtful case. . . . The opposition between the Constitution and the law should be such that the judge feels a clear and strong conviction of their incompatibility with each other.

More recently, in *Sinking Fund Cases,* 99 U.S. 718, we said:

It is our duty, when required in the regular course of judicial proceedings, to declare an act of Congress void if not within the legislative power of the **United States**, but this declaration should never be made except in a clear case. Every possible presumption is [p*28] in favor of the validity of a statute, and this continues until the contrary is shown beyond a rational doubt. One branch of the government cannot encroach on the domain of another without danger. The safety of our institutions depends in no small degree on a strict observance of this salutary rule.

Before considering the language and scope of these amendments, it will be proper to recall the relations subsisting, prior to their adoption, between the national government and the institution of **SLAVERY**, as indicated by the provisions of the Constitution, the legislation of Congress, and the decisions of this court. In this mode, we may obtain keys with which to open the mind of the people and discover the thought intended to be expressed.

In section 2 of article IV of the Constitution, it was provided that

no person held to service or labor in one State, under the laws thereof, escaping into another, shall, in consequence of any law or regulation therein, be discharged from such service or labor, but shall be delivered up on claim of the party to whom such service or labor may be due.

Under the authority of this clause, Congress passed the Fugitive Slave Law of 1793, establishing a mode for the recovery of fugitive slaves and prescribing a penalty against any person who should knowingly and willingly obstruct or hinder the master, his agent, or attorney in seizing, arresting, and recovering the fugitive, or who should rescue the fugitive from him, or who should harbor or conceal the slave after notice that he was a fugitive.

In *Prigg v. Commonwealth of Pennsylvania,* 16 Pet. 539, this court had occasion to define the powers and duties of

Congress in reference to fugitives from labor. Speaking by MR. JUSTICE STORY, it laid down these propositions:

That a clause of the Constitution conferring a right should not be so construed as to make it shadowy or unsubstantial, or leave the citizen without a remedial power adequate for its protection when another construction equally accordant with the words and the sense in which they were used would enforce and protect the right granted;

That Congress is not restricted to legislation for the execution [p*29] of its expressly granted powers, but, for the protection of rights guaranteed by the Constitution, may employ such means, not prohibited, as are necessary and proper, or such as are appropriate, to attain the ends proposed;

That the Constitution recognized the master's right of property in his fugitive slave, and, as incidental thereto, the right of seizing and recovering him, regardless of any State law or regulation or local custom whatsoever; and,

That the right of the master to have his slave, thus escaping, delivered up on claim, being guaranteed by the Constitution, the fair implication was that the national government was clothed with appropriate authority and functions to enforce it.

The court said

The fundamental principle, applicable to all cases of this sort, would seem to be that, when the end is required the means are given, and when the duty is enjoined, the ability to perform it is contemplated to exist on the part of the functionary to whom it is entrusted.

Again, It would be a strange anomaly and forced construction to suppose that the national government meant to rely for the due fulfillment of its own proper duties, and the rights which it intended to secure, upon State legislation, and not upon that of the Union. *A fortiori,* it would be more objectionable to suppose that a power which was to be the same throughout the Union should be confided to State sovereignty, which could not rightfully act beyond its own territorial limits

The act of 1793 was, upon these grounds, adjudged to be a constitutional exercise of the powers of Congress.

It is to be observed from the report of Priggs' case that Pennsylvania, by her attorney general, pressed the argument that the obligation to surrender fugitive slaves was on the States and for the States, subject to the restriction that they should not pass laws or establish regulations liberating such fugitives; that the Constitution did not take from the States the right to determine the status of all persons within their respective jurisdictions; that it was for the State in which the alleged fugitive was found to determine, through her courts or in such modes as she prescribed, whether the person arrested was, in fact, a freeman or a fugitive slave; that the sole power [p*30] of the general government in the premises was, by judicial instrumentality, to restrain and correct, not to forbid and prevent in the absence of hostile State action, and that, for the general government to assume primary authority to legislate on the subject of fugitive slaves, to the exclusion of the States, would be a dangerous encroachment on State sovereignty. But to such suggestions, this court turned a deaf ear, and adjudged that primary legislation by Congress to enforce the master's right was authorized by the Constitution.

We next come to the **Fugitive Slave Act of 1850**, the constitutionality of which rested, as did that of 1793, solely upon the implied power of Congress to enforce the master's rights. The provisions of that act were far in advance of previous legislation. They placed at the disposal of the master seeking to recover his fugitive slave substantially the whole power of the nation. It invested commissioners, appointed under the act, with power to summon the *posse comitatus* for the enforcement of its provisions, and commanded all good citizens to assist in its prompt and efficient execution whenever their services were required as part of the *posse comitatus*. Without going into the details of that act, it is sufficient to say that Congress omitted from it nothing which the utmost ingenuity could suggest as essential to the successful enforcement of the master's claim to recover his fugitive slave. And this court, in *Ableman v. Booth,* 21 How. 506 , adjudged it to be "in all of its provisions, fully authorized by the Constitution of the **United States**."

The only other case, prior to the adoption of the recent amendments, to which reference will be made, is that of *Dred Scott v. Sanford,* 19 How. 399 . That case was instituted in a circuit court of the **United States** by Dred Scott, claiming to be a citizen of Missouri, the defendant being a citizen of another State. Its object was to assert the title of himself and family to freedom. The defendant pleaded in abatement that Scott -- being of **AFRICAN** descent, whose ancestors, of pure **AFRICAN** blood, were brought into this country and sold as slaves -- was not a citizen. The only matter in issue, said the court, was whether the descendants of slaves thus imported [p*31] and sold, when they should be emancipated, or who were born of parents who had become free before their birth, are citizens of a State in the sense in which the word "citizen" is used in the Constitution of the **United States**.

In determining that question, the court instituted an inquiry as to who were citizens of the several States at the adoption of the Constitution and who at that time were recognized as the people whose rights and liberties had been violated by the British government. The result was a declaration by this court, speaking by Chief Justice Taney, that the legislation and histories of the times, and the language used in the Declaration of Independence, showed

that neither the class of persons who had been imported as slaves nor their descendants, whether they had become free or not, were then acknowledged as a part of the people, nor intended to be included in the general words used in that instrument;that

they had for more than a century before been regarded as beings of an inferior race, and altogether unfit to associate with the white race either in social or political relations, and so far inferior that they had no rights which the white man was bound to respect, and that the negro might justly and lawfully be reduced to **SLAVERY** for his benefit;

that he was "bought and sold, and treated as an ordinary article of merchandise and traffic, whenever a profit could be made by it;" and, that

this opinion was at that time fixed and universal in the civilized portion of the white race. It was regarded as an axiom in morals, as well as in politics, which no one thought of disputing, or supposed to be open to dispute, and men in every grade and position in society daily and habitually acted upon it in their private pursuits, as well as in matters of public concern, without for a moment doubting the correctness of this opinion.

The judgment of the court was that the words "people of the **United States**" and "citizens" meant the same thing, both describing

The political body who, according to our republican institutions, form the sovereignty and hold the power and conduct the government through their representatives; that they are what we familiarly call the "sovereign people," and [p*32] every citizen is one of this people and a constituent member of this sovereignty;

but that the class of persons described in the plea in abatement did not compose a portion of this people, were not "included, and were not intended to be included, under the word `citizens' in the Constitution;" that, therefore, they could "claim none of the rights and privileges which that instrument provides for and secures to citizens of the **United States**;" that,

on the contrary, they were at that time considered as a subordinate and inferior class of beings who had been subjugated by the dominant race and, whether emancipated or not, yet remained subject to their authority, and had no rights or privileges but such as those who held the power and the government might choose to grant them

Such were the relations which formerly existed between the government, whether national or state, and the descendants, whether free or in bondage, of those of **AFRICAN** blood who had been imported into this country and sold as slaves. The first section of the Thirteenth Amendment provides that neither **SLAVERY** nor involuntary servitude, except as a punishment for crime, whereof the party shall have been duly convicted, shall exist within the **United States**, or any place subject to their jurisdiction.

Its second section declares that "Congress shall have power to enforce this article by appropriate legislation." This amendment was followed by the Civil Rights Act of April 9, 1866, which, among other things, provided that

all persons born in the **United States**, and not subject to any foreign power, excluding Indians not taxed, are hereby declared to be citizens of the **United States**.

14 Stat. 27. The power of Congress, in this mode, to elevate the enfranchised race to national citizenship was maintained by the supporters of the act of 1866 to be as full and complete as its power, by general statute, to make the children, being of full age, of persons naturalized in this country, citizens of the **United States** without going through the process of naturalization. The act of 1866 in this respect was also likened to that of 1843, in which Congress declared

that the Stockbridge tribe of Indians, and each and every one of them, shall be deemed to be and are hereby declared to be, citizens of the **United States** to [p*33] all intents and purposes, and shall be entitled to all the rights, privileges, and immunities of such citizens, and shall in all respects be subject to the laws of the **United States**.

If the act of 1866 was valid in conferring national citizenship upon all embraced by its terms, then the colored race, enfranchised by the Thirteenth Amendment, became citizens of the **United States** prior to the adoption of the Fourteenth Amendment. But, in the view which I take of the present case, it is not necessary to examine this question.

The terms of the Thirteenth Amendment are absolute and universal. They embrace every race which then was, or might thereafter be, within the **United States**. No race, as such, can be excluded from the benefits or rights thereby conferred. Yet it is historically true that that amendment was suggested by the condition, in this country, of that race which had been declared by this court to have had -- according to the opinion entertained by the most civilized portion of the white race at the time of the adoption of the Constitution -- "no rights which the white man was bound to respect," none of the privileges or immunities secured by that instrument to citizens of the **United States**. It had reference, in peculiar sense, to a people which (although the larger part of them were in **SLAVERY**) had been invited by an act of Congress to aid in saving from overthrow a government which, theretofore, by all of its departments, had treated them as an inferior race, with no legal rights or privileges except such as the white race might choose to grant them.

These are the circumstances under which the Thirteenth Amendment was proposed for adoption. They are now recalled only that we may better understand what was in the minds of the people when that amendment was considered, and what were the mischiefs to be remedied and the grievances to be redressed by its adoption.

We have seen that the power of Congress, by legislation, to enforce the master's right to have his slave delivered up on claim was *implied* from the recognition of that right in the national Constitution. But the power conferred by the

Thirteenth Amendment does not rest upon implication or [p*34] inference. Those who framed it were not ignorant of the discussion, covering many years of our country's history, as to the constitutional power of Congress to enact the Fugitive Slave Laws of 1793 and 1850. When, therefore, it was determined, by a change in the fundamental law, to uproot the institution of **SLAVERY** wherever it existed in the land and to establish universal freedom, there was a fixed purpose to place the authority of Congress in the premises beyond the possibility of a doubt. Therefore, *ex industria,* power to enforce the Thirteenth Amendment by appropriate legislation was expressly granted. Legislation for that purpose, my brethren concede, may be direct and primary. But to what specific ends may it be directed? This court has uniformly held that the national government has the power, whether expressly given or not, to secure and protect rights conferred or guaranteed by the Constitution. **United States** *v. Reese,* 92 U.S. 214; *Strauder v. West Virginia,* 100 U.S. 303 . That doctrine ought not now to be abandoned when the inquiry is not as to an implied power to protect the master's rights, but what may Congress, under powers expressly granted, do for the protection of freedom and the rights necessarily inhering in a state of freedom.

The Thirteenth Amendment, it is conceded, did something more than to prohibit **SLAVERY** as an *institution* resting upon distinctions of race and upheld by positive law. My brethren admit that it established and decreed universal *civil freedom* throughout the **United States**. But did the freedom thus established involve nothing more than exemption from actual **SLAVERY**? Was nothing more intended than to forbid one man from owning another as property? Was it the purpose of the nation simply to destroy the institution, and then remit the race, theretofore held in bondage, to the several States for such protection, in their civil rights, necessarily growing out of freedom, as those States, in their discretion, might choose to provide? Were the States against whose protest the institution was destroyed to be left free, so far as national interference was concerned, to make or allow discriminations against that race, as such, in the enjoyment of those fundamental rights which, by universal concession, inhere in a state of freedom? [p*35] Had the Thirteenth Amendment stopped with the sweeping declaration in its first section against the existence of **SLAVERY** and involuntary servitude except for crime, Congress would have had the power, by implication, according to the doctrines of *Prigg v. Commonwealth of Pennsylvania,* repeated in *Strauder v. West Virginia,* to protect the freedom established, and consequently, to secure the enjoyment of such civil rights as were fundamental in freedom. That it can exert its authority to that extent is made clear, and was intended to be made clear, by the express grant of power contained in the second section of the Amendment.

That there are burdens and disabilities which constitute badges of **SLAVERY** and servitude, and that the power to enforce by appropriate legislation the Thirteenth Amendment may be exerted by legislation of a direct and primary character for the eradication not simply of the institution, but of its badges and incidents, are propositions which ought to be deemed indisputable. They lie at the foundation of the Civil Rights Act of 1866. Whether that act was authorized by the Thirteenth Amendment alone, without the support which it subsequently received from the Fourteenth Amendment, after the adoption of which it was reenacted with some additions, my brethren do not consider it necessary to inquire. But I submit, with all respect to them, that its constitutionality is conclusively shown by their opinion. They admit, as I have said, that the Thirteenth Amendment established freedom; that there are burdens and disabilities, the necessary incidents of **SLAVERY**, which constitute its substance and visible form; that Congress, by the act of 1866, passed in view of the Thirteenth Amendment, before the Fourteenth was adopted, undertook to remove certain burdens and disabilities, the necessary incidents of **SLAVERY**, and to secure to all citizens of every race and color, and without regard to previous servitude, those fundamental rights which are the essence of civil freedom, namely, the same right to make and enforce contracts, to sue, be parties, give evidence, and to inherit, purchase, lease, sell, and convey property as is enjoyed by white citizens; that, under the Thirteenth Amendment, Congress has to do with **SLAVERY** and [p*36] its incidents, and that legislation, so far as necessary or proper to eradicate all forms and incidents of slaver and involuntary servitude, may be direct and primary, operating upon the acts of individuals, whether sanctioned by State legislation or not. These propositions being conceded, it is impossible, as it seems to me, to question the constitutional validity of the Civil Rights Act of 1866. I do not contend that the Thirteenth Amendment invests Congress with authority, by legislation, to define and regulate the entire body of the civil rights which citizens enjoy, or may enjoy, in the several States. But I hold that, since **SLAVERY**, as the court has repeatedly declared, *Slaughterhouse Cases,* 16 Wall. 36 ; *Strauder West Virginia,* 100 U.S. 303 , was the moving or principal cause of the adoption of that amendment, and since that institution rested wholly upon the inferiority, as a race, of those held in bondage, their freedom necessarily involved immunity from, and protection against, all discrimination against them, because of their race, in respect of such civil rights as belong to freemen of other races. Congress, therefore, under its express power to enforce that amendment by appropriate legislation, may enact laws to protect that people against the deprivation, *because of their race,* of any civil rights granted to other freemen in the same State, and such legislation may be of a direct and primary character, operating upon States, their officers and agents, and also upon at least such individuals and corporations as exercise public functions and wield power and authority under the State.

To test the correctness of this position, let us suppose that, prior to the adoption of the Fourteenth Amendment, a State had passed a statute denying to freemen of **AFRICAN** descent, resident within its limits, the same right which was accorded to white persons of making and enforcing contracts and of inheriting, purchasing, leasing, selling and conveying property; or a statute subjecting colored people to severer punishment for particular offences than was prescribed for white persons, or excluding that race from the benefit of the laws exempting homesteads from execution. Recall the legislation of 1865-1866 in some of the States, of which this court in the *Slaughterhouse* [p*37]

*Cases* said that it imposed upon the colored race onerous disabilities and burdens; curtailed their rights in the pursuit of life, liberty and property to such an extent that their freedom was of little value; forbade them to appear in the towns in any other character than menial servants; required them to reside on and cultivate the soil, without the right to purchase or own it; excluded them from many occupations of gain, and denied them the privilege of giving testimony in the courts where a white man was a party. 16 Wall. 57. Can there be any doubt that all such enactments might have been reached by direct legislation upon the part of Congress under its express power to enforce the Thirteenth Amendment? Would any court have hesitated to declare that such legislation imposed badges of servitude in conflict with the civil freedom ordained by that amendment? That it would have been also in conflict with the Fourteenth Amendment because inconsistent with the fundamental rights of American citizenship does not prove that it would have been consistent with the Thirteenth Amendment.

What has been said is sufficient to show that the power of Congress under the Thirteenth Amendment is not necessarily restricted to legislation against **SLAVERY** as an institution upheld by positive law, but may be exerted to the extent, at least, of protecting the liberated race against discrimination in respect of legal rights belonging to freemen where such discrimination is based upon race.

It remains now to inquire what are the legal rights of colored persons in respect of the accommodations, privileges and facilities of public conveyances, inns, and places of public amusement?

*First,* as to public conveyances on land and water. In *New Jersey Steam Navigation Co. v. Merchants' Bank,* 6 How. 344, this court, speaking by Mr. Justice Nelson, said that a common carrier is

in the exercise of a sort of public office, and has public duties to perform, from which he should not be permitted to exonerate himself without the assent of the parties concerned.

To the same effect is *Munn v. Illinois,* 94 U.S. 113 . In *Olcott v. Supervisor,* 16 Wall. 678, it was ruled that [p*38] railroads are public highways, established by authority of the State for the public use; that they are nonetheless public highways because controlled and owned by private corporations; that it is a part of the function of government to make and maintain highways for the convenience of the public; that no matter who is the agent, or what is the agency, the function performed is *that of the State;* that, although the owners may be private companies, they may be compelled to permit the public to use these works in the manner in which they can be used; that, upon these grounds alone have the courts sustained the investiture of railroad corporations with the State's right of eminent domain, or the right of municipal corporations, under legislative authority, to assess, levy and collect taxes to aid in the construction of railroads. So in *Township of Queensbury v. Culver,* 19 Wall. 83, it was said that a municipal subscription of railroad stock was in aid of the construction and maintenance of a public highway, and for the promotion of a public use. Again, in *Township of Pine Grove v. Talcott,* 19 Wall. 666: "Though the corporation [railroad] was private, its work was public, as much so as if it were to be constructed by the State." To the like effect are numerous adjudications in this and the State courts with which the profession is familiar. The **Supreme** Judicial Court of Massachusetts, in *Inhabitants of Worcester v. The Western R.R. Corporation,* 4 Met. 564, said in reference to a railroad:

The establishment of that great thoroughfare is regarded as a public work, established by public authority, intended for the public use and benefit, the use of which is secured to the whole community, and constitutes, therefore, like a canal, turnpike, or highway, a public easement. . . . It is true that the real and personal property, necessary to the establishment and management of the railroad is vested in the corporation, but it is in trust for the public.

In *Erie, Etc., R.R. Co. v. Casey,* 26 Penn. St. 287, the court, referring to an act repealing the charter of a railroad, and under which the State took possession of the road, said:

It is a public highway, solemnly devoted to public use. When the lands were taken, it was for such use, or they could not have been taken at all. . . . Railroads established [p*39] upon land taken by the right of eminent domain by authority of the commonwealth, created by her laws as thoroughfares for commerce, are her highways. No corporation has property in them, though it may have franchises annexed to and exercisable within them.

In many courts it has been held that, because of the public interest in such a corporation, the land of a railroad company cannot be levied on and sold under execution by a creditor. The sum of the adjudged cases is that a railroad corporation is a governmental agency, created primarily for public purposes and subject to be controlled for the public benefit. Upon this ground, the State, when unfettered by contract, may regulate, in its discretion, the rates of fares of passengers and freight. And upon this ground, too, the State may regulate the entire management of railroads in all matters affecting the convenience and safety of the public, as, for example, by regulating speed, compelling stops of prescribed length at stations, and prohibiting discriminations and favoritism. If the corporation neglect or refuse to discharge its duties to the public, it may be coerced to do so by appropriate proceedings in the name or in behalf of the State.

Such being the relations these corporations hold to the public, it would seem that the right of a colored person to use an improved public highway upon the terms accorded to freemen of other races is as fundamental, in the state of freedom established in this country, as are any of the rights which my brethren concede to be so far fundamental as to be deemed the essence of civil freedom. "Personal liberty consists," says Blackstone,

in the power of locomotion, of changing situation, or removing one's person to whatever places one's own inclination may direct, without restraint unless by due course of law.

But of what value is this right of locomotion if it may be clogged by such burdens as Congress intended by the act of 1875 to remove? They are burdens which lay at the very foundation of the institution of **SLAVERY** as it once existed. They are not to be sustained except upon the assumption that there is, in this land of universal liberty, a class which may still be discriminated against, even in respect of rights of a character [p*40] so necessary and **Supreme** that, deprived of their enjoyment in common with others, a freeman is not only branded as one inferior and infected, but, in the competitions of life, is robbed of some of the most essential means of existence, and all this solely because they belong to a particular race which the nation has liberated. The Thirteenth Amendment alone obliterated the race line so far as all rights fundamental in a state of freedom are concerned.

*Second,* as to inns. The same general observations which have been made as to railroads are applicable to inns. The word "inn" has a technical legal signification. It means, in the act of 1875, just what it meant at common law. A mere private boarding house is not an inn, nor is its keeper subject to the responsibilities, or entitled to the privileges, of a common innkeeper.

To constitute one an innkeeper within the legal force of that term, he must keep a house of entertainment or lodging for all travelers or wayfarers who might choose to accept the same, being of good character or conduct.

Redfield on Carriers, etc., § 7. Says Judge Story:

An innkeeper may be defined to be the keeper of a common inn for the lodging and entertainment of travelers and passengers, their horses and attendants. An innkeeper is bound to take in all travelers and wayfaring persons, and to entertain them, if he can accommodate them, for a reasonable compensation, and he must guard their goods with proper diligence. . . . If an innkeeper improperly refuses to receive or provide for a guest, he is liable to be indicted therefor. . . . They (carriers of passengers) are no more at liberty to refuse a passenger, if they have sufficient room and accommodations, than an innkeeper is to refuse suitable room and accommodations to a guest.

Story on Bailments §§ 475-476.

In *Rex v. Ivens,* 7 Carrington & Payne 213, 32 E.C.L. 49, the court, speaking by Mr. Justice Coleridge, said:

An indictment lies against an innkeeper who refuses to receive a guest, he having at the time room in his house and either the price of the guest's entertainment being tendered to him or such circumstances occurring as will dispense with that [p*41] tender. This law is founded in good sense. The innkeeper is not to select his guest. He has no right to say to one, you shall come to my inn, and to another, you shall not, as everyone coming and conducting himself in a proper manner has a right to be received, and, for this purpose innkeepers are a sort of public servants, they having, in return a kind of privilege of entertaining travelers and supplying them with what they want.

These authorities are sufficient to show that a keeper of an inn is in the exercise of a *quasi*-public employment. The law gives him special privileges. and he is charged with certain duties and responsibilities to the public. The public nature of his employment forbids him from discriminating against any person asking admission as a guest on account of the race or color of that person.

*Third.* As to places of public amusement. It may be argued that the managers of such places have no duties to perform with which the public are, in any legal sense, concerned, or with which the public have any right to interfere, and that the exclusion of a black man from a place of public amusement on account of his race, or the denial to him on that ground of equal accommodations at such places, violates no legal right for the vindication of which he may invoke the aid of the courts. My answer is that places of public amusement, within the meaning of the act of 1875, are such as are established and maintained under direct license of the law. The authority to establish and maintain them comes from the public. The colored race is a part of that public. The local government granting the license represents them as well as all other races within its jurisdiction. A license from the public to establish a place of public amusement imports in law equality of right at such places among all the members of that public. This must be so unless it be -- which I deny -- that the common municipal government of all the people may, in the exertion of its powers, conferred for the benefit of all, discriminate or authorize discrimination against a particular race solely because of its former condition of servitude.

I also submit, whether it can be said -- in view of the doctrines of this court as announced in *Munn v. State of Illinois,* [p*42] 94 U.S. 113 , and reaffirmed in *Peik v. Chicago & N.W. Railway Co.,* 94 U.S. 169, that the management of places of public amusement is a purely private matter, with which government has no rightful concern? In the *Munn* case, the question was whether the State of Illinois could fix, by law, the maximum of charges for the storage of grain in certain warehouses in that State -- the *private property of individual citizens.* After quoting a remark attributed to Lord Chief Justice Hale, to the effect that, when private property is "affected with a public interest, it ceases to be *juris privati* only," the court says:

Property does become clothed with a public interest when used in a manner to make it of public consequence and affect the community at large. When, therefore, one devotes his property to a use in which the public has an interest, he, in effect, grants to the public an interest in that use, and must submit to be controlled by the public for the common good to the extent of the interest he has thus created. He may withdraw his grant by discontinuing the use, but, so long as he maintains the use, he must submit to the control.

The doctrines of *Munn v. Illinois* have never been modified by this court, and I am justified upon the authority of that case in saying that places of public amusement, conducted under the authority of the law, are clothed with a public interest because used in a manner to make them of public consequence and to affect the community at large. The law may therefore regulate, to some extent, the mode in which they shall be conducted, and, consequently, the public have rights in respect of such places which may be vindicated by the law. It is consequently not a matter purely of private concern.

Congress has not, in these matters, entered the domain of State control and supervision. It does not, as I have said, assume to prescribe the general conditions and limitations under which inns, public conveyances, and places of public amusement shall be conducted or managed. It simply declares, in effect, that, since the nation has established universal freedom in this country for all time, there shall be no discrimination, based merely upon race or color, in respect of the accommodations [p*43] and advantages of public conveyances, inns, and places of public amusement.

I am of the opinion that such discrimination practised by corporations and individuals in the exercise of their public or *quasi*-public functions is a badge of servitude the imposition of which Congress may prevent under its power, by appropriate legislation, to enforce the Thirteenth Amendment; and consequently, without reference to its enlarged power under the Fourteenth Amendment, the act of March 1, 1875, is not, in my judgment, repugnant to the Constitution.

It remains now to consider these cases with reference to the power Congress has possessed since the adoption of the Fourteenth Amendment. Much that has been said as to the power of Congress under the Thirteenth Amendment is applicable to this branch of the discussion, and will not be repeated.

Before the adoption of the recent amendments, it had become, as we have seen, the established doctrine of this court that negroes, whose ancestors had been imported and sold as slaves, could not become citizens of a State, or even of the **United States**, with the rights and privileges guaranteed to citizens by the national Constitution; further, that one might have all the rights and privileges of a citizen of a State without being a citizen in the sense in which that word was used in the national Constitution, and without being entitled to the privileges and immunities of citizens of the several States. Still further, between the adoption of the Thirteenth Amendment and the proposal by Congress of the Fourteenth Amendment, on June 16, 1866, the statute books of several of the States, as we have seen, had become loaded down with enactments which, under the guise of Apprentice, Vagrant, and contract regulations, sought to keep the colored race in a condition, practically, of servitude. It was openly announced that whatever might be the rights which persons of that race had as freemen, under the guarantees of the national Constitution, they could not become citizens of a State, with the privileges belonging to citizens, except by the consent of such State; consequently, that their civil rights as citizens of the State depended entirely upon State legislation. To meet this new peril to the black race, that the [p*44] purposes of the nation might not be doubted or defeated, and by way of further enlargement of the power of Congress, the Fourteenth Amendment was proposed for adoption.

Remembering that this court, in the *Slaughterhouse Cases,* declared that the one pervading purpose found in all the recent amendments, lying at the foundation of each and without which none of them would have been suggested, was

the freedom of the slave race, the security and firm establishment of that freedom, and the protection of the newly made freeman and citizen from the oppression of those who had formerly exercised unlimited dominion over him

-- that each amendment was addressed primarily to the grievances of that race -- let us proceed to consider the language of the Fourteenth Amendment.

Its first and fifth sections are in these words:

SEC. 1. All persons born or naturalized in the **United States**, and subject to the jurisdiction thereof, are citizens of the **United States** and of the State wherein they reside. No State shall make or enforce any law which shall abridge the privileges or immunities of citizens of the **United States**; nor shall any State deprive any person of life, liberty, or property, without due process of law; nor deny to any person within its jurisdiction the equal protection of the laws.

\* \* \* \*

SEC. 5. That Congress shall have power to enforce, by appropriate legislation, the provisions of this article.

It was adjudged in *Strauder v. West Virginia,* 100 U.S. 303 , and *Ex parte Virginia,* 100 U.S. 339, and my brethren concede, that positive rights and privileges were intended to be secured, and are, in fact, secured, by the Fourteenth Amendment.

But when, under what circumstances, and to what extent may Congress, by means of legislation, exert its power to enforce the provisions of this amendment? The theory of the opinion of the majority of the court -- the foundation upon which their reasoning seems to rest -- is that the general government cannot, in advance of hostile State laws or hostile State [p*45] proceedings, actively interfere for the protection of any of the rights, privileges, and immunities secured by the Fourteenth Amendment. It is said that such rights, privileges, and immunities are secured by way of *prohibition* against State laws and State proceedings affecting such rights and privileges, and by power given to Congress to legislate for the purpose of carrying *such prohibition* into effect; also, that congressional legislation must necessarily be predicated upon such supposed State laws or State proceedings, and be directed to the correction of their operation and effect.

In illustration of its position, the court refers to the clause of the Constitution forbidding the passage by a State of any law impairing the obligation of contracts. That clause does not, I submit, furnish a proper illustration of the scope and effect of the fifth section of the Fourteenth Amendment. No express power is given Congress to enforce, by primary direct legislation, the prohibition upon State laws impairing the obligation of contracts. Authority is, indeed, conferred to enact all necessary and proper laws for carrying into execution the enumerated powers of Congress and all other powers vested by the Constitution in the government of the **United States** or in any department or officer thereof. And, as heretofore shown, there is also, by necessary implication, power in Congress, by legislation, to protect a right derived from the national Constitution. But a prohibition upon a State is not a power in *Congress* or *in the national government.* It is simply a *denial of power* to the State. And the only mode in which the inhibition upon State laws impairing the obligation of contracts can be enforced is indirectly, through the courts in suits where the parties raise some question as to the constitutional validity of such laws. The judicial power of the **United States** extends to such suits for the reason that they are suits arising under the Constitution. The Fourteenth Amendment presents the first instance in our history of the investiture of Congress with affirmative power, by *legislation,* to *enforce* an express prohibition upon the States. It is not said that the *judicial* power of the nation may be exerted for the enforcement of that amendment. No enlargement of the judicial power was required, for it is clear [p*46] that, had the fifth section of the Fourteenth Amendment been entirely omitted, the judiciary could have stricken down all State laws and nullified all State proceedings in hostility to rights and privileges secured or recognized by that amendment. The power given is, in terms, by congressional legislation, to enforce the provisions of the amendment.

The assumption that this amendment consists wholly of prohibitions upon State laws and State proceedings in hostility to its provisions is unauthorized by its language. The first clause of the first section --

All persons born or naturalized in the **United States**, and subject to the jurisdiction thereof, are citizens of the **United States**, and of the State wherein they reside

-- is of a distinctly affirmative character. In its application to the colored race, previously liberated, it created and granted as well citizenship of the **United States** as citizenship of the State in which they respectively resided. It introduced all of that race whose ancestors had been imported and sold as slaves at once into the political community known as the "People of the **United States**." They became instantly citizens of the **United States** and of their respective States. Further, they were brought by this **Supreme** act of the nation within the direct operation of that provision of the Constitution which declares that "the citizens of each State shall be entitled to all privileges and immunities of citizens in the several States." Art. 4, § 2.

The citizenship thus acquired by that race in virtue of an affirmative grant from the nation may be protected not alone by the judicial branch of the government, but by congressional legislation of a primary direct character, this because the power of Congress is not restricted to the enforcement of prohibitions upon State laws or State action. It is, in terms distinct and positive, to enforce "the *provisions of this article*" of amendment; not simply those of a prohibitive character, but the provisions -- *all* of the provisions -- affirmative and prohibitive, of the amendment. It is, therefore, a grave misconception to suppose that the fifth section of the amendment has reference exclusively to express prohibitions upon State laws or State action. If any right was created by that amendment, the [p*47] grant of power through appropriate legislation to enforce its provisions authorizes Congress, by means of legislation operating throughout the entire Union, to guard, secure, and protect that right.

It is therefore an essential inquiry what, if any, right, privilege or immunity was given, by the nation to colored persons when they were made citizens of the State in which they reside? Did the constitutional grant of State citizenship to that race, of its own force, invest them with any rights, privileges and immunities whatever? That they became entitled, upon the adoption of the Fourteenth Amendment, "to all privileges and immunities of citizens in the several States," within the meaning of section 2 of article 4 of the Constitution, no one, I suppose, will for a moment question. What are the privileges and immunities to which, by that clause of the Constitution, they became entitled? To this it may be answered generally, upon the authority of the adjudged cases, that they are those which are fundamental in citizenship in a free republican government, such as are "common to the citizens in the latter States under their constitutions and laws by virtue of their being citizens." Of that provision it has been said, with the approval of this court, that no other one in the Constitution has tended so strongly to constitute the citizens of the **United States** one people. *Ward v. Maryland,* 12 Wall. 418; *Corfield v.*

*Coryell,* 4 Wash.C.C. 371; *Paul v. Virginia,* 8 Wall. 168; *Slaughterhouse Cases,* 16 *id.* 36 .

Although this court has wisely forborne any attempt by a comprehensive definition to indicate all of the privileges and immunities to which the citizen of a State is entitled of right when within the jurisdiction of other States, I hazard nothing, in view of former adjudications, in saying that no State can sustain her denial to colored citizens of other States, while within her limits, of privileges or immunities fundamental in republican citizenship upon the ground that she accords such privileges and immunities only to her white citizens, and withholds them from her colored citizens. The colored citizens of other States, within the jurisdiction of that State, could claim, in virtue of section 2 of article 4 of the Constitution, every privilege and immunity [p*48] which that State secures to her white citizens. Otherwise it would be in the power of any State, by discriminating class legislation against its own citizens of a particular race or color, to withhold from citizens of other States belonging to that proscribed race, when within her limits, privileges and immunities of the character regarded by all courts as fundamental in citizenship, and that too when the constitutional guaranty is that the citizens of each State shall be entitled to "all privileges and immunities of citizens of the several States." No State may, by discrimination against a portion of its own citizens of a particular race, in respect of privileges and immunities fundamental in citizenship, impair the constitutional right of citizens of other States, of whatever race, to enjoy in that State all such privileges and immunities as are there accorded to her most favored citizens. A colored citizen of

Ohio or Indiana, while in the jurisdiction of Tennessee, is entitled to enjoy any privilege or immunity, fundamental in citizenship, which is given to citizens of the white race in the latter State. It is not to be supposed that anyone will controvert this proposition.

But what was secured to colored citizens of the **United States** -- as between them and their respective States -- by the national grant to them of State citizenship? With what rights, privileges, or immunities did this grant invest them? There is one, if there be no other -- exemption from race discrimination in respect of any civil right belonging to citizens of the white race in the same State. That, surely, is their constitutional privilege when within the jurisdiction of other States. And such must be their constitutional right in their own State, unless the recent amendments be splendid baubles thrown out to delude those who deserved fair and generous treatment at the hands of the nation. Citizenship in this country necessarily imports at least equality of civil rights among citizens of every race in the same State. It is fundamental in American citizenship that, in respect of such rights, there shall be no discrimination by the State, or its officers, or by individuals or corporations exercising public functions or authority, against any citizen because of his race or previous condition of servitude. In ***United States*** *v. Cruikshank,* 92 U.S. 542, it was said at page 555, that the [p*49] rights of life and personal liberty are natural rights of man, and that "the equality of the rights of citizens is a principle of republicanism." And in *Ex parte Virginia,* 100 U.S. 334, the emphatic language of this court is that
one great purpose of these amendments was to raise the colored race from that condition of inferiority and servitude

in which most of them had previously stood into perfect equality of civil rights with all other persons within the jurisdiction of the States.

So, in *Strauder v. West Virginia,* 100 U.S. 306, the court, alluding to the Fourteenth Amendment, said:

This is one of a series of constitutional provisions having a common purpose, namely, securing to a race recently emancipated, a race that, through many generations, had been held in **SLAVERY**, all the civil rights that the superior race enjoy.

Again, in *Neal v. Delaware,* 103 U.S. 386, it was ruled that this amendment was designed primarily

to secure to the colored race, thereby invested with the rights, privileges, and responsibilities of citizenship, the enjoyment of all the civil rights that, under the law, are enjoyed by white persons.

The language of this court with reference to the Fifteenth Amendment adds to the force of this view. In ***United States*** *v. Cruikshank,* it was said:

In ***United States*** *v. Reese,* 92 U.S. 214, we held that the Fifteenth Amendment has invested the citizens of the **United States** with a new constitutional right, which is exemption from discrimination in tho exercise of the elective franchise, on account of race, color, or previous condition of servitude. From this it appears that the right of suffrage is not a necessary attribute of national citizenship, but that exemption from discrimination in the exercise of that right on account of race, &c., is. The right to vote in the States comes from the States, but the right of exemption from the prohibited discrimination comes from the **United**

**States**. The first has not been granted or secured by the Constitution of the **United States**, but the last has been.

Here, in language at once clear and forcible, is stated the principle for which I contend. It can scarcely be claimed that exemption from race discrimination, in respect of civil rights, against those to whom State citizenship was granted by the [p*50] nation, is any less, for the colored race, a new constitutional right, derived from and secured by the national Constitution, than is exemption from such discrimination in the exercise of the elective franchise. It cannot be that the latter is an attribute of national citizenship, while the other is not essential in national citizenship or fundamental in State citizenship.

If, then, exemption from discrimination in respect of civil rights is a new constitutional right, secured by the grant of State citizenship to colored citizens of the **United States** -- and I do not see how this can now be questioned -- why may not the nation, by means of its own legislation of a primary direct character, guard, protect, and enforce that right? It is a right and privilege which the nation conferred. It did not come from the States in which those colored citizens reside. It has been the established doctrine of this court during all its history, accepted as essential to the national supremacy, that Congress, in the absence of a positive delegation of power to the State legislatures, may, by its own legislation, enforce and protect any right derived from or created by the national Constitution. It was so declared in *Prigg v. Commonwealth of Pennsylvania.* It was reiterated in ***United States** v. Reese,* 92 U.S. 214, where the court said that rights and immunities created by and dependent upon the Constitution of the **United States** can be protected by Congress. The form and manner of the protection may be such as Congress, in the legitimate exercise of its discretion, shall provide. These may be varied to meet the necessities of the particular right to be protected.

It was distinctly reaffirmed in *Strauder v. West Virginia,* 100 U.S. 310, where we said that

a right or immunity created by the Constitution or only guaranteed by it, even without any express delegation of power, may be protected by Congress.

How then can it be claimed, in view of the declarations of this court in former cases, that exemption of colored citizens, within their States, from race discrimination in respect of the civil rights of citizens is not an immunity created or derived from the national Constitution?

This court has always given a broad and liberal construction to the Constitution, so as to enable Congress, by legislation, to [p*51] enforce rights secured by that instrument. The legislation which Congress may enact in execution of its power to enforce the provisions of this amendment is such as may be appropriate to protect the right granted. The word appropriate was undoubtedly used with reference to its meaning, as established by repeated decisions of this court. Under given circumstances, that which the court characterizes as corrective legislation might be deemed by Congress appropriate and entirely sufficient. Under other circumstances, primary direct legislation may be required. But it is for Congress, not the judiciary, to say that legislation is appropriate -- that is, best adapted to the end to be attained. The judiciary may not, with safety to our institutions, enter the domain of legislative discretion and dictate the means which Congress shall employ in the exercise of its granted powers. That would be sheer usurpation of the functions of a coordinate department, which, if often repeated, and permanently acquiesced in, would work a radical change in our system of government. In *United States* v. *Fisher,* 2 Cr. 38, the court said that

Congress must possess the choice of means, and must be empowered to use any means which are, in fact, conducive to the exercise of a power granted by the Constitution. . . . The sound construction of the Constitution,

said Chief Justice Marshall,

must allow to the national legislature that discretion, with respect to the means by which the powers it confers are to be carried into execution, which will enable that body to perform the high duties assigned to it in the manner most beneficial to the people. Let the end be legitimate, let it be within the scope of the Constitution, and all means which are appropriate, which are plainly adapted to that end, which are not prohibited, but consist with the letter and spirit of the Constitution, are constitutional.

*McCulloch v. Maryland,* 4 Wheat. 421.

Must these rules of construction be now abandoned? Are the powers of the national legislature to be restrained in proportion as the rights and privileges, derived from the nation, are valuable? Are constitutional provisions, enacted to secure the dearest rights of freemen and citizens, to be subjected to that rule of construction, applicable to private instruments, [p*52] which requires that the words to be

interpreted must be taken most strongly against those who employ them? Or shall it be remembered that
a constitution of government, founded by the people for themselves and their posterity and for objects of the most momentous nature -- for perpetual union, for the establishment of justice, for the general welfare, and for a perpetuation of the blessings of liberty -- necessarily requires that every interpretation of its powers should have a constant reference to these objects? No interpretation of the words in which those powers are granted can be a sound one which narrows down their ordinary import so as to defeat those objects.

The opinion of the court, as I have said, proceeds upon the ground that the power of Congress to legislate for the protection of the rights and privileges secured by the Fourteenth Amendment cannot be brought into activity except with the view, and as it may become necessary, to correct and annul State laws and State proceedings in hostility to such rights and privileges. In the absence of State laws or State action adverse to such rights and privileges, the nation may not actively interfere for their protection and security, even against corporations and individuals exercising public or *quasi*-public functions. Such I understand to be the position of my brethren. If the grant to colored citizens of the **United States** of citizenship in their respective States imports exemption from race discrimination in their States in respect of such civil rights as belong to citizenship, then to hold that the amendment remits that right to the States for their protection, primarily, and stays the hands of the nation until it is assailed by State laws or State proceedings is to adjudge that the amendment, so far from enlarging the powers of Congress -- as we have heretofore said it did -- not only curtails them, but reverses the policy which the general government has pursued from its very organization. Such an interpretation of the amendment is a denial to Congress of the power, by appropriate legislation, to enforce one of its provisions. In view of the circumstances under which the recent amendments were incorporated into the Constitution, and especially in view of the peculiar character of the new [p*53] rights they created and secured, it ought not to be presumed that the general government has abdicated its authority, by national legislation, direct and primary in its character, to guard and protect privileges and immunities secured by that instrument. Such an interpretation of the Constitution ought not to be accepted if it be possible to avoid it. Its acceptance would lead to this anomalous result: that, whereas, prior to the amendments, Congress, with the sanction of this court, passed the most stringent laws -- operating directly and primarily upon States and their officers and agents, as well as upon individuals -- in vindication of **SLAVERY** and the right of the master, it may not now, by legislation of a like primary and direct character, guard, protect, and secure the freedom established, and the most essential right of the citizenship granted, by the constitutional amendments. With all respect for the opinion of others, I insist that the national legislature may, without transcending the limits of the Constitution, do for human liberty and the fundamental rights of American citizenship what it did, with the sanction of this court, for the protection of **SLAVERY** and the rights of the masters of fugitive slaves. If fugitive slave laws, providing modes and prescribing penalties whereby the master could seize and recover his fugitive slave, were legitimate exercises of an implied power to protect and enforce a right recognized by the Constitution, why shall the hands of Congress be tied so that -- under an express power, by appropriate legislation, to enforce a constitutional provision granting citizenship -- it may not, by means of direct legislation, bring the whole power of this nation to bear upon States and their officers and upon such individuals and corporations exercising public functions as assume to abridge, impair, or deny rights confessedly secured by the **Supreme** law of the land?

It does not seem to me that the fact that, by the second clause of the first section of the Fourteenth Amendment, the States are expressly prohibited from making or enforcing laws abridging the privileges and immunities of citizens of the **United States** furnishes any sufficient reason for holding or maintaining that the amendment was intended to deny Congress the power, by general, primary, and direct legislation, of [p*54] protecting citizens of the several States, being also citizens of the **United States**, against all discrimination in respect of their rights as citizens which is founded on race, color, or previous condition of servitude.

Such an interpretation of the amendment is plainly repugnant to its fifth section, conferring upon Congress power, by appropriate legislation, to enforce not merely the provisions containing prohibitions upon the States, but all of the provisions of the amendment, including the provisions, express and implied, in the first clause of the first section of the article granting citizenship. This alone is sufficient for holding that Congress is not restricted to the enactment of laws adapted to counteract and redress the operation of State legislation, or the action of State officers, of the character prohibited by the amendment. It was perfectly well known that the great danger to the equal enjoyment by citizens of their rights as citizens was to be apprehended not altogether from unfriendly State legislation, but from the hostile action of corporations and individuals in the States. And it is to be presumed that it was intended by that section to clothe Congress with power and authority to meet that danger. If the rights intended to be secured by the act of 1875 are such as belong to the citizen in common or equally with other citizens in the same State, then it is not to be denied that such legislation is peculiarly appropriate to the end which Congress is authorized to accomplish, *viz.,* to protect the citizen, in respect of such rights, against discrimination on account of his race. Recurring to the specific prohibition in the Fourteenth Amendment upon the making or enforcing of State laws abridging the privileges of citizens of the **United States**, I remark that if, as held in the *Slaughterhouse Cases,* the privileges here referred to were those which belonged to citizenship of the **United States**, as distinguished from those belonging to State citizenship, it was impossible for any State prior to the adoption of that amendment to have enforced laws of that character. The judiciary could have annulled all such legislation under the provision that the Constitution shall be the **Supreme** law of the land, anything in the constitution or laws of any State to the contrary notwithstanding. The States were [p*55] already under an implied prohibition not to abridge any privilege or immunity belonging to citizens of the **United States** as such. Consequently, the prohibition upon State laws in hostility to rights belonging to citizens of the **United States** was intended -- in view of the introduction into the body of citizens of a race formerly denied the essential rights of citizenship -- only as an express limitation on the powers of the States, and was not intended to diminish in the slightest degree the authority which the nation has always exercised of protecting, by means of its own direct legislation, rights created or secured by the Constitution. Any purpose to diminish the national authority in respect of privileges derived from the nation is distinctly negatived by the express grant of power by legislation to enforce every provision of the amendment, including that which, by the grant of citizenship in the State, secures exemption from race discrimination in respect of the civil rights of citizens.

It is said that any interpretation of the Fourteenth Amendment different from that adopted by the majority of the court would imply that Congress had authority to enact a municipal code for all the States covering every matter affecting the life, liberty, and property of the citizens of the several States Not so. Prior to the adoption of that amendment, the constitutions of the several States, without perhaps an exception, secured all *persons* against deprivation of life, liberty, or property otherwise than by due process of law, and, in some form, recognized the right of all *persons* to the equal protection of the laws. Those rights therefore existed before that amendment was proposed or adopted, and were not created by it. If, by reason of that fact, it be assumed that protection in these rights of persons still rests primarily with the States, and that Congress may not interfere except to enforce, by means of corrective legislation, the prohibitions upon State laws or State proceedings inconsistent with those rights, it does not at all follow that privileges which have been *granted by the nation* may not be protected by primary legislation upon the part of Congress. The personal rights and immunities recognized in the prohibitive clauses of the amendment were, prior to its adoption, [p*56] under the protection, primarily, of the States, while rights, created by or derived from the **United States** have always been and, in the nature of things, should always be, primarily under the protection of the general government. Exemption from race discrimination in respect of the civil rights which are fundamental in *citizenship* in a republican government, is, as we have seen, a new right, created by the nation, with express power in Congress, by legislation, to enforce the constitutional provision from which it is derived. If, in some sense, such race discrimination is, within the letter of the last clause of the first section, a denial of that equal protection of the laws which is secured against State denial to all persons, whether citizens or not, it cannot be possible that a mere prohibition upon such State denial, or a prohibition upon State laws abridging the privileges and immunities of citizens of the **United States**, takes from the nation the power which it has uniformly exercised of protecting, by direct primary legislation, those privileges and immunities which existed under the Constitution before the adoption of the Fourteenth Amendment or have been created by that amendment in behalf of those thereby made *citizens* of their respective States.

This construction does not in any degree intrench upon the just rights of the States in the control of their domestic affairs. It simply recognizes the enlarged powers conferred by the recent amendments upon the general government. In the view which I take of those amendments, the States possess the same authority which they have always had to define and regulate the civil rights which their own people, in virtue of State citizenship, may enjoy within their respective limits, except that its exercise is now subject to the expressly granted power of Congress, by legislation, to enforce the provisions of such amendments -- a power which necessarily carries with it authority, by national legislation, to protect and secure the privileges and immunities which are created by or are derived from those amendments. That exemption of citizens from discrimination based on race or color, in respect of civil rights, is one of those privileges or immunities can no longer be deemed an open question in this court. [p*57]

It was said of the case of *Dred Scott v. Sandford* that this court there overruled the action of two generations, virtually inserted a new clause in the Constitution, changed its character, and made a new departure in the workings of the federal government. I may be permitted to say that, if the recent amendments are so construed that Congress may not, in its own discretion and independently of the action or nonaction of the States, provide by legislation of a direct character for the security of rights created by the national Constitution, if it be adjudged that the obligation to protect the fundamental privileges and immunities granted by the

Fourteenth Amendment to citizens residing in the several States rests primarily not on the nation, but on the States, if it be further adjudged that individuals and corporations exercising public functions or wielding power under public authority may, without liability to direct primary legislation on the part of Congress, make the race of citizens the ground for denying them that equality of civil rights which the Constitution ordains as a principle of republican citizenship, then not only the foundations upon which the national supremacy has always securely rested will be materially disturbed, but we shall enter upon an era of constitutional law when the rights of freedom and American citizenship cannot receive from the nation that efficient protection which heretofore was unhesitatingly accorded to **SLAVERY** and the rights of the master.

But if it were conceded that the power of Congress could not be brought into activity until the rights specified in the act of 1875 had been abridged or denied by some State law or State action, I maintain that the decision of the court is erroneous. There has been adverse State action within the Fourteenth Amendment as heretofore interpreted by this court. I allude to *Ex parte Virginia, supra.* It appears in that case that one Cole, judge of a county court, was charged with the duty by the laws of Virginia of selecting grand and petit jurors. The law of the State did not authorize or permit him, in making such selections, to discriminate against colored citizens because of their race. But he was indicted in the federal court, under the act of 1875, for making such discriminations. [p*58] The attorney general of Virginia contended before us that the State had done its duty, and had not authorized or directed that county judge to do what he was charged with having done; that the State had not denied to the colored race the equal protection of the laws, and that consequently the act of Cole must be deemed his individual act, in contravention of the will of the State. Plausible as this argument was, it failed to convince this court, and after saying that the Fourteenth Amendment had reference to the political body denominated a State "by whatever instruments or in whatever modes that action may be taken," and that a State acts by its legislative, executive, and judicial authorities, and can act in no other way, we proceeded:

The constitutional provision, therefore, must mean that no agency of the State or of the officers or agents by whom its powers are exerted shall deny to any person within its jurisdiction the equal protection of the laws. Whoever, by virtue of public position under a State government, deprives another of property, life, or liberty without due process of law, or denies or takes away the equal protection of the laws, violates the constitutional inhibition; and, as he acts under the name and for the State, and is clothed with the State's power, his act is that of the State. This must be so, or the constitutional prohibition has no meaning. Then the State has clothed one of its agents with power to annul or evade it. But the constitutional amendment was ordained for a purpose. It was to secure equal rights to all persons, and, to insure to all persons the enjoyment of such rights, power was given to Congress to enforce its provisions by appropriate legislation. Such legislation must act upon persons, not upon the abstract thing denominated a State, but upon the persons who are the agents of the State in the denial of the rights which were intended to be secured.

*Ex parte Virginia,* 100 U.S. 346-347.

In every material sense applicable to the practical enforcement of the Fourteenth Amendment, railroad corporations, keepers of inns, and managers of places of public amusement are agents or instrumentalities of the State, because they are charged with [p*59] duties to the public and are amenable, in respect of their duties and functions, to governmental regulation. It seems to me that, within the principle settled in *Ex parte Virginia,* a denial by these instrumentalities of the State to the citizen, because of his race, of that equality of civil rights secured to him by law is a denial by the State within the meaning of the Fourteenth Amendment. If it be not, then that race is left, in respect of the civil rights in question, practically at the mercy of corporations and individuals wielding power under the States.

But the court says that Congress did not, in the act of 1866, assume, under the authority given by the Thirteenth Amendment, to adjust what may be called the social rights of men and races in the community. I agree that government has nothing to do with social, as distinguished from technically legal, rights of individuals. No government ever has brought, or ever can bring, its people into social intercourse against their wishes. Whether one person will permit or maintain social relations with another is a matter with which government has no concern. I agree that, if one citizen chooses not to hold social intercourse with another, he is not and cannot be made amenable to the law for his conduct in that regard, for even upon grounds of race, no legal right of a citizen is violated by the refusal of others to maintain merely social relations with him. What I affirm is that no State, nor the officers of any State, nor any corporation or individual wielding power under State authority for the public benefit or the public convenience, can, consistently either with the freedom established by the fundamental law or with that equality of civil rights which now belongs to every citizen, discriminate against freemen or citizens in those rights because of their race, or because they once labored under the disabilities of **SLAVERY** imposed upon them as a race. The rights which Congress, by the act of 1875, endeavored to secure and protect are legal, not social, rights. The right, for instance, of a colored citizen to use the accommodations of a public highway upon the same terms as are permitted to white citizens is no more a social right than his right under the law to use the public streets of a city or a town, or a turnpike road, or a public market, or a post office, or his right to sit [p*60] in a public building with others, of whatever race, for the purpose of hearing the political questions of the day discussed. Scarcely a day passes without our seeing in this courtroom citizens of the white and black races sitting side by side, watching the progress of our business. It would never occur to anyone that the presence of a colored citizen in a courthouse, or courtroom, was an invasion of the social rights of white persons who may frequent such places. And yet such a suggestion would be quite as sound in law -- I say it with all respect -- as is the suggestion that the claim of a colored citizen to use, upon the same terms as is permitted to white citizens, the accommodations of public highways, or public inns, or places of public amusement, established under the license of the law, is an invasion of the social rights of the white race.

The court, in its opinion, reserves the question whether Congress, in the exercise of its power to regulate commerce amongst the several States, might or might not pass a law regulating rights in public conveyances passing from one State to another. I beg to suggest that that precise question was substantially presented here in the only one of these cases relating to railroads -- *Robinson and Wife v. Memphis & Charleston Railroad Company.* In that case, it appears that Mrs. Robinson, a citizen of Mississippi, purchased a railroad ticket entitling her to be carried from Grand Junction, Tennessee, to Lynchburg, Virginia. Might not the act of 1875 be maintained in that case as applicable at least to commerce between the States, notwithstanding it does not, upon its face, profess to have been passed in pursuance of the power of Congress to regulate commerce? Has it ever been held that the judiciary should overturn a statute because the legislative department did not accurately recite therein the particular provision of the Constitution authorizing its enactment? We have often enforced municipal bonds in aid of railroad subscriptions where they failed to recite the statute authorizing their issue, but recited one which did not sustain their validity. The inquiry in such cases has been was there, in any statute, authority for the execution of the bonds? Upon this branch of the case, it may be remarked that the State of Louisiana, in 1869, passed a statute [p*61] giving to passengers, without regard to race or color, equality of right in the accommodations of railroad and street cars, steamboats or other watercrafts, stage coaches, omnibuses, or other vehicles. But in *Hall v. De Cuir,* 95 U.S. 487, that act was pronounced unconstitutional so far as it related to commerce between the States, this court saying that, "if the public good requires such legislation, it must come from Congress, and not from the States." I suggest, that it may become a pertinent inquiry whether Congress may, in the exertion of its power to regulate commerce among the States, enforce among passengers on public conveyances equality of right, without regard to race, color or previous condition of servitude, if it be true -- which I do not admit -- that such legislation would be an interference by government with the social rights of the people.

My brethren say that, when a man has emerged from **SLAVERY**, and by the aid of beneficent legislation has shaken off the inseparable concomitants of that state, there must be some stage in the progress of his elevation when he takes the rank of a mere citizen, and ceases to be the special favorite of the laws, and when his rights as a citizen or a man are to be protected in the ordinary modes by which other men's rights are protected. It is, I submit, scarcely just to say that the colored race has been the special favorite of the laws. The statute of 1875, now adjudged to be unconstitutional, is for the benefit of citizens of every race and color. What the nation, through Congress, has sought to accomplish in reference to that race is what had already been done in every State of the Union for the white race -- to secure and protect rights belonging to them as freemen and citizens, nothing more. It was not deemed enough "to help the feeble up, but to support him after." The one underlying purpose of congressional legislation has been to enable the black race to take the rank of mere citizens. The difficulty has been to compel a recognition of the legal right of the black race to take the rank of citizens, and to secure the enjoyment of privileges belonging, under the law, to them as a component part of the people for whose welfare and happiness government is ordained. [p*62] At every step in this direction, the nation has been confronted with class tyranny, which a contemporary English historian says is, of all tyrannies, the most intolerable,

for it is ubiquitous in its operation and weighs perhaps most heavily on those whose obscurity or distance would withdraw them from the notice of a single despot.

Today it is the colored race which is denied, by corporations and individuals wielding public authority, rights fundamental in their freedom and citizenship. At some future time, it may be that some other race will fall under the ban of race discrimination. If the constitutional amendments be enforced according to the intent with which, as I conceive, they were adopted, there cannot be, in this republic, any class of human beings in practical subjection to another class with power in the latter to dole out to the former just such privileges as they may choose to grant. The **Supreme** law of the land has decreed that no authority shall be exercised in this country upon the basis of discrimination, in respect of civil rights, against freemen and citizens because of their race, color, or previous condition of servitude. To that decree -- for the due enforcement of which, by appropriate legislation, Congress has been invested with express power -- everyone must bow, whatever may have been, or whatever now are, his individual views as to the wisdom or policy either of the recent changes in the fundamental law or of the legislation which has been enacted to give them effect.

For the reasons stated, I feel constrained to withhold my assent to the opinion of the court.

**Booker T. Washington**
**1854-1915**
**Founder of Tuskegee Institute**
**Delivered Atlanta Compromise Address in 1895**

### Booker T. Washington's Appeal to Pragmatism (1895)

As you read the final documents, Booker T. Washington's Atlanta Compromise speech and the **US Supreme Court**'s 1896 *Plessy v. Ferguson* ruling, I challenge you to carefully review the manipulative wiles of the **ANGLO-AMERICAN LEGAL TRADITION**, by reviewing the **Freedman's Bureau Act of 1865**,[1] the **Enforcement Act of 1870**, the **Civil Rights Act of 1875**, and the **Supreme Court**'s ruling on its constitutionality in 1883. With the collapse of Reconstruction, there would be one final appeal on the part of the **AFRICAN**, the appeal to Southern pragmatism. Booker T. Washington in his famous, Atlanta Compromise Speech best articulated this appeal in 1895.

Washington, a former slave, had recently founded the Tuskegee Institute in Alabama. It was a school designed exclusively for **AFRICANS**. It also reflected its founder's belief that **AFRICANS** would survive if they appealed to the worst instincts of the **ANGLO-AMERICAN LEGAL TRADITION**—the **AFRICAN** was guilty by virtue of the fact of his **AFRICANITY**. The speech, delivered at the Cotton States and International Exposition, served as a watershed appeal to the prejudices of his white audience of nearly 2000. It was a watershed, because Washington took it upon himself to speak for *all* **AFRICANS** in the South by agreeing to accept second-class citizenship and in turn

---

[1] See a copy of the Act in *No Rights And No Respect*, 179-182.

"earn" the right of full citizenship by the adoption of an ethic that basically endorsed American Society's "guilty" verdict relative to the **AFRICAN**. Washington's success at implementing his strategy was mixed, he was able to curry the favor of Northern liberals and industrialists, and like minded whites in the South, but even he could not escape the color of his skin. The Nineteenth Century Mississippi politician, J.K. Vardeman, perhaps best summarized the uselessness of any appeal. Said Vardeman, of Washington, "I am just as opposed to Booker Washington as a voter, with all his Anglo-Saxon re-enforcements as I am opposed to the coconut-headed, chocolate-colored, typical little coon, Andy Dotson, who blacks my shoes every morning. Neither is fit to [vote]."[2]

Washington was later accused of assaulting a white woman in New York in 1911. Washington was never convicted, but the specter of a "hulking" **AFRICAN** male attempting to *rape a white woman*, damaged his credibility, and haunted him for the rest of his life.[3]

---

[2] Franklin, *From **SLAVERY** to Freedom*, 275. Vardaman would say of Washington's attempts at educating African students at Tuskegee in 1907 in an interview, [Washington is a] fraud & a liar; a smart man; training social parasites; you never heard of a student of his school who ever did anything useful except teach school. BTW has one practice in the South another in the North—showing him a hypocrite." Louis R. Harlan, *Booker T. Washington: The Wizard of Tuskegee, 1901-1915* (New York: Oxford University Press, 1983)

[3] Ibid. 379-404.

## Booker T. Washington's Atlanta Compromise Speech (1895)

Mr. President and gentlemen of the Board of Directors and citizens. One third of the population of the South is of the Negro race. No enterprise seeking the material, civil, or moral welfare of this section can disregard this element of our population and reach the highest success. I must convey to you, Mr. President and Directors, and Secretaries and masses of my race, when I say that in no way have the value and manhood of the American Negro been more fittingly and generously recognized, than by the managers of this magnificent exposition at every stage of its progress. It is a recognition that will do more to cement the friendship of the two races than any occurrence since the dawn of our freedom. Not only this, but the opportunities here afforded will awaken among us a new era of industrial progress.

Ignorant and inexperienced, it is not strange that in the first years of our new life we began at the top instead of the bottom, that a seat in Congress or the state legislature was more sought than real estate or industrial skill, that the political convention of some teaching had more attraction than starting a dairy farm or a stockyard.

A ship lost at sea for many days suddenly sighted a friendly vessel. From the mast of the unfortunate vessel was seen a signal: "Water, water. We die of thirst." The answer from the friendly vessel at once came back: "Cast down your bucket where you are." A second time, the signal, "Water, send us water!" went up from the distressed vessel. And was answered: "Cast down your bucket where you are." A third and fourth signal for water was answered: "Cast down your bucket where you are." The captain of the distressed vessel, at last heeding the injunction, cast down his bucket and it came up full of fresh, sparkling water from the mouth of the Amazon River.

To those of my race who depend on bettering their condition in a foreign land, or who underestimate the importance of preserving friendly relations with the southern white man who is their next door neighbor, I would say: "Cast down your bucket where you are." Cast it down, making friends in every manly way of the people of all races, by whom you are surrounded.

To those of the white race who look to the incoming of those of foreign birth and strange tongue and habits for the prosperity of the South, were I permitted, I would repeat what I have said to my own race: "Cast down your bucket where you are." Cast it down among the eight millions of Negroes whose habits you know, whose fidelity and love you have tested in days when to have proved treacherous meant the ruin of your fireside. Cast down your bucket among these people who have without strikes and labor wars tilled your fields, cleared your forests, built your railroads and cities, brought forth treasures from the bowels of the earth, just to make possible this magnificent representation of the progress of the South.

### More Than A Street Car Ride: Plessy v. Ferguson (1896)

On the Legislative level, the **Civil Rights Act of 1875** was passed in Congress and signed into law by President Grant. In 1883, the **United States Supreme Court** declared the Act to be unconstitutional! In 1896, the **Supreme Court** handed down its infamous verdict in the case of *Plessy v. Ferguson*. The case involved an **AFRICAN** shoemaker named Homer Plessy. Plessy was jailed on June 7, 1892 for sitting in the "white" section of a streetcar in New Orleans. Plessy was asked by the conductor to move to the "colored" section of the streetcar. Plessy refused, claiming that since, by his own calculation, he was 7/8 white and only 1/8 **AFRICAN**. He foolishly believed that his mathematics would afford him the seat he desired. It did not! A local judge, John Howard Ferguson, ruled against Plessy. Plessy fought all the way to the **Supreme Court** and lost! *Plessy v. Ferguson* is available for your reading also! The upshot of the ruling was that "Separate but Equal" would be given Constitutional sanction, by the nation's highest court! *Twist! Twist! Twist!*

## U.S. Supreme Court
## PLESSY v. FERGUSON, 163 U.S. 537 (1896)
## 163 U.S. 537
## PLESSY
## v.
## FERGUSON.
## No. 210.

May 18, 1896. [163 U.S. 537, 538] This was a petition for writs of prohibition and certiorari originally filed in the **Supreme Court** of the state by Plessy, the plaintiff in error, against the Hon. John H. Ferguson, judge of the criminal district court for the parish of Orleans, and setting forth, in substance, the following facts:

That petitioner was a citizen of the **United States** and a resident of the state of Louisiana, of mixed descent, in the proportion of seven-eighths Caucasian and one-eighth **AFRICAN** blood; that the mixture of colored blood was not discernible in him, and that he was entitled to every recognition, right, privilege, and immunity secured to the citizens of the **United States** of the white race by its constitution and laws; that on June 7, 1892, he engaged and paid for a first-class passage on the East Louisiana Railway, from New Orleans to Covington, in the same state, and thereupon entered a passenger train, and took possession of a vacant seat in a coach where passengers of the white race were accommodated; that such railroad company was incorporated by the laws of Louisiana as a common carrier, and was not authorized to distinguish between citizens according to their race, but, notwithstanding this, petitioner was required by the conductor, under penalty of ejection from said train and imprisonment, to vacate said coach, and occupy another seat, in a coach assigned by said company for persons not of the white race, and for no other reason than that petitioner was of the colored race; that, upon petitioner's refusal to comply with such order, he was, with the aid of a police officer, forcibly ejected from said coach, and hurried off to, and imprisoned in, the parish jail of [163 U.S. 537, 539] New Orleans, and there held to answer a charge made by such officer to the effect that he was guilty of having criminally violated an act of the general assembly of the state, approved July 10, 1890, in such case made and provided.

The petitioner was subsequently brought before the recorder of the city for preliminary examination, and committed for trial to the criminal district court for the parish of Orleans, where an information was filed against him in the matter above set forth, for a violation of the above act, which act the petitioner affirmed to be null and void, because in conflict with the constitution of the **United States**; that petitioner interposed a plea to such information, based upon the unconstitutionality of the act of the general assembly, to which the district attorney, on behalf of the state, filed a demurrer; that, upon issue being joined upon such demurrer and plea, the court sustained the demurrer, overruled the plea, and ordered petitioner to plead over to the facts set forth in the information, and that, unless the judge of the said court be enjoined by a writ of prohibition from further proceeding in such case, the court will proceed to fine and sentence petitioner to imprisonment, and thus deprive him of his constitutional rights set forth in his said plea, notwithstanding the unconstitutionality of the act under which he was being prosecuted; that no appeal lay from such sentence, and petitioner was without relief or remedy except by writs of prohibition and certiorari. Copies of the information and other proceedings in the criminal district court were annexed to the petition as an exhibit.

Upon the filing of this petition, an order was issued upon the respondent to show cause why a writ of prohibition should not issue, and be made perpetual, and a further order that the record of the proceedings had in the criminal cause be certified and transmitted to the **Supreme Court**.

To this order the respondent made answer, transmitting a certified copy of the proceedings, asserting the constitutionality of the law, and averring that, instead of pleading or admitting that he belonged to the colored race, the said Plessy declined and refused, either by pleading or otherwise, to ad- [163 U.S. 537, 540] mit that he was in any sense or in any proportion a colored man.

The case coming on for hearing before the **Supreme Court**, that court was of opinion that the law under which the prosecution was had was constitutional and denied the relief prayed for by the petitioner (Ex parte Plessy, 45 La. Ann. 80, 11 South. 948); whereupon petitioner prayed for a writ of error from this court, which was allowed by the chief justice of the **Supreme Court** of Louisiana.

Mr. Justice Harlan dissenting.

A. W. Tourgee and S. F. Phillips, for plaintiff in error.

Alex. Porter Morse, for defendant in error.

Mr. Justice BROWN, after stating the facts in the foregoing language, delivered the opinion of the court.

This case turns upon the constitutionality of an act of the general assembly of the state of Louisiana, passed in 1890, providing for separate railway carriages for the white and colored races. Acts 1890, No. 111, p. 152.

The first section of the statute enacts 'that all railway companies carrying passengers in their coaches in this state, shall provide equal but separate accommodations for the white, and colored races, by providing two or more passenger coaches for each passenger train, or by dividing the passenger coaches by a partition so as to secure separate accommodations: provided, that this section shall not be construed to apply to street railroads. No person or persons shall be permitted to occupy seats in coaches, other than the ones assigned to them, on account of the race they belong to.'

By the second section it was enacted 'that the officers of such passenger trains shall have power and are hereby required [163 U.S. 537, 541] to assign each passenger to the coach or compartment used for the race to which such passenger belongs; any passenger insisting on going into a coach or compartment to which by race he does not belong, shall be liable to a fine of twenty-five dollars, or in lieu thereof to imprisonment for a period of not more than twenty days in the parish prison, and any officer of any railroad insisting on assigning a passenger to a coach or compartment other than the one set aside for the race to which said passenger belongs, shall be liable to a fine of twenty-five dollars, or in lieu thereof to imprisonment for a period of not more than twenty days in the parish prison; and should any passenger refuse to occupy the coach or compartment to which he or she is assigned by the officer of such railway, said officer shall have power to refuse to carry such passenger on his train, and for such refusal neither he nor the railway company which he represents shall be liable for damages in any of the courts of this state.' The third section provides penalties for the refusal or neglect of the officers, directors, conductors, and employees of railway companies to comply with the act, with a proviso that 'nothing in this act shall be construed as applying to nurses attending children of the other race.' The fourth section is immaterial.

The information filed in the criminal district court charged, in substance, that Plessy, being a passenger between two stations within the state of Louisiana, was assigned by officers of the company to the coach used for the race to which he belonged, but he insisted upon going into a coach used by the race to which he did not belong. Neither in the information nor plea was his particular race or color averred.

The petition for the writ of prohibition averred that petitioner was seven-eights Caucasian and one-eighth **AFRICAN** blood; that the mixture of colored blood was not discernible in him; and that he was entitled to every right, privilege, and immunity secured to citizens of the **United States** of the white race; and that, upon such theory, he took possession of a vacant seat in a coach where passengers of the white race were accommodated, and was ordered by the conductor to vacate [163 U.S. 537, 542] said coach, and take a seat in another, assigned to persons of the colored race, and, having refused to comply with such demand, he was forcibly ejected, with the aid of a police officer, and imprisoned in the parish jail to answer a charge of having violated the above act.

The constitutionality of this act is attacked upon the ground that it conflicts both with the thirteenth amendment of the constitution, abolishing **SLAVERY**, and the fourteenth amendment, which prohibits certain restrictive legislation on the part of the states.

**1.** That it does not conflict with the thirteenth amendment, which abolished **SLAVERY** and involuntary servitude, except a punishment for crime, is too clear for argument. **SLAVERY** implies involuntary servitude,-a state of bondage; the ownership of mankind as a chattel, or, at least, the control of the labor and services of one man for the benefit of another, and the absence of a legal right to the disposal of his own person, property, and services. This amendment was said in the Slaughter-House Cases, 16 Wall. 36, to have been intended primarily to abolish **SLAVERY**, as it had been previously known in this country, and that it equally forbade Mexican peonage or the Chinese coolie trade, when they amounted to **SLAVERY** or involuntary servitude, and that the use of the word 'servitude' was intended to prohibit the use of all forms of involuntary **SLAVERY**, of whatever class or name. It was intimated, however, in that case, that this amendment was regarded by the statesmen of that day as insufficient to protect the colored race from certain laws which had been enacted in the Southern states, imposing upon the colored race onerous disabilities and burdens, and curtailing their rights in the pursuit of life, liberty, and property to such an extent that their freedom was of little value; and that the fourteenth amendment was devised to meet this exigency.

So, too, in the Civil Rights Cases, 109 U.S. 3 , 3 Sup. Ct. 18, it was said that the act of a mere individual, the owner of an inn, a public conveyance or place of amusement, refusing accommodations to colored people, cannot be justly regarded as imposing any badge of **SLAVERY** or servitude upon the applicant, but [163 U.S. 537, 543] only as involving an ordinary civil injury, properly cognizable by the laws of the state, and presumably subject to redress by those laws until the contrary appears. 'It would be running the **SLAVERY** question into the ground,' said Mr. Justice Bradley, 'to make it apply to every act of discrimination which a person may see fit to make as to the guests he will entertain, or as to the people he will take into his coach or cab or car, or admit to his concert or theater, or deal with in other matters of intercourse or business.'

A statute which implies merely a legal distinction between the white and colored races-a distinction which is founded in the color of the two races, and which must always exist so long as white men are distinguished from the other race by color-has no tendency to destroy the legal equality of the two races, or re-establish a state of involuntary servitude. Indeed, we do not understand that the thirteenth amendment is strenuously relied upon by the plaintiff in error in this connection.

**2.** By the fourteenth amendment, all persons born or naturalized in the **United States**, and subject to the jurisdiction thereof, are made citizens of the **United States** and of the state wherein they reside; and the states are forbidden from making or enforcing any law which shall abridge the privileges or immunities of citizens of the **United States**, or shall deprive any person of life, liberty, or property without due process of law, or deny to any person within their jurisdiction the equal protection of the laws.

The proper construction of this amendment was first called to the attention of this court in the Slaughter-House Cases, 16 Wall. 36, which involved, however, not a question of race, but one of exclusive privileges. The case did not call for any expression of opinion as to the exact rights it was intended to secure to the colored race, but it was said generally that its main purpose was to establish the citizenship of the negro, to give definitions of citizenship of the **United States** and of the states, and to protect from the hostile legislation of the states the privileges and immunities of citizens of the **United States**, as distinguished from those of citizens of the states. [163 U.S. 537, 544] The object of the amendment was undoubtedly to enforce the absolute equality of the two races before the law, but, in the nature of things, it could not have been intended to abolish distinctions based upon color, or to enforce social, as distinguish d from political, equality, or a commingling of the two races upon terms unsatisfactory to either. Laws permitting, and even requiring, their separation, in places where they are liable to be brought into contact, do not necessarily imply the inferiority of either race to the other, and have been generally, if not universally, recognized as within the competency of the state legislatures in the exercise of their police power. The most common instance of this is connected with the establishment of separate schools for white and colored children, which have been held to be a valid exercise of the legislative power even by courts of states where the political rights of the colored race have been longest and most earnestly enforced.

One of the earliest of these cases is that of Roberts v. City of Boston, 5 Cush. 198, in which the **Supreme** judicial court of Massachusetts held that the general school committee of Boston had power to make provision for the instruction of colored children in separate schools established exclusively for them, and to prohibit their attendance upon the other schools. 'The great principle,' said Chief Justice Shaw, 'advanced by the learned and eloquent advocate for the plaintiff [Mr. Charles Sumner], is that, by the constitution and laws of Massachusetts, all persons, without distinction of age or sex, birth or color, origin or condition, are equal before the law. ... But, when this great principle comes to be applied to the actual and various conditions of persons in society, it will not warrant the assertion that men and women are legally clothed with the same civil and political powers, and that children and adults are legally to have the same functions and be subject to the same treatment; but only that the rights of all, as they are settled and regulated by law, are equally entitled to the paternal consideration and protection of the law for their maintenance and security.' It was held that the powers of the committee extended to the establish- [163 U.S. 537, 545] ment of separate schools for children of different ages, sexes and colors, and that they might also establish special schools for poor and neglected children, who have become too old to attend the primary school, and yet have not acquired the rudiments of learning, to enable them to enter the ordinary schools. Similar laws have been enacted by congress under its general power of legislation over the

District of Columbia (sections 281- 283, 310, 319, Rev. St. D. C.), as well as by the legislatures of many of the states, and have been generally, if not uniformly, sustained by the courts. State v. McCann, 21 Ohio St. 210; Lehew v. Brummell (Mo. Sup.) 15 S. W. 765; Ward v. Flood, 48 Cal. 36; Bertonneau v. Directors of City Schools, 3 Woods, 177, Fed. Cas. No. 1,361; People v. Gallagher, 93 N. Y. 438; Cory v. Carter, 48 Ind. 337; Dawson v. Lee, 83 Ky. 49.

Laws forbidding the intermarriage of the two races may be said in a technical sense to interfere with the freedom of contract, and yet have been universally recognized as within the police power of the state. State v. Gibson, 36 Ind. 389.

The distinction between laws interfering with the political equality of the negro and those requiring the separation of the two races in schools, theaters, and railway carriages has been frequently drawn by this court. Thus, in Strauder v. West Virginia, 100 U.S. 303 , it was held that a law of West Virginia limiting to white male persons 21 years of age, and citizens of the state, the right to sit upon juries, was a discrimination which implied a legal inferiority in civil society, which lessened the security of the right of the colored race, and was a step towards reducing them to a condition of servility. Indeed, the right of a colored man that, in the selection of jurors to pass upon his life, liberty, and property, there shall be no exclusion of his race, and no discrimination against them because of color, has been asserted in a number of cases. Virginia v. Rivers, 100 U.S. 313 ; Neal v. Delaware, 103 U.S. 370 ; ush v. Com., 107 U.S. 110 , 1 Sup. Ct. 625; Gibson v. Mississippi, 162 U.S. 565 , 16 Sup. Ct. 904. So, where the laws of a particular locality or the charter of a particular railway corporation has provided that no person shall be excluded from the cars on account of [163 U.S. 537, 546] color, we have held that this meant that persons of color should travel in the same car as white ones, and that the enactment was not satisfied by the company providing cars assigned exclusively to people of color, though they were as good as those which they assigned exclusively to white persons. Railroad Co. v. Brown, 17 Wall. 445.

Upon the other hand, where a statute of Louisiana required those engaged in the transportation of passengers among the states to give to all persons traveling within that state, upon vessels employed in that business, equal rights and privileges in all parts of the vessel, without distinction on account of race or color, and subjected to an action for damages the owner of such a vessel who excluded colored passengers on account of their color from the cabin set aside by him for the use of whites, it was held to be, so far as it applied to interstate commerce, unconstitutional and void. Hall v. De Cuir, 95 U.S. 485 . The court in this case, however, expressly disclaimed that it had anything whatever to do with the statute as a regulation of internal commerce, or affecting anything else than commerce among the states.

In the Civil Rights Cases, 109 U.S. 3 , 3 Sup. Ct. 18, it was held that an act of congress entitling all persons within the jurisdiction of the **United States** to the full and equal enjoyment of the accommodations, advantages, facilities, and privileges of inns, public conveyances, on land or water, theaters, and other places of public amusement, and made applicable to citizens of every race and color, regardless of any previous condition of servitude, was unconstitutional and void, upon the ground that the fourteenth amendment was prohibitory upon the states only, and the legislation authorized to be adopted by congress for enforcing it was not direct legislation on matters respecting which the states were prohibited from making or enforcing certain laws, or doing certain acts, but was corrective legislation, such as might be necessary or proper for counter-acting and redressing the effect of such laws or acts. In delivering the opinion of the court, Mr. Justice Bradley observed that the fourteenth amendment 'does not invest congress with power to legislate upon subjects that are within the [163 U.S. 537, 547] domain of state legislation, but to provide modes of relief against state legislation or state action of the kind referred to. It does not authorize congress to create a code of municipal law for the regulation of private rights, but to provide modes of redress against the operation of state laws, and the action of state officers, executive or judicial, when these are subversive of the fundamental rights specified in the amendment. Positive rights and privileges are undoubtedly secured by the fourteenth amendment; but they are secured by way of prohibition against state laws and state proceedings affecting those rights and privileges, and by power given to congress to legislate for the purpose of carrying such prohibition into effect; and such legislation must necessarily be predicated upon such supposed state laws or state proceedings, and be directed to the correction of their operation and effect.'

Much nearer, and, indeed, almost directly in point, is the case of the Louisville, N. O. & T. Ry. Co. v. State, 133

U.S. 587 , 10 Sup. Ct. 348, wherein the railway company was indicted for a violation of a statute of Mississippi, enacting that all railroads carrying passengers should provide equal, but separate, accommodations for the white and colored races, by providing two or more passenger cars for each passenger train, or by dividing the passenger cars by a partition, so as to secure separate accommodations. The case was presented in a different aspe t from the one under consideration, inasmuch as it was an indictment against the railway company for failing to provide the separate accommodations, but the question considered was the constitutionality of the law. In that case, the **Supreme Court** of Mississippi (66 Miss. 662, 6 South. 203) had held that the statute applied solely to commerce within the state, and, that being the construction of the state statute by its highest court, was accepted as conclusive. 'If it be a matter,' said the court (page 591, 133 U. S., and page 348, 10 Sup. Ct.), 'respecting commerce wholly within a state, and not interfering with commerce between the states, then, obviously, there is no violation of the commerce clause of the federal constitution. ... No question arises under this section as to the power of the state to separate in different compartments interstate pas- [163 U.S. 537, 548] sengers, or affect, in any manner, the privileges and rights of such passengers. All that we can consider is whether the state has the power to require that railroad trains within her limits shall have separate accommodations for the two races. That affecting only commerce within the state is no invasion of the power given to congress by the commerce clause.'

A like course of reasoning applies to the case under consideration, since the **Supreme Court** of Louisiana, in the case of State v. Judge, 44 La. Ann. 770, 11 South. 74, held that the statute in question did not apply to interstate passengers, but was confined in its application to passengers traveling exclusively within the borders of the state. The case was decided largely upon the authority of Louisville, N. O. & T. Ry. Co. v. State, 66 Miss. 662, 6 South, 203, and affirmed by this court in 133 U.S. 587 , 10 Sup. Ct. 348. In the present case no question of interference with interstate commerce can possibly arise, since the East Louisiana Railway appears to have been purely a local line, with both its termini within the state of Louisiana. Similar statutes for the separation of the two races upon public conveyances were held to be constitutional in Railroad v. Miles, 55 Pa. St. 209; Day v. Owen 5 Mich. 520; Railway Co. v. Williams, 55 Ill. 185; Railroad Co. v. Wells, 85 Tenn. 613; 4 S. W. 5; Railroad Co. v. Benson, 85 Tenn. 627, 4 S. W. 5; The Sue, 22 Fed. 843; Logwood v. Railroad Co., 23 Fed. 318; McGuinn v. Forbes, 37 Fed. 639; People v. King ( N. Y. App.) 18 N. E. 245; Houck v. Railway Co., 38 Fed. 226; Heard v. Railroad Co., 3 Inter St. Commerce Com. R. 111, 1 Inter St. Commerce Com. R. 428.

While we think the enforced separation of the races, as applied to the internal commerce of the state, neither abridges the privileges or immunities of the colored man, deprives him of his property without due process of law, nor denies him the equal protection of the laws, within the meaning of the fourteenth amendment, we are not prepared to say that the conductor, in assigning passengers to the coaches according to their race, does not act at his peril, or that the provision of the second section of the act that denies to the passenger compensa- [163 U.S. 537, 549] tion in damages for a refusal to receive him into the coach in which he properly belongs is a valid exercise of the legislative power. Indeed, we understand it to be conceded by the state's attorney that such part of the act as exempts from liability the railway company and its officers is unconstitutional. The power to assign to a particular coach obviously implies the power to determine to which race the passenger belongs, as well as the power to determine who, under the laws of the particular state, is to be deemed a white, and who a colored, person. This question, though indicated in the brief of the plaintiff in error, does not properly arise upon the record in this case, since the only issue made is as to the unconstitutionality of the act, so far as it requires the railway to provide separate accommodations, and the conductor to assign passengers according to their race.

It is claimed by the plaintiff in error that, in an mixed community, the reputation of belonging to the dominant race, in this instance the white race, is 'property,' in the same sense that a right of action or of inheritance is property. Conceding this to be so, for the purposes of this case, we are unable to see how this statute deprives him of, or in any way affects his right to, such property. If he be a white man, and assigned to a colored coach, he may have his action for damages against the company for being deprived of his so-called 'property.' Upon the other hand, if he be a colored man, and be so assigned, he has been deprived of no property, since he is not lawfully entitled to the reputation of being a white man.

In this connection, it is also suggested by the learned counsel for the plaintiff in error that the same argument that will justify the state legislature in requiring railways to provide separate accommodations for the two races will also authorize them to require separate cars to be provided for people whose hair is of a certain color, or who are aliens, or who belong to certain nationalities, or to enact laws requiring colored people to walk upon one side of the street, and white people upon the other, or requiring white men's houses to be painted white, and colored men's black, or their vehicles or business signs to be of different colors, upon the theory that one side [163 U.S. 537, 550] of the street is as good as the other, or that a house or vehicle of one color is as good as one of another color. The reply to all this is that every exercise of the police power must be reasonable, and extend only to such laws as are enacted in good faith for the promotion of the public good, and not for the annoyance or oppression of a particular class. Thus, in Yick Wo v. Hopkins, 118 U.S. 356, 6 Sup. Ct. 1064, it was held by this court that a municipal ordinance of the city of San Francisco, to regulate the carrying on of public laundries within the limits of the municipality, violated the provisions of the constitution of the **United States**, if it conferred upon the municipal authorities arbitrary power, at their own will, and without regard to discretion, in the legal sense of the term, to give or withhold consent as to persons or places, without regard to the competency of the persons applying or the propriety of the places selected for the carrying on of the business. It was held to be a covert attempt on the part of the municipality to make an arbitrary and unjust discrimination against the Chinese race. While this was the case of a municipal ordinance, a like principle has been held to apply to acts of a state legislature passed in the exercise of the police power. Railroad Co. v. Husen, 95 U.S. 465 ; Louisville & N. R. Co. v. Kentucky, 161 U.S. 677 , 16 Sup. Ct. 714, and cases cited on page 700, 161 U. S., and page 714, 16 Sup. Ct.; Daggett v. Hudson, 43 Ohio St. 548, 3 N. E. 538; Capen v. Foster, 12 Pick. 485; State v. Baker, 38 Wis. 71; Monroe v. Collins, 17 Ohio St. 665; Hulseman v. Rems, 41 Pa. St. 396; Osman v. Riley, 15 Cal. 48.

So far, then, as a conflict with the fourteenth amendment is concerned, the case reduces itself to the question whether the statute of Louisiana is a reasonable regulation, and with respect to this there must necessarily be a large discretion on the part of the legislature. In determining the question of reasonableness, it is at liberty to act with reference to the established usages, customs, and traditions of the people, and with a view to the promotion of their comfort, and the preservation of the public peace and good order. Gauged by this standard, we cannot say that a law which authorizes or even requires the separation of the two races in public conveyances [163 U.S. 537, 551] is unreasonable, or more obnoxious to the fourteenth amendment than the acts of congress requiring separate schools for colored children in the District of Columbia, the constitutionality of which does not seem to have been questioned, or the corresponding acts of state legislatures.

We consider the u derlying fallacy of the plaintiff's argument to consist in the assumption that the enforced separation of the two races stamps the colored race with a badge of inferiority. If this be so, it is not by reason of anything found in the act, but solely because the colored race chooses to put that construction upon it. The argument necessarily assumes that if, as has been more than once the case, and is not unlikely to be so again, the colored race should become the dominant power in the state legislature, and should enact a law in precisely similar terms, it would thereby relegate the white race to an inferior position. We imagine that the white race, at least, would not acquiesce in this assumption. The argument also assumes that social prejudices may be overcome by legislation, and that equal rights cannot be secured to the negro except by an enforced commingling of the two races. We cannot accept this proposition. If the two races are to meet upon terms of social equality, it must be the result of natural affinities, a mutual appreciation of each other's merits, and a voluntary consent of individuals. As was said by the court of appeals of New York in People v. Gallagher, 93 N. Y. 438, 448: 'This end can neither be accomplished nor promoted by laws which conflict with the general sentiment of the community upon whom they are designed to operate. When the government, therefore, has secured to each of its citizens equal rights before the law, and equal opportunities for improvement and progress, it has accomplished the end for which it was organized, and performed all of the functions respecting social advantages with which it is endowed.' Legislation is powerless to eradicate racial instincts, or to abolish distinctions based upon physical differences, and the attempt to do so can only result in accentuating the difficulties of the present situation. If the civil and political rights of both races be equal, one cannot be inferior to the other civilly [163 U.S. 537, 552] or politically. If one race be inferior to the other socially, the constitution of the **United States** cannot put them upon the same plane.

It is true that the question of the proportion of colored blood necessary to constitute a colored person, as distinguished from a white person, is one upon which there is a difference of opinion in the different states; some holding that any visible admixture of black blood stamps the person as belonging to the colored race (State v. Chavers, 5 Jones [N. C.] 1); others, that it depends upon the preponderance of blood (Gray v. State, 4 Ohio, 354; Monroe v. Collins, 17 Ohio St. 665); and still others, that the predominance of white blood must only be in the proportion of three-fourths (People v. Dean, 14 Mich. 406; Jones v. Com., 80 Va. 544). But these are questions to be determined under the laws of each state, and are not properly put in issue in this case. Under the allegations of his petition, it may undoubtedly become a question of importance whether, under the laws of Louisiana, the petitioner belongs to the white or colored race.

The judgment of the court below is therefore affirmed.

Mr. Justice BREWER did not hear the argument or participate in the decision of this case.

Mr. Justice HARLAN dissenting.

By the Louisiana statute the validity of which is here involved, all railway companies (other than street-railroad companies) carry passengers in that state are required to have separate but equal accommodations for white and colored persons, 'by providing two or more passenger coaches for each passenger train, or by dividing the passenger coaches by a partition so as to secure separate accommodations.' Under this statute, no colored person is permitted to occupy a seat in a coach assigned to white persons; nor any white person to occupy a seat in a coach assigned to colored persons. The managers of the railroad are not allowed to exercise any discretion in the premises, but are required to assign each passenger to some coach or compartment set apart for the exclusive use of is race. If a passenger insists upon going into a coach or compartment not set apart for persons of his race, [163 U.S. 537, 553] he is subject to be fined, or to be imprisoned in the parish jail. Penalties are prescribed for the refusal or neglect of the officers, directors, conductors, and employees of railroad companies to comply with the provisions of the act

Only 'nurses attending children of the other race' are excepted from the operation of the statute. No exception is made of colored attendants traveling with adults. A white man is not permitted to have his colored servant with him in the same coach, even if his condition of health requires the constant personal assistance of such servant. If a colored maid insists upon riding in the same coach with a white woman whom she has been employed to serve, and who may need her personal attention while traveling, she is subject to be fined or imprisoned for such an exhibition of zeal in the discharge of duty.

While there may be in Louisiana persons of different races who are not citizens of the **United States**, the words in the act 'white and colored races' necessarily include all citizens of the **United States** of both races residing in that state. So that we have before us a state enactment that compels, under penalties, the separation of the two races in railroad passenger coaches, and makes it a crime for a citizen of either race to enter a coach that has been assigned to citizens of the other race.

Thus, the state regulates the use of a public highway by citizens of the **United States** solely upon the basis of race.

However apparent the injustice of such legislation may be, we have only to consider whether it is consistent with the constitution of the **United States**.

That a railroad is a public highway, and that the corporation which owns or operates it is in the exercise of public functions, is not, at this day, to be disputed. Mr. Justice Nelson, speaking for this court in New Jersey Steam Nav. Co. v. Merchants' Bank, 6 How. 344, 382, said that a common carrier was in the exercise 'of a sort of public office, and has public duties to perform, from which he should not be permitted to exonerate himself without the assent of the parties concerned.' Mr. Justice Strong, delivering the judgment of [163 U.S. 537, 554] this court in Olcott v. Supervisors, 16 Wall. 678, 694, said: 'That railroads, though constructed by private corporations, and owned by them, are public highways, has been the doctrine of nearly all the courts ever since such conveniences for passage and transportation have had any existence. Very early the question arose whether a state's right of eminent domain could be exercised by a private corporation created for the purpose of constructing a railroad. Clearly, it could not, unless taking land for such a purpose by such an agency is taking land for public use. The right of eminent domain nowhere justifies taking property for a private use. Yet it is a doctrine universally accepted that a state legislature may authorize a private corporation to take land for the construction of such a road, making compensation to the owner. What else does this doctrine mean if not that building a railroad, though it be built by a private corporation, is an act done for a public use?' So, in Township of Pine Grove v. Talcott, 19 Wall. 666, 676: 'Though the corporation [a railroad company] was private, its work was public, as much so as if it were to be constructed by the state.' So, in Inhabitants of Worcester v. Western R. Corp., 4 Metc. (Mass.) 564: 'The establishment of that great thoroughfare is regarded as a public work, established by public authority, intended for the public use and benefit, the use of which is secured to the whole community, and constitutes, therefore, like a canal, turnpike, or highway, a public easement.' 'It is true that the real and personal property, necessary to the establishment and management of the railroad, is vested in the corporation; but it is in trust for the public.'

In respect of civil rights, common to all citizens, the constitution of the **United States** does not, I think, permit any public authority to know the race of those entitled to be protected in the enjoyment of such rights. Every true man has pride of race, and under appropriate circumstances, when the rights of others, his equals before the law, are not to be affected, it is his privilege to express such pride and to take such action based upon it as to him seems proper. But I deny that any legislative body or judicial tribunal may have regard to the [163 U.S. 537, 555] race of citizens when the civil rights of those citizens are involved. Indeed, such legislation as that here in question is inconsistent not only with that equality of rights which pertains to citizenship, national and state, but with the personal liberty enjoyed by every one within the **United States**.

The thirteenth amendment does not permit the withholding or the deprivation of any right necessarily inhering in freedom. It not only struck down the institution of **SLAVERY** as previously existing in the **United States**, but it prevents the imposition of any burdens or disabilities that constitute badges of **SLAVERY** or servitude. It decreed universal civil freedom in this country. This court has so adjudged. But, that amendment having been found inadequate to the protection of the rights of those who had been in **SLAVERY**, it was followed by the fourteenth amendment, which added greatly to the dignity and glory of American citizenship, and to the security of personal liberty, by declaring that 'all persons born or naturalized in the **United States**, and subject to the jurisdiction thereof, are citizens of the **United States** and of the state wherein they reside,' and that 'no state shall make or enforce any law which shall abridge the privileges or immunities of citizens of the **United States**; nor shall any state deprive any person of life, liberty or property without due process of law, nor deny to any person within its jurisdiction the equal protection of the laws.' These two amendments, if enforced according to their true intent and meaning, will protect all the civil rights that pertain to freedom and citizenship. Finally, and to the end that no citizen should be denied, on account of his race, the privilege of participating in the political control of his country, it was declared by the fifteenth amendment that 'the right of citizens of the **United States** to vote shall not be denied or abridged by the **United States** or by any state on account of race, color or previous condition of servitude.'

These notable additions to the fundamental law were welcomed by the friends of liberty throughout the world. They removed the race line from our governmental systems. They had, as this court has said, a common purpose, namely, to secure 'to a race recently emancipated, a race that through [163 U.S. 537, 556] many generations have been held in **SLAVERY**, all the civil rights that the superior race enjoy.' They declared, in legal effect, this court has further said, 'that the law in the states shall be the same for the black as for the white; that all persons, whether colored or white, shall stand equal before the laws of the states; and in regard to the colored race, for whose protection the amendment was primarily designed, that no discrimination shall be made against them by law because of their color.' We also said: 'The words of the amendment, it is true, are prohibitory, but they contain a necessary implication of a positive immunity or right, most valuable to the colored race,-the right to exemption from unfriendly legislation against them distinctively as colored; exemption from legal discriminations, implying inferiority in civil society, lessening the security of their enjoyment of the rights which others enjoy; and discriminations which are steps towards reducing them to the condition of a subject race.' It was, consequently, adjudged that a state law that excluded citizens of the colored race from juries, because of their race, however well qualified in other respects to dischar e the duties of jurymen, was repugnant to the fourteenth amendment. Strauder v. West Virginia, 100 U.S. 303, 306 , 307 S.; Virginia v. Rives, Id. 313; Ex parte Virginia, Id. 339; Neal v. Delaware, 103 U.S. 370 , 386; Bush v. Com., 107 U.S. 110, 116 , 1 S. Sup. Ct. 625. At the present term, referring to the previous adjudications, this court declared that 'underlying all of those decisions is the principle that the constitution of the **United States**, in its present form, forbids, so far as civil and political rights are concerned, discrimination by the general government or the states against any citizen because of his race. All citizens are equal before the law.' Gibson v. State, 162 U.S. 565 , 16 Sup. Ct. 904.

The decisions referred to show the scope of the recent amendments of the constitution. They also show that it is not within the power of a state to prohibit colored citizens, because of their race, from participating as jurors in the administration of justice.

It was said in argument that the statute of Louisiana does [163 U.S. 537, 557] not discriminate against either race, but prescribes a rule applicable alike to white and colored citizens. But this argument does not meet the difficulty. Every one knows that the statute in question had its origin in the purpose, not so much to exclude white persons from railroad cars occupied by blacks, as to exclude colored people from coaches occupied by or assigned to white persons. Railroad corporations of Louisiana did not make discrimination among whites in the matter of commodation for travelers. The thing to accomplish was, under the guise of giving equal accommodation for whites and blacks, to compel the latter to keep to themselves while traveling in railroad passenger coaches. No one would be so wanting in candor as to assert the contrary. The fundamental objection, therefore, to the statute, is that it interferes with the personal freedom of citizens. 'Personal liberty,' it has been well said, 'consists in the power of locomotion, of changing situation, or removing one's person to whatsoever places one's own inclination may direct, without imprisonment or restraint, unless by due course of law.' 1 Bl. Comm. *134. If a white man and a black man choose to occupy the same public conveyance on a public highway, it is their right to do so; and no government, proceeding alone on grounds of race, can prevent it without infringing the personal liberty of each.

It is one thing for railroad carriers to furnish, or to be required by law to furnish, equal accommodations for all whom they are under a legal duty to carry. It is quite another thing for government to forbid citizens of the white and black races from traveling in the same public conveyance, and to punish officers of railroad companies for permitting persons of the two races to occupy the same passenger coach. If a state can prescribe, as a rule of civil conduct, that whites and blacks shall not travel as passengers in the same railroad coach, why may it not so regulate the use of the streets of its cities and towns as to compel white citizens to keep on one side of a street, and black citizens to keep on the other? Why may it not, upon like grounds, punish whites and blacks who ride together in street cars or in open vehicles on a public road [163 U.S. 537, 558] or street? Why may it not require sheriffs to assign whites to one side of a court room, and blacks to the other? And why may it not also prohibit the commingling of the two races in the galleries of legislative halls or in public assemblages convened for the consideration of the political questions of the day? Further, if this statute of Louisiana is consistent with the personal liberty of citizens, why may not the state require the separation in railroad coaches of native and naturalized citizens of the **United States**, or of Protestants and Roman Catholics?

The answer given at the argument to these questions was that regulations of the kind they suggest would be unreasonable, and could not, therefore, stand before the la . Is it meant that the determination of questions of legislative power depends upon the inquiry whether the statute whose validity is questioned is, in the judgment of the courts, a reasonable one, taking all the circumstances into consideration? A statute may be unreasonable merely because a sound public policy forbade its enactment. But I do not understand that the courts have anything to do with the policy or expediency of legislation. A statute may be valid, and yet, upon grounds of public policy, may well be characterized as unreasonable. Mr. Sedgwick correctly states the rule when he says that, the legislative intention being clearly ascertained, 'the courts have no other duty to perform than to execute the legislative will, without any regard to their views as to the wisdom or justice of the particular enactment.' Sedg. St. & Const. Law, 324. There is a dangerous tendency in these latter days to enlarge the functions of the courts, by means of judicial interference with the will of the people as expressed by the legislature. Our institutions have the distinguishing characteristic that the three departments of government are co-ordinate and separate. Each much keep within the limits defined by the constitution. And the courts best discharge their duty by executing the will of the law-making power, constitutionally expressed, leaving the results of legislation to be dealt with by the people through their representatives. Statutes must always have a reasonable construction.

Sometimes they are to be construed strictly, sometimes literally, in order to carry out the legisla- [163 U.S. 537, 559] tive will. But, however construed, the intent of the legislature is to be respected if the particular statute in question is valid, although the courts, looking at the public interests, may conceive the statute to be both unreasonable and impolitic. If the power exists to enact a statute, that ends the matter so far as the courts are concerned. The adjudged cases in which statutes have been held to be void, because unreasonable, are those in which the means employed by the legislature were not at all germane to the end to which the legislature was competent.

The white race deems itself to be the dominant race in this country. And so it is, in prestige, in achievements, in education, in wealth, and in power. So, I doubt not, it will continue to be for all time, if it remains true to its great heritage, and holds fast to the principles of constitutional liberty. But in view of the constitution, in the eye of the law, there is in this country no superior, dominant, ruling class of citizens. There is no caste here. Our constitution is color-blind, and neither knows nor tolerates classes among citizens. In respect of civil rights, all citizens are equal before the law. The humblest is the peer of the most powerful. The law regards man as man, and takes no account of his surroundings or of his color when his civil rights as guarantied by the spreme law of the land are involved. It is therefore to be regretted that this high tribunal, the final expositor of the fundamental law of the land, has reached the conclusion that it is competent for a state to regulate the enjoyment by citizens of their civil rights solely upon the basis of race.

In my opinion, the judgment this day rendered will, in time, prove to be quite as pernicious as the decision made by this tribunal in the Dred Scott Case.

It was adjudged in that case that the descendants of **AFRICANS** who were imported into this country, and sold as slaves, were not included nor intended to be included under the word 'citizens' in the constitution, and could not claim any of the rights and privileges which that instrument provided for and secured to citizens of the **United States**; that, at time of the adoption of the constitution, they were 'considered as a subordinate and inferior class of beings, who had been subjugated by the dominant [163 U.S. 537, 560] race, and, whether emancipated or not, yet remained subject to their authority, and had no rights or privileges but such as those who held the power and the government might choose to grant them.' 17 How. 393, 404. The recent amendments of the constitution, it was supposed, had eradicated these principles from our institutions. But it seems that we have yet, in some of the states, a dominant race,-a superior class of citizens,-which assumes to regulate the enjoyment of civil rights, common to all citizens, upon the basis of race. The present decision, it may well be apprehended, will not only stimulate aggressions, more or less brutal and irritating, upon the admitted rights of colored citizens, but will encourage the belief that it is possible, by means of state enactments, to defeat the beneficent purposes which the people of the **United States** had in view when they adopted the recent amendments of the constitution, by one of which the blacks of this country were made citizens of the **United States** and of the states in which they respectively reside, and whose privileges and immunities, as citizens, the states are forbidden to abridge. Sixty millions of whites are in no danger from the presence here of eight millions of blacks. The destinies of the two races, in this country, are indissolubly linked together, and the interests of both require that the common government of all shall not permit the seeds of race hate to be planted under the sanction of law. What can more certainly arouse race hate, what more certainly create and perpetuate a feeling of distrust between these races, than state enactments which, in fact, proceed on the ground that colored citizens are so inferior and degraded that they cannot be allowed to sit in public coaches occupied by white citizens? That, as all will admit, is the real meaning of such legislation as was enacted in Louisiana.

The sure guaranty of the peace and security of each race is the clear, distinct, unconditional recognition by our governments, national and state, of every right that inheres in civil freedom, and of the equality before the law of all citizens of the **United States**, without regard to race. State enactments regulating the enjoyment of civil rights upon the basis of race, and cunningly devised to defeat legitimate results of the [163 U.S. 537, 561] war, under the pretense of recognizing equality of rights, can have no other result than to render permanent peace impossible, and to keep alive a conflict of races, the continuance of which must do harm to all concerned. This question is not met by the suggestion that social equality cannot exist between the white and black races in this country. That argument, if it can be properly regarded as one, is scarcely worthy of consideration; for social equality no more exists between two races when traveling in a passenger coach or a public highway than when members of the same races sit by each other in a street car or in the jury box, or stand or sit with each other in a political assembly, or when they use in common the streets of a city or town, or when they are in the same room for the purpose of having their names placed on the registry of voters, or when they approach the ballot box in order to exercise the high privilege of voting.

There is a race so different from our own that we do not permit those belonging to it to become citizens of the **United States**. Persons belonging to it are, with few exceptions, absolutely excluded from our country. I allude to the Chinese race. But, by the statute in question, a Chinaman can ride in the same passenger coach with white citizens of the **United States**, while citizens of the black race in Louisiana, many of whom, perhaps, risked their lives for the preservation of the Union, who are entitled, by law, to participate in the political control of the state and nation, who are not excluded, by law or by reason of their race, from public stations of any kind, and who have all the legal rights that belong to white citizens, are yet declared to be criminals, liable to imprisonment, if they ride in a public coach occupied by citizens of the white race. It is scarcely just to say that a colored citizen should not object to occupying a public coach assigned to his own race. He does not object, nor, perhaps, would he object to separate coaches for his race if his rights under the law were recognized. But he does object, and he ought never to cease objecting, that citizens of the white and black races can be adjudged criminals because they sit, or claim the right to sit, in the same public coach on a public highway. [163 U.S. 537, 562] The arbitrary separation of citizens, on the basis of race, while they are on a public highway, is a badge of servitude wholly inconsistent with the civil freedom and the equality before the law established by the constitution. It cannot be justified upon any legal grounds.

If evils will result from the commingling of the two races upon public highways established for the benefit of all, they will be infinitely less than those that will surely come from state legislation regulating the enjoyment of civil rights upon the basis of race. We boast of the freedom enjoyed by our people above all other peoples. But it is difficult to reconcile that boast with a state of the law which, practically, puts the brand of servitude and degradation upon a large class of our fellow citizens,-our equals before the law. The thin disguise of 'equal' accommodations for passengers in railroad coaches will not mislead any one, nor atone for the wrong this day done.

The result of the whole matter is that while this court has frequently adjudged, and at the present term has recognized the doctrine, that a state cannot, consistently with the constitution of the **United States**, prevent white and black citizens, having the required qualifications for jury service, from sitting in the same jury box, it is now solemnly held that a state may prohibit white and black citizens from sitting in the same passenger coach on a public highway, or may require that they be separated by a 'partition' when in the same passenger coach. May it not now be reasonably expected that astute men of the dominant race, who affect to be disturbed at the possibility that the integrity of the white race may be corrupted, or that its supremacy will be imperiled, by contact on public highways with black people, will endeavor to procure statutes requiring white and black jurors to be separated in the jury box by a 'partition,' and that, upon retiring from the court room to consult as to their verdict, such partition, if it be a movable one, shall be taken to their consultation room, and set up in such way as to prevent black jurors from coming too close to their brother jurors of the white race. If the 'partition' used in the court room happens to be stationary, provision could be made for screens with openings through [163 U.S. 537, 563] which jurors of the two races could confer as to their verdict without coming into personal contact with each other. I cannot see but that, according to the principles this day announced, such state legislation, although conceived in hostility to, and enacted for the purpose of humiliating, citizens of the **United States** of a particular race, would be held to be consistent with the constitution.

I do not deem it necessary to review the decisions of state courts to which reference was made in argument. Some, and the most important, of them, are wholly inapplicable, because rendered prior to the adoption of the last amendments of the constitution, when colored people had very few rights which the dominant race felt obliged to respect. Others were made at a time when public opinion, in many localities, was dominated by the institution of **SLAVERY**; when it would not have been safe to do justice to the black man; and when, so far as the rights of blacks were concerned, race prejudice was, practically, the **Supreme** law of the land. Those decisions cannot be guides in the era introduced by the recent amendments of the **Supreme** law, which established universal civil freedom, gave citizenship to all born or naturalized in the **United States**, and residing ere, obliterated the race line from our systems of governments, national and state, and placed our free institutions upon the broad and sure foundation of the equality of all men before the law.

I am of opinion that the state of Louisiana is inconsistent with the personal liberty of citizens, white and black, in that state, and hostile to both the spirit and letter of the constitution of the **United States**. If laws of like character should be enacted in the several states of the Union, the effect would be in the highest degree mischievous. **SLAVERY**, as an institution tolerated by law, would, it is true, have disappeared from our country; but there would remain a power in the states, by sinister legislation, to interfere with the full enjoyment of the blessings of freedom, to regulate civil rights, common to all citizens, upon the basis of race, and to place in a condition of legal inferiority a large body of American citizens, now constituting a part of the political community, called the [163 U.S. 537, 564] 'People of the **United States**,' for whom, and by whom through representatives, our government is administered. Such a system is inconsistent with the guaranty given by the constitution to each state of a republican form of government, and may be stricken down by congressional action, or by the courts in the discharge of their solemn duty to maintain the **Supreme** law of the land, anything in the constitution or laws of any state to the contrary notwithstanding.

For the reason stated, I am constrained to withhold my assent from the opinion and judgment of the majority.

## Conclusion

In *No Rights and No Respect, A Documentary Commentary on **AFRICAN** Life In America*[1], I concluded with a speech given by Frederick Douglas which exposed the hypocrisy of celebrating the 4$^{th}$ of July while there still existed **SLAVERY** in America. I also predicted America's dissolution. America, because of its criminality (*legal* yet!), will not stand! I believe that at some point in time, it will come crashing down upon all of us! The persons that will be startled are the slave masters (keepers of the **ANGLO-AMERICAN LEGAL TRADITION**) and their "House" Slaves.

This revision to *Twisting in the Wind* is written in the aftermath of "9-11." The sitting Attorney General, John Ashcroft, has unilaterally introduced directives aimed at curbing Civil Liberties. The range and scope of which are too great to relate in detail here. Suffice it to say, that this draconian approach to *counter-terrorism* is an example of *state sponsored terrorism!* It has had a ripple effect throughout the law enforcement "community." On January 21, 2002, elements of the San Francisco Police Department allegedly beat and fondled several African youth around mid-night on Martin Luther King, Jr.'s birthday. The incident occurred on Kiska Road in the City's

---

[1] Williams, *No Rights And No Respect*, Begin on Page 190.

predominantly African public housing development, Hunters Point. What follows is a letter I wrote to the following persons. They were:

*Mr. Sidney Chan*
**Chairman**
**San Francisco Police Commission**

*Ms. Donna Medley*
**Office of Citizens Complaints**

*Police Chief Fred Lau*
**San Francisco Police Department**

And
*Mr. Terrance Hallinan*
**District Attorney**
*For The*
**City and County of San Francisco**

Knowing what I know about the draconian mood of "the powers that be," I struggled as to whether I should send the letter. Nevertheless, in the end, I decided to do so. Without going into detail, my family has suffered greatly of late at the hands of American "Justice." Nevertheless, after further reflection, I asked myself the rhetorical question, "what else can they do?" Therefore, I sent the letter the persons listed above. The inferences drawn from the incident support my view that persons of African descent in America live in a society hostile to their very presence! Although the incident occurred in San Francisco on

Monday, January 21, 2002, it could have just as well happened anywhere in America! The attitude of the San Francisco Police Department is symptomatic of all law "enforcement" personnel! I present the letter to you!

++++++++++++++++++++++++++++++++++++++++++++++

**Saint James Missionary Baptist Church**

1470 Hudson Avenue
San Francisco, California 94124

Telephone 415-648-5995
Fax 415-468-6387
Email PMSW46@AOL.COM

March 21, 2002

My name is Michael S. Williams. I currently serve as the pastor of the Saint James Missionary Baptist Church located in the Bayview District.

Ms. "X", one of the principals in the now well known Martin Luther King, Jr. Day incident, which occurred on Kiska Road, is one of my parishioners. I must commend Ms. "X" for having the presence of mind to take pictures of the incident.

I am writing this letter, not to get a response; after all, due to statue issues, that will not happen. I am writing this letter, and as a consumer of police services, to share some observations.

I am a native San Franciscan. I am also rapidly approaching the half-century mark. I am not in a habit of "bashing" public servants. I would hope this missive would not be construed as such. However, I would say the following. Perhaps one reason the community has risen in such virulent protest is the historic tensions that have existed between the African community in America and governmental structures. American governmental units, Federal, State, county, and local have had a historical advantage over us. Therefore, we may have a tendency to view your legal system with suspicion. I will give some examples of what I mean and conclude this matter.

First, by way of your Constitution, in 1787, we were declared, as **Article I, Section 2, Clause 3** so eloquently (still) states 3/5 human, and that for census reasons. Our less than human status was given the US Supreme Court's Imprimatur in 1856, when the Chief Justice, writing for the majority, declared in the matter of *Scott v. Sanford*, that we had no rights that the greater society was bound to respect. In fact the Chief Justice even went so far to argue that when the framers of the Constitution wrote, "we the people..." persons of African descent were not included.

You might argue that such conditions do not exist today. We have seen your government give and take away rights at a whim! If the Voters/Civil Rights Acts can be passed, it can be *un*passed. I firmly believe that your government can do whatever it wants to do. A case in point is the recent erosion of civil liberties in the wake of 9-11—all in the name of protecting our way of life. For the record, I do not feel safe.

Second, I was raised in the Bayview by my Grandmother, now of blessed memory. She had a morbid fear of uniformed authority. Her fear dated back to the early part of the last century when the state militia would ride through her small town in the American South on horse back and murder at will any black person that dared not show the proper deference. In fact, the Black town's folk called the militia "the malicious."

During the 1960s, she did not want me to dress in a certain way to attract the attention of the police and therefore have them shoot me. We were ignorant of the abuses of COINTELPRO. However, she instinctively knew that something was wrong, and she did not want me to be causality.

Third, such activities as the infamous Tuskegee Experiment, funded by the Federal Government have not engendered a sense of trust between your government and our people. In fact no charges were ever filed, why should they have been? It was legal!

All of the examples I cited above were legal, and passed constitutional muster. They were legal because governing authority said so. We can buy that! What choice do we have? Many of us are aware that we are profitable commodities. Based upon figures complied by the Washington based Sentencing Report, out of the nearly 2,000,000 persons involved in your Criminal Justice System, i.e., probation, parole, jail, prison, etc., 800,000 of them are males of African descent. We are also aware that the Criminal Justice System is a vital part of the American economy. Therefore, if African Americans, specifically males refrained from conflicting with your laws, a serious strain would be put on your economic system.

Finally, I would like to echo the thoughts expressed at the last Police Commission meeting by one of the fathers, whose son was beaten. My late Grandmother raised this same point with me back in the 1960s. She argued that if she were to administer corporal punishment upon me, she could go to jail for child abuse, if a law enforcement officer did it, it would be considered resisting arrest.

I close with this statement. I have sat at the table of your justice of late, and found that money dictates the service and choice of meals served by the blindfolded European woman with the scales in her hand. She is blindfolded, but she does have a tendency to peek through her mask and see who stands before her. This confirmed Chief Justice Taney's observations concerning us.

I really doubt that a Kiska type incident would have occurred in Pacific Heights, Sea Cliff, or the Marina District. However, I am eager to be proven wrong. At the risk of overstatement, I would argue that not looking at this problem closely and dealing with it, should the facts support the community's observations, will do nothing more than confirm our worst opinions, that as Taney said, "we have nor rights and are due no respect." Additionally, if "state sponsored terrorism" is defined as government sanctioned, as well as funded, use of overwhelming force to destroy or debilitate an unsuspecting people, the Kiska Road incident may be a text book example.

You might argue that there is a significant African presence on your force, in the prosecutor's office, the judiciary, etc., that is true, but even they take their lives in their hands when they are caught in the wrong place at the wrong time. That place/time could be getting into his/her car late at night! The car could be an expensive one, one that a person like him/her "wouldn't drive," therefore it must be stolen! Law enforcement officers of African descent are often seriously injured or killed by their "colleagues," sometimes during undercover operations. The "findings" usually support the incident as being "accidental." African American law enforcement, at all levels, local, state and Federal, must constantly "watch their backs," and simultaneously strive for "acceptance." The recent Federal Court battles waged by Black FBI and Secret Service Agents are cases in point. In fact, when one ranking African American SFPD officer made a politically incorrect, but socially accurate, statement about racism and the social tight rope he had to walk as a Black person, he was promptly censured. Since I expect nothing from you, but surveillance and the like, a job loss is not my fear!

I realize that this letter could have me "put on your list." I do not know everything that you know, because I do not possess the necessary "clearance." I do not need to know what you know, I just know your capabilities, and that is enough. I also realize that you have a constituency to answer to, the politically powerful, to whom you owe your appointments. Such power keeps their peccadilloes from being considered "crimes." No! Their "peculiarities" are tolerated with a wink and a nod! If the deviancies are considered too outrageous, they are quietly moved from one position to another, or quietly "retired." After all, it has to be done that way for the sake of "friendship" or to save the institution, to say nothing of careers from embarrassment and ruin. If they are publicly exposed, "friendship" not withstanding, they will be sacrificed without mercy. Finally, when persons with meager resources are "caught up," justice must be done! We realize that and accept it!

Our community will watch this process very closely. We will see if Mr. Taney's dictum was correct. We would hope it is not, but such processes are not in our hands. In closing, one positive result of one of the officers allegedly addressing the persons on Kiska Road that night as you people is that it seems to have elevated us higher than even Chief Justice Taney would have had us to go.


Sincerely,


Pastor Michael S. Williams, D.Min

In light of the material presented in this book, as well as the above letter, I close with chillingly prophetic words from the nation's third and sixteenth presidents respectively, Thomas Jefferson and Abraham Lincoln.

Said Jefferson in his *Notes on the State of Virginia*,

> And can the liberties of a nation be thought secure, when we have removed their only firm basis, a conviction in the minds of the people that these liberties are of the gift of God? That they are not to be violated but with his wrath? Indeed I tremble for my country when I reflect that God is just: that his justice cannot sleep forever....[2]

Lincoln stated in a speech given in Illinois in 1838,

> Shall we expect some transatlantic military giant, to step the Ocean, and crush us at a blow? Never! --All the armies of Europe, Asia and Africa combined, with all the treasure of the earth (our own excepted) in their military chest; with a [Napoleon] Buonaparte for a commander, could not by force, take a drink from the Ohio, or make a track on the Blue Ridge, in a trial of a thousand years.
>
> At what point then is the approach of danger to be expected? I answer, if it ever reach us,

---

[2] Ibid. 40.

> it must spring up amongst us. It cannot come from abroad. If destruction be our lot, we must ourselves be its author and finisher. As a nation of freemen, we must live through all time, or die by suicide.

In other words, America will implode; it will collapse under its own weight! It will one day hear the Almighty Judge of History intone, using the **ANGLO-AMERICAN TRADITION'S** formula for pronouncing the death penalty, *You will hang by the neck until your are Dead! Dead! Dead! America you will Twist! Twist! Twist!*

## A Response by Rev. John Brinson, M.Div.

There are literally hundreds of books written and published daily for the consumption of an ever growing and avid **AFRICAN** reading community. However, most of them are either mundane or written to satisfy the author's need for money. There are however, a few written to illume our minds. *Twisting in the Wind,* is one of those illuminating books that appear on the scene inducing profound changes in how man views himself and society.

Dr. Williams examines some of the Laws of the Land that directly impact on the **AFRICAN** Community and the **Supreme Court** opinions on these Laws in the context of changing political realities. He exposes the notion of the non- citizen and obsolete status of **AFRICANS** in America and what that signifies in its ultimate reality.

Dr. Michael Williams approaches his task as a skilled surgeon whose aim is to expose what produces the sickness so it can be effectively neutralized and the sick person can begin healing process. He accomplishes this by allowing the documents (laws, opinions, writings) to speak for themselves, which adds power to his persuasive presentation. He has woven a tapestry of history and social consciousness that informs **AFRICANS** in American that the laws that govern this land are projections of the Euro-

American's mind and that their interpretation is riding on the crest of his flip flopping inclinations.

The author not only draws upon historical documents per se, but also uses some powerful, common daily incidents in the lives of **AFRICANS** in America to illuminate the fact of the treatment of them as contrary to that of real citizens. The evidence he uses illustrates concisely the point he seeks to make. **AFRICANS** in America are *not, nor have they ever been, citizens.*

Dr. Williams sees no hope for **AFRICANS** under the present scheme of things, as a matter of fact because he indicates their economic obsolescence there appears a dark cloud over their future horizon. He claims preparations at one time or another have been made for the final solution to the problem. The most notable ones are the "King Alfred Plan," the "Aids Biological Warfare" and the "Tuskegee Experiment."

If you have ever needed to read a book, you need to read this one. Dr. Williams is sounding an alarm so that those who hear and heed may prepare for survival. I believe I am better of by having read this book than not, and so shall you.

John D Brinson, M/Div.

## Biographical Sketch of Dr. Michael S. Williams

Pastor Michael S. Williams, D.Min. is a native of San Francisco, California. He is a product of San Francisco's public school system. He received his **Bachelor of Arts** degree *cum laude*, from **Bishop College**, formerly of Dallas, Texas, in 1976. He earned the **Masters of Divinity and Doctor of Ministry** degrees from the world-renown **Pacific School of Religion, Berkeley, California in 1979 and 1996 respectively.**

### Professional/Fraternal Activities

He served as the **Assistant to the President of the Graduate Theological Union from 1996-1997** and holds dual membership with the **American Academy of Religion** and the **Society of Biblical Literature**. Dr. Williams holds the rank of **Professor of Biblical Studies and Vice President for Development at the Southern Marin Bible Institute**. Dr. Williams is a member of **Alpha Phi Alpha, Inc.**

### Denominational Activities

Dr. Williams has been in parish ministry for over a quarter century. He is a respected leader within his denomination, the **National Baptist Convention, USA, Inc.** He is a certified instructor through the **National Baptist Convention's (USA, Inc.) Department of Christian Education.** He served in a variety of pastoral and staff positions within the **United Methodist Church**, the **AFRICAN Methodist Episcopal Zion Church**, the **National Baptist Convention of America,** and the **National Baptist Convention, USA, Inc**. Since 1989, Dr. Williams has served as **Pastor of the Saint James Missionary Baptist Church of San Francisco**. He served as the **Moderator of the Bay Area Baptist District Association (1995-99).**

## Dr. Williams' Published Writings Are Below:

"The Book of Job as a Reflection on the Practice of Ministry" *The Journal of Religious Thought* 54:2/55:1 (Spring/Fall 1998): 53-59.

Sermon entitled, "Holding Up Your End" (*The **African** American Pulpit,* Summer 2000 Issue, Judson Press).

*If You Want to go to the Left, Then I'll Go to the Right, If You want to Go to the Right, Then, I'll Go to the Left: A Church Member's Guide to Conflict Resolution.*

*Some Thoughts For The Journey To Cana: Christian Matrimony: Choice Or Chance.*

*From Eden to Egypt: The Book of Genesis Revisited.*

*No Rights and No Respect: A Documentary Commentary on **AFRICAN** Life in America.*

**The City Church Publication Society** published all of Dr. Williams's writings, with the exception of his journal publications

## Family

Since 1984, Pastor Williams has been married to the former Patricia A. Andrews. They are the parents of two children, Marthaa, and Timothy.

## DID YOU KNOW:

- The tradition of enslaving Africans in America grew out of their low "LEGAL" status?
- An African, Benjamin Banneker, literally "saved the day" in 1791 as well as the Federal Government from embarrassment when he produced the plans for the nation's capital from memory after the French army officer originally hired by George Washington, over a pay dispute, returned to France –with the plans?
- That same year Banneker wrote a long letter to Thomas Jefferson requesting Constitutional rights for Africans——only to have Jefferson "brush him off?" In addition, George Washington signed the Fugitive Slave Act of 1793 in the very city whose plans Banneker reproduced from memory?
- An African preacher, Nat Turner, struck fear in the hearts of the Slave Regime when he unsuccessfully led a bloody revolt against the "legally" sanctioned slave system in Virginia?
- Like the recent theft of the Presidential election in 2000, a similar occurrence happened in 1876, and that the winner—Rutherford B. Hayes, withdrew Federal Troops from the South thereby ensuring African subjugation—and that it is LEGAL?
- No *Negro* Federal Judge has/is ever been recommended for confirmation by the traditionally all Euro-American US Senate's Judiciary Committee—unless the person is considered "safe"?
- *Negro* Federal Law Enforcement Agents have to "sue" their employer—the United States Government in order to be considered members of the "team"?

*Pastor Michael S. Williams, D.Min.* has done the unthinkable! He has surpassed his previous work, *No Rights and No Respect: A Documentary Commentary on African Life in America.* He uses his pervious work as a point of reference as he exposes the predatory nature of America's LEGAL *SYSTEM*, as reflected in its LEGAL *TRADITION*, which was inherited from its "Mother Country," England! He does this by carefully analyzing selected documents form America's parasitic past. In this volume, he finishes the job he began in No Rights and No Respect. He lets Africans know that regardless of their perceived "status" as American "citizens," the Anglo-American Legal tradition has tried and convicted them and has left them *TWISTING IN THE WIND* by using the **United States Constitution** as a rope!

www.ingramcontent.com/pod-product-compliance
Lightning Source LLC
Chambersburg PA
CBHW051629230426
43669CB00013B/2236